The Last Word

BOOKS BY LOUIS KRONENBERGER

A Mania for Magnificence
Animal, Vegetable, Mineral
No Whippings, No Gold Watches
The Polished Surface
The Cart and the Horse
A Month of Sundays
Marlborough's Duchess
The Republic of Letters
Company Manners
The Thread of Laughter
Grand Right and Left
Kings and Desperate Men
The Grand Manner

EDITED OR TRANSLATED BY LOUIS KRONENBERGER

Atlantic Brief Lives
The Cutting Edge
Quality: Its Image in the Arts
The Viking Book of Aphorisms
(with W. H. Auden)
Novelists on Novelists
The Great World: From Greville's Memoirs
The Maxims of La Rochefoucauld
The Pleasure of Their Company
Anouilh's Mademoiselle Colombe
Cavalcade of Comedy
The Portable Johnson and Boswell
Selected Works of Alexander Pope
The Plays of Sheridan
The Best Plays of 1952–53 through 1960–61
Shaw: A Critical Survey

Louis Kronenberger

THE LAST WORD

Portraits
of Fourteen
Master Aphorists

The Macmillan Company, New York, New York
Collier-Macmillan Limited, London

To my granddaughter

Amy Sachs Wanklyn

Contents

ᴐᴥ *Author's Note*

The subtitle of this book, I would hope, reveals something of its intentions, which were to set down, at modest length, the lives, personalities and achievements of fourteen distinguished men who have one great gift in common—a mastery of the aphorism. There was never any thought of an exhaustive treatment of the aphorism, or an extensive list of aphorists. Nor would the book, while exhibiting the talent that all fourteen men share, hurry past what makes all fourteen of them different—what has brought them fame as poets or playwrights, statesmen or physicists, courtiers or radicals, pacifists or warriors, diners-out or madmen. I have accordingly tried to convey what they were and did as well as what they said. And it has seemed to me that a book of this sort, presenting many variations on a single theme, should not run on too long. Certainly other distinguished aphorists might have been chosen, but these fourteen seemed to me to lend themselves best to this kind of biographical treatment.

I would thank Arthur Gregor for his proposing that I write this book, and Ray Roberts for his kindness and care in watching over its publication, and for suggesting the title.

I

La Rochefoucauld

FRANÇOIS, sixth Duc de La Rochefoucauld, wrote one of the shortest and one of the most enduring of classics: after three hundred years his *Maxims* remain unrivaled in their kind. In him we have a concentrated, detailed, participant's insight into worldly conduct and motivations; from him descend many writers of aphorisms who clearly show his influence and, in great or small degree, assent to his conclusions.

He was born in Paris in 1613, the son of the fifth Comte de La Rochefoucauld and the scion of a very old family; on his mother's side he came of the noble and wealthy Liancourts. The La Rochefoucaulds had a number of habitations in the west of France—a chateau in a village that bore their name; a castle in Marcillac, which bestowed its name on the heir to the future dukedom; a townhouse in Fontenay-le-Comte; and a castle at Verteuil. François was the eldest of fourteen children, who for the most part were brought up in the country by their mother, their father being often in Paris, where he led the frivolous, unfettered, not very noble life of the nobly born; where in the presence of the young Louis XIII he clicked his heels and bowed low; raised his glass and drank deep; drew his sword in brawls and fracases; and paid his court—that he might win their favor—to obliging ladies of fashion. Such was his frivolousness that, in order to take part in a ballet, he refused an ambassadorship; such was his assiduity, however, that the king made him lieutenant general of a province and, in 1620, elevated him from *comte* to *duc et pair*, the highest of nonroyal titles. But such were the king's tactics that long years went by without the dukedom being registered by the Parlement—in other words, without its being made legal.

François, now the Prince de Marcillac as heir to the unregistered dukedom, was taken by his mother to the Fontenay-le-Comte townhouse, where he was tutored in Latin and mathematics, learned how to fence and dance, probably how to snub, and certainly how to show great pride of rank and to acquire an air of assurance. He further learned that above all stood the Family and that he should strive to make his family, wherever possible, stand above all others. Precedence, at the French court, whether in walking six inches ahead of other people, or in sitting six inches above them at table, or being seated in a slightly larger chair, or being privileged to go through a more widely opened door, was with most members of the nobility an ambition that could verge on obsession: the tricks they played to outwit people in order to outrank them produced some of the most solemn, idiotic farces in the annals of society. And in forwarding their ambitions or frustrating other people's, in indulging their tastes or engineering their revenges, the *noblesse* could be as brutal and cutthroat in manner as they were ridiculous and childish in intent. Nor did the young king set a highbred example—he chiefly liked sports, he also liked to make jam and to market vegetables, or to cut his courtiers' hair, or to imitate the agonized look on the faces of dying men. Moreover, he set no standards of virility: his marriage to Anne of Austria (actually of Spain) went unconsummated for years, and produced no child until, twenty-three years after marriage, the future Louis XIV was born. In addition, as a weak king willing to let someone else rule, Louis XIII had granted the lowborn, fiercely ambitious Cardinal Richelieu more and more power, and more and more opportunities for power, enough to thwart, to threaten, to punish the outraged nobility, and to install lieutenants and sycophants of his own.

Richelieu even set up as royal matchmaker: he wanted Louis XIII's brother, Gaston d'Orléans, to marry an immensely rich royal heiress, Mademoiselle de Montpensier, which the royal bastards and the princes of the blood conspiratorially opposed for personal reasons—such as marrying her themselves. Gaston also opposed it, having been reminded that, should the sickly king die, *he* might marry the queen. Richelieu, getting wind of the plot, got the king to sanction a number of arrests, and then compelled Gaston to marry the heiress, best known as La Grande Mademoiselle. This typical, overbearing procedure of Richelieu's infuriated the adolescent François, and his head spinning with chivalric dreams, he was roused to a great devotion for a member of the conspiracy, the beautiful Duchesse de Chevreuse. In François's future life the villainous prime minister and the beautiful duchess would both play significant roles; as of the moment, François's father, troubled by his son's reveries, decided to marry him off. He was barely fourteen, but the duke contrived a good match that worked out well enough as a marriage. Meanwhile, the young couple were connubially a little confused and a little unsure of each other; but, sent to Paris to live, they had the life of the capital, and its exacting pleasures, to exhilarate and to educate them.

François, with continuing romantic fervor, became devoted to the queen, who loved her dreary, ailing husband and was rewarded with his neglect; her great friend, Madame de Chevreuse, was François's other dream princess, who, at the moment because of the conspiracy, was an exile in Lorraine.

THE LAST WORD

But with Richelieu ensaddled with ship and spurs, François had no future at court and went off to war—the Thirty Years' War—winning a regiment which he clothed, fed, and fee'd: a plundering, scoundrelly gang who used a Christ on the Cross for their target practice. François, having helped fight a battle and been foiled of another, came back from the wars and a year later sold his regiment and resigned his commission. For the first time, it appears, the romantic dreamer had seen some of the horrors of war and the harshness of existence. On returning to Paris, he found that the king's mother, Marie de Médicis, had bade her son choose between Richelieu and herself; that the son had agreed to oust Richelieu but then so strongly changed his mind that the Queen Mother, ordered to a distant country house, had fled the country, never to return. Richelieu became more powerful than before, and one of his victims, as an adherent of Marie de Médicis, was François's father, who was banished to an estate and deprived of his governorship of Poitou. François himself remained at court— at eighteen, a good-looking, well-mannered, witty courtier, but intelligent enough to stray off to the fashionable salons, where he could hear distinguished people converse. His heart and his homage, however, went to the queen, who in return was friendly and unreserved with him; and when Madame de Chevreuse returned from exile, he came to worship her as well and to enter into a charmingly informal friendship. The young Marcillac came to be a good friend also of Mademoiselle de Hauteforte, a very virtuous young girl the king had fallen very virtuously in love with. Soon enough, amid a nest of intrigues and uprisings which Richelieu quashed, the Duchesse de Chevreuse was once again exiled—to a chateau near Paris, where she was caught out being disobedient, and this time exiled at a distance. François acted as courier for secret letters between the queen and her: in her far-off habi-

4

tation, her drawing room little visited, her bedroom un-
shared, she very likely had François share it with her. A little
later he again set off for the wars and, on returning, found
himself banished from court, ostensibly for being indiscreet
about military maneuvers, more credibly for being a friend of
the king's neglected wife and the king's virtuous lady love.
François went to his country place and to *his* neglected wife;
but when a Spanish army invaded France, he joined up, only
to find himself, at the end of the war, banished once again. But
first he managed to see his adored queen, who was violent
about Richelieu and involved in conspiracies. He came away a
knight-errant, carrying a letter from the queen to Madame de
Chevreuse, which he delivered and was suitably thanked for.
But he began to find la Chevreuse rather imperious and
difficult.

Soon after, family matters took a favorable turn: his father's
dukedom was formalized, and the ban for both father and son
on living at court was lifted. But now the queen was treason-
ably implicated when a letter of hers to Madame de Chevreuse
was intercepted. François professed his loyalty, but it was by
Mademoiselle de Hauteforte that her treasonable Majesty
was saved. The king forgave the queen by humiliating her;
yet soon after, being forced one night to share her bed if he
was to have a bed at all, he begot *le Roi-Soleil*-to-be.

Marcillac, charged by the queen with keeping Madame de
Chevreuse informed of various matters, was warned by his
father that every step he took was charted, and that he would
be in trouble if he did not shun the duchess. Taking a first
step in prudence, François arranged to have his information
delivered at second hand. But a scared Duchesse de Chevreuse, successfully fleeing in male disguise to Spain, and
making use of François on the way, got him sufficiently involved in the general hue and cry to be sent by Richelieu to

the Bastille. When released, he got involved with having la Chevreuse's jewels in his keeping, and was so fed up with the lady that he refused to deliver her letters to the queen. Meanwhile, the queen was showing less affection toward *him* and made him refuse a good military post. Retiring to his chateau, he exchanged the sword for the pen and—one way of starting a literary career—drew up a document arguing that the La Rochefoucauld dukedom should by rights stand before, not lag behind, two other dukedoms. When, a year or two later, the king's dashing young companion, Cinq-Mars—along with the king's brother, the queen, and other highborn figures —plotted against Richelieu, François refused to be drawn in. Richelieu quashed the conspiracy and soon after, he died. He had been the great obstruction to François's ambitions, but in his *Memoirs* François himself acknowledges that Richelieu's masterly planning as prime minister and adroit execution of his plans worked great good for France.

Five months later Louis XIII died. His forty-two-year-old queen, ruling with the advice of a council, would now become regent for the four-year-old Louis XIV; and François, long the queen's knight-errant, hoped he might notably prosper. The Queen Regent was far from universally popular, and was surrounded by very ambitious, royal-blooded grandees— Condés, Vendômes, and Louis XIII's brother, Gaston. But at her right hand she had a former protégé of Richelieu's, the handsome, Italian-born Giulio Mazarini, whom Richelieu, a year before his death, had turned into Cardinal Mazarin and into prime minister of France. Mazarin, unlike Richelieu, was gentle, courteous, self-depreciatory, with tactics so velvety as to muffle his stratagems and to be looked on with scorn. He himself lived up to one of La Rochefoucauld's most-quoted aphorisms—indeed he may have inspired it: "It is exceedingly clever to know how to hide your cleverness." The queen's friends were at once Mazarin's friends, and he clearly strove to become her greatest friend of all. That they in later days became lovers seems very probable; that they secretly became husband and wife is rather in doubt. Meanwhile, with Mazarin playing Her Majesty's servant, they became stanch, co-governing allies. Very deferential to François, Mazarin was in no way any help to him. And the queen was far from the kindly self she had once been, all too often finding things to reproach François with, and reasons to withhold the honors he had been promised. She also ordered him to break with Madame de Chevreuse—by now the queen's enemy— and to seek the friendship of Mazarin. And though François may not have involved himself in the plots against her or Mazarin, neither was he altogether guiltless. By way of those plots, moreover, Mazarin strengthened his position and François was left more or less out in the cold, enough to be looked askance at by people at court. Beginning now to distrust others, he was distrusted in turn. As part of a world it would be hard to surpass in emulousness and treachery—with the polish the mere hilt of the *poignard*—François was learning its import and discovering its tactics but not yet practicing what he would someday preach, or eschewing what he would some day condemn.

Cold-shouldered at court, he turned to the salon—the famous Madame de Rambouillet's—for company. Here were gathered the *précieux*, who sought to refine speech, to elevate manners, to liberate women and enlarge their role. The members quite soon created a too-utterly-utter preciosity which Molière satirically pounced on: people fainted because a dog was naked, people collapsed because someone's grammar was faulty. Still, they had cultivated interests: discoursed on the arts, listened to music, wrote maxims. Finding this attractive, François also wrote maxims. By now his romanticism had dried up, and love was for him a game or an art, with its various forms to be differentiated and defined. "No disguise," to quote a few from his lifetime's hoard, "can long conceal love where it exists, or long feign it where it is lacking." "What keeps lovers and mistresses from tiring of being together is that they talk of nothing but themselves." "There are successful marriages but no blissful ones." "What counts least of all in conventional love-making is love." And finally: "When we are weary of love, we welcome infidelity: it absolves us of having to be faithful ourselves." Though pursuing culture in Madame de Rambouillet's drawing room, François indulged elsewhere in rakish amours and courtly misconduct—exploits neither constituting happiness nor conducive to it, exploits that intensified disillusionment and led to self-disgust.

Presently, ambition linking arms with amour, François was seized with the desire to become the lover of a great beauty who bore a very great name: the proud Duchesse de Longueville. Born a Condé, she came of a tremendously devoted family and was married to a man twenty-four years her elder. But François's desire was not easy to attain, for the lady's friendship, not to say her favor, was widely besought. But he had rendered Madame de Longueville a service, which doubtless proved of advantage at the outset of his courtship; his courtliness, worldliness, and wit doubtless counted even more: and though no date can be put upon it, François's desire was gratified.

In time the liaison became known to everyone except the Duc de Longueville, and appeared to be a happy one. Yet love, in such an age and between two such people, far from conquering all, set going other goals. François and the duchess were both immensely ambitious, but at different altitudes. She was very proud and very grand; she was drawn to intrigue and intent on domination. Born close to the throne, the Condés endlessly eyed it. François, with merely minor credentials, eyed, for his wife, a *tabouret*—the right to sit in the presence of the queen. Indeed, he sought this *of* the queen: both she and Mazarin were friendly about it, but extremely vague, and at length gave six other wives footstools, but not François's.

At the level of the Condés, the objective was not winning footstools, but waging wars. The famous warrior—the "Great Condé"—was loyal to the queen, but his *intrigante* sister, Madame de Longueville, rather lusted after rebellion and got François to join her. This brings us to the conspiratorial, sanguinary years of the Fronde—of the rebellious opposition to Mazarin and the court—with its mass of incident, its back-stabbings and reshufflings, its petty complications and large gambles, which not even the most aphoristic style could sufficiently condense. In the course of it François—who also in the course of it became Duc de La Rochefoucauld—tended to reverse roles and shift ground. He joined Madame de Longueville, who was pregnant with his child, in a cabal to overthrow Mazarin and the regency. When at the outset of action Mazarin, the queen, and the boy king fled, Madame de Longueville's two brothers went with them, as did her husband; and when the Parlement, and rebellious nobles like Madame de Longueville, took over Paris, François was deputed to bring her husband and brothers back into the cabal. For such *lèse-majesté* François, should he fail of his mission, might forfeit his head. He won back the duchess's husband and her weaker brother, but not the Great Condé, who in fact surrounded Paris with his troops, in an attempt to starve it out. François, despite his efforts, won no high place among the rebels; later, by being badly wounded, he may well have escaped a grim indictment. Peace was made between Mazarin and the Parlement, Mazarin giving in to certain highborn demands (among them, giving François back the La Rochefoucauld governorship of Poitou) but continuing as prime minister.

Soon there were new intrigues, with once more a role for François. Once more his duchess was a kind of ringleader, this time with her great brother siding with her, but with new figures, including the Duchesse de Chevreuse, against them. Condé was tricked by Mazarin into getting arrested and, along with his brother and the Duc de Longueville, was imprisoned in a fortress. Warned that he must flee, François rushed to the duchess and they fled together: repulsed at Rouen, refused an audience at Le Havre, the duchess finally took to the sea, while François went to Poitou, where he found his father dying. But François had no sooner become a duke than he learned he was charged with *lèse-majesté* and might die on the scaffold. He continued active, sharing the command of a rebel army that took over Bordeaux, only to be attacked by the royal army and defeated. The royal army had succeeded generally in the west of France; but elsewhere the warriors were ready to shift from Mazarin's side to Condé's. To La Rochefoucauld, the wiser procedure was to make peace between Mazarin and Condé, but getting no support for this, he accepted the proposed plan. There was by now a great cry to release the Condés and Longueville from prison and a reaction against Mazarin so intense that he took flight. But La Rochefoucauld, on the way to have the prisoners released, came upon them at dinner in a chateau: armed with an order from the queen, Mazarin had got them released before him.

Condé, returning to Paris, was huzza'd as a hero and, with Mazarin fleeing and the queen in a fright, was in a position to seize the reins. But, far more warrior than statesman, he vacillated; and when the Frondeurs proposed a *people's* revolt against the queen, he sniffed that he had no experience of fighting with chamber pots. Madame de Longueville, having come back to Paris with Condé, was reunited with La Rochefoucauld, but this time with a lover fed up with politics and war, and rather resentful of his arrogant, war-loving mistress. She now urged Condé, whom the Frondeurs were hostile to, to lead a civil-war rebellion, which La Rochefoucauld opposed but could not come out against; and Condé, fearful of arrest and assassination, went to his chateau, summoning a Madame de Longueville who was all for action and a La Rochefoucauld who favored a settlement with the queen. La Rochefoucauld fiddle-faddled to no effect; Condé, very grand and scornful, returned to Paris and, with La Rochefoucauld's support, made accusations in the Parlement against the future Cardinal de Retz. La Rochefoucauld then idiotically pinioned the cardinal in a doorway and unsuccessfully ordered him murdered—a piece of bravura that rebounded harshly against him. Out of favor, Condé skipped attendance at Louis XIV's thirteen-year-old "coming of age," having his brother and François represent him, and then ordering them both to join him at the Condé fortress near Bourges. There, where Madame de Longueville had arrived earlier, the four of them—debating the choice between reconciliation with the court and rebellion against it—chose, thanks to Madame de Longueville's ambitions, rebellion. Thus ensued the third and last embroilment of the Fronde, full of the same political intrigues, military mistakes, and human mischances, La Rochefoucauld in the course of it breaking with a Madame de Longueville who had disparaged him behind his back and found other lovers. A badly off Condé finally sought peace, agreeing that Mazarin should return to power in exchange for handsome compensations, which La Rochefoucauld would share in. Matters dragged on, Condé lost popular favor, it came again to arms and bloodshed, with the great Condé opposed by the great Turenne, with the great Condé just saved from defeat, and with François suffering a face wound that left him half blind. Thus François's career as courtier and conspirator, as soldier and seeker after power came— when he was forty years old—to a disappointed end. When the king proposed an amnesty to the rebels, La Rochefoucauld haughtily refused it and was again found guilty of *lèse-majesté*; but Mazarin eventually smothered the verdict and restored François's estates. The war struggled to a conclusion, with Condé decamping to Spain to command its legions against his native France.

Though thwarted in his ambitions, La Rochefoucauld had enjoyed the entrée into the great world at its most splendid, most tumultuous, most perilous and deceitful. He had been the young friend of the queen, the lover of two influential great ladies, the companion of a great general. He had gained certain honors and rewards; he had felt the knout of one tremendous prime minister and had crossed swords with another; he had stood in the shadow of the scaffold, but, more than once, had also glimpsed the Promised Land. This see-sawing career that was thought to have produced a thorough cynic had in itself—as it changed color and acquired scars and shed ideals—been opulently cinematic. The rest of La Rochefoucauld's life was to be spent in comparative retirement, but not without social activity and not, it would seem, without amorous rewards. During the first years François spent much time at his country house, became the father of an eighth and final child, took to reading the classical moralists, reflected on mankind, scrutinized himself, and set about writing his memoirs. In them he revisited his early life, his earlier, knightlier self, and moved on from gallantry and amour to the days of the Fronde and the downfall of the nobility's ambitions. On all this he moralized; over all this—along with his disillusioned comments—he spread a defensive glaze: like most autobiography, his is a form of apologia. After a while he went back, unmenaced, to Paris, saw his old friends and his old mistress, Ninon de Lenclos, paid considerable court to the visiting Queen of Sweden, frequented the salon of Mademoiselle de Scudéry, where the assembled guests played literary games and wrote their own portraits. As the years went by, he was forgiven his past: Mazarin got him a pension, the king awarded him an honor. He became a habitué of the famous salon of Madame de Sablé, who so feared infection that her guests had to submit to an examination on arriving. Once admitted, the guests among other things put together and pulled apart proverbs and epigrams, and La Rochefoucauld composed, revised, and polished many of his own. In 1663 appeared a book of pirated and anonymous maxims, including some two hundred of La Rochefoucauld's; he set matters straight by issuing some three hundred on his own initiative. But though he was by now famous for his aphorisms, the notable last chapter—his relationship with Madame de La Fayette—still lay ahead.

This lady, the intimate friend of Madame de Sévigné and the author of the still greatly esteemed *La Princesse de Clèves*, was married to a dullard peer, was never financially well off, and had perforce to be something of a climber. She managed in time to attract La Rochefoucauld to her house, her brilliance attracted him to come again and again, each satisfied a need in the other, and their friendship led to much gossip and eventual celebrity. Whether it went beyond friendship remains, now as long ago, unanswered; but whatever its nature, it was important to La Rochefoucauld. After going briefly to war at the age of fifty-three—still seeking glory? still com-

bating cynicism?—he came back, listlessly, to Madame de La
Fayette, who in a sense took care of him; he mingled with
old friends and old enemies; he tried in vain to be the
Dauphin's tutor; he had a hand in the writing, or rewriting,
of Madame de La Fayette's immediately successful *Princesse*
(someone, while praising their collaboration, remarked that
they were no longer able to do anything else together). La
Rochefoucauld's unsung faithful wife, to whom he was endlessly unfaithful and about whom he is virtually silent, died
in 1670; his mother, whom he loved, died soon after; his
children, except for his oldest son—and heir—he largely
neglected. He composed new maxims and reworked the old
ones, and as further editions appeared, his fame increased.
In 1680, when he was sixty-six, he died. The "widowed"
Madame de La Fayette mourned him deeply; by La Rochefoucauld's cynical aphoristic lights, no doubt she did so for
self-regardful reasons.

If we read La Rochefoucauld's *Maxims* knowing virtually
nothing of his life, one of our strongest reactions is how
detached, indeed how clinical, we find them; even granting
the objective nature of aphorisms, his seem as much de-
personalized in origin as in effect. Their overwhelming
burden, of course, is how vain, foolish, faithless, envious,
selfish, and ambitious men and women can be—the findings,
it appears, of a reflective, observant student who sees the
dross and dirt of mankind that underlie its trappings and
glitter. Even so, we are surprised to find here so much that
smacks of dross and dirt coupled with so much that seems
cut in marble. It is only when we have come to know La
Rochefoucauld's life—or, more accurately, his life and times
—that we realize how much of what he says is not just the
offshoot of observation and reflection; is, indeed, the fruit of

intimate experience. Aware that he was a duke, we might have assumed that he had seen, and even minutely studied, the ways of the great world: its ambitions, its hypocrisies, its deceits, and had fitted them to his own strong sense of human failings. But once we are conscious of the role he played in that way of life and of all its temptations and corruptions, we cannot but regard the *Maxims* as something of a mirror as well as a microscope; we cannot but see, in La Rochefoucauld's reaching a verdict on mankind (as he knew it), that his own motives and rationalizations provide a very substantial part of the evidence.

His intense disillusionment was, of course, partly the classic reaction to his early idealism; but the very idealism—call it romantic and naïve—contained a strong element of selfish dreaming; of becoming, in chivalrous fashion, beloved, be-medaled, exalted. Our ideals, La Rochefoucauld *might* have said, are seldom at variance with our ambitions. But romantically *and* realistically, he seems embittered by how little life bore out what he had conceived it to be. And, following him through all the years that he participated in court life, political life, military life—not just participated, but plotted; not just strove, but double-dealt—we see how he came to use the treacherous tactics of the world he strove in as both weapons to defeat others and armor for himself. In this there was inevitably a good deal of the dyer's hand being subdued to what it works in; of worldly values born of a worldling life. Morris Bishop, to whose biography of La Rochefoucauld I am much indebted, sees the *Maxims*, indeed, as an autobiographical confession wherein La Rochefoucauld, with grand impersonality, Told All. Certainly, I think, we must see in them something of self-indictment bred of self-searching, as well as an indictment of mankind bred of perception and experience.

We must emphasize *perception* here, for though La Roche-foucauld's disillusion and cynicism are intense, and though he made vanity and self-interest the basis for almost all our thought and action, he was never the mere propagandist, or extremist, for this contention. He was the careful, shrewd psychologist, piercing below the bland or deceptive surface; puncturing the glib, factitious explanation; rooting out what underlies the seemingly kind deed or benevolent gesture, until he demonstrated that not just all our bad quali-ties stem from vanity and self-interest, but so, in a disguised form, do our good qualities as well. Here indeed, and twice over, stands forth La Rochefoucauld's great distinction: for not only is he a notable psychologist (one who in some ways anticipated the Freudians) but he is, among aphorists, really the first. Before him there were countless pithy sayings, pro-verbial and philosophic truths, and sound popular generali-ties; but no systematic examination of men's motives and maneuvers, and of their efforts to conceal them—whether from the world or from themselves.

La Rochefoucauld's investigation, augmented by his ex-perience, becomes a massive assault on what we are ashamed of or touchy about, but hardly less on what we are proud of and praise ourselves for. Let us hear him on men's mere mis-demeanors: "If we resist our passions, it is oftener because they are weak than because we are strong." Again: "We confess to small faults to create the impression that we have no great ones." Once more: "Virtue would not go nearly so far if vanity did not keep it company." We may question comments like these in bulk, but we cannot quite shrug them off. And we can hardly question one of the most famous, and doubtless most cynical, of La Rochefoucauld's maxims: "We all have strength enough to endure the misfortunes of others." And here, though a little too cynical, La Rochefoucauld is, about "most men," psychologically sound: "Love of justice, in most men, is only a fear of encountering injustice."

We can, of course, defend or exonerate ourselves from a good many of his accusations by laying stress on the milieu in which he works—the privileged, peremptory court life, its pleasure-loving pursuits, its need—for self-preservation as well as self-interest—to deceive and to betray; its fear of ridicule, of punishment, of disgrace. And it is true that life, even for dukes, under a relentless Richelieu, or a superlatively slippery Mazarin, or a *l'état-c'est-moi* Louis XIV, had its constant threats and terrors.* All the same, by way of ambitions and intrigues, there are analogies enough between seventeenth-century courts and twentieth-century corporations, between suppliant, sycophant courtiers and hideously competitive rat races. The upper levels, for example, of the television industry often suggest a Richelieu-like kindliness or a Mazarin-like candor. But from a great many of La Rochefoucauld's contentions about our vanity, our self-interest, our self-deceptions, we cannot claim exclusion, though the prick of conscience, the sense of decency, and our very special twentieth-century guilt feelings act as an un-La Rochefoucauldian restraint. And at times La Rochefoucauld, in his cynicism, clearly goes astray; in his obsession, goes too far. The psychologist's microscope becomes a crude magnifying

---

* It is, I think, worth mentioning just how La Rochefoucauld differs from his fellow duke of genius, Saint-Simon, whose vast *Mémoires*, written two generations later, bear out in their panoramic view of life under Louis XIV so much that La Rochefoucauld distills into his maxims. Beyond the distinct difference in style—Saint-Simon being as pungently slapdash as La Rochefoucauld is scrupulously polished—there is the curious fact that, where La Rochefoucauld was a decided participant in all forms of the high life of his times, his approach seems that of a detached observer; while Saint-Simon, foiled of any significant participation, and playing the ubiquitous busybody, eavesdropper, and detective, brought the world of Louis XIV intimately and unforgettably alive—a life in which every reader tremendously participates.

glass, the aphorisms become commonplaces or the merest verbiage. But when the psychologist is predominant and we tend to dispute or doubt him, we do well to ask ourselves whether our own vanity or self-interest doesn't motivate our objection or influence our judgment. One very important thing more must be said of La Rochefoucauld: beyond the worldling participant, the keen observer, the acute psychologist, he is—in his aphorisms—a great lapidary artist, a polished master of style.

Aphorisms

Self-interest speaks all sorts of languages and plays all sorts of roles, even that of disinterestedness.

Self-love is the greatest of all flatterers.

It is a form of coquetry to emphasize the fact that you do not indulge in it.

We make promises to the extent that we hope, and keep them to the extent that we fear.

We are more often treacherous through weakness than through calculation.

LA ROCHEFOUCAULD

Old men love to give good advice to console themselves for not being able to set bad examples.

We are never so ridiculous for the qualities we have as for those we pretend to.

To establish oneself in the world, one does all one can to seem established there already.

We behave politely to be treated politely, and to be considered polite.

Flattery is counterfeit money which, but for vanity, would have no circulation.

Pride does not wish to owe and vanity does not wish to pay.

We refuse praise from a desire to be praised twice.

As for women who spend their lives making love, making love is the least of their faults.

Hypocrisy is the homage that vice offers to virtue.

There are bad people who would be less dangerous if they had no good in them.

THE LAST WORD

Why is our memory good enough to recall to the last detail things that have happened to us, yet not good enough to recall how often we have told them to the same person?

Weakness, not vice, is virtue's worst enemy.

It takes greater character to carry off good fortune than bad.

How can we expect someone else to keep our secret if we cannot keep it ourselves?

II

The Marquis of Halifax

GEORGE SAVILE, first Marquis of Halifax, occupies in the world of politics a substantial yet rather singular place, one which gained him influence and admiration, distrust and dislike, and has left him a somewhat disputed and ambiguous figure, thanks in part to his self-made alliance with an ambiguous role, that of "Trimmer." His career, like La Rochefoucauld's in France, involved him—though with much more significance—in the countless intrigues, tergiversations, and upheavals of seventeenth-century England; his nature, like the later La Rochefoucauld's, was skeptical and unillusioned, and his commentary often stinging and tart. But he can boast a solid role in history, where La Rochefoucauld is a recurrent and picturesque minor character; and Halifax's aphorisms— as pointed as La Rochefoucauld's, and mostly as well put —can be biting without being embittered, and full of practical wisdom and veteran worldliness.

Born in 1633, he came of an old Yorkshire family that had grown rich and made profitable marriages. His father, Sir William Savile, who took up arms on the Royalist side during the Civil War, died when George, who succeeded him as fourth baronet, was ten. George's education, supervised by his mother, was neither very English nor very extensive, and acquired mostly through tutoring and travel—Angers, Leghorn, Naples; and Rome, where he may have remained until close to his coming of age, at which time, unlike most Royalists, he became a very rich man. At twenty-three he married into another established and Royalist family: his wife was a Spencer and a daughter of the Earl of Sunderland; his charming mother-in-law, born a Sidney, had been the celebrated Sacharissa of the poet Waller. At the start of his career, in 1660, Sir George represented Pontefract in the Convention Parliament, this his only appearance in the House of Commons. In the years immediately following, when his wife bore him several children, he began an "orderly and splendid way of living," at his country place at Rufford in Nottinghamshire. By his gifts of intellect and conversation he attracted attention; he attached himself politically to the brilliant, courtly, profligate Duke of Buckingham, thanks to which he won, largely by association, the name of atheist. (Accused of atheism in later years, he answered that "he believed as much as he could, and he hoped God would not lay it to his charge that he could not digest iron, as an ostrich did." On the other hand, when Halifax spoke of Charles II as the head of the church he belonged to, Charles replied that "he did not desire to be the head of Nothing.") Sir George must have benefited from the knowledge and experience of his mother's statesmanlike brother, Sir William Coventry, through whom he got to know—"and sumptuously entertain"—the king's brother, the future James II, who in turn sought, of Charles II, a peerage for Sir George. The peerage was not bestowed, however, until 1668, when Sir George was appointed by the House of Commons a commissioner to investigate the scandalous expenditures of Charles's regime: to propitiate him, he was created Baron Savile of Eland, and Viscount Halifax. Though the new viscount made light of titles and other honors, he far from disdained them: "When he talked to me as a philosopher," wrote the famous Bishop Burnet long after, "of his contempt of the world, I asked him what he meant by getting so many new titles, which I called the hanging himself about with bells and tinsel. He had no other excuse for it but that since the world were such fools as to value these matters, a man must be a fool for company"—adding that "titles might be of use to his family." Halifax, like La Rochefoucauld, had a strong, ingrained sense of family and of wishing to advance it.

His peerage had a real importance, however, for giving him a seat in the House of Lords and a voice in political matters. For the first few years he played no palpable speaking part in the Lords; but the 1670's in England would bring on crises, conspiracies, and wars of various sorts, to arouse in Halifax various reactions and allegiances. During those years Charles II—no mere fribble and witty rake, but a shrewd, brilliant, and treacherous monarch—though officially allied by the Triple Alliance with Holland, was actually taking bribes that called for betrayals, from Louis XIV. In return for Charles's promoting the safety and welfare of Roman Catholics, and sometimes of France, Louis agreed to pay most of Charles's bills. Hence England was virtually fighting Holland while fighting on her side, and France was her ally while officially her enemy. Charles's illegal Declaration of Indulgence to all nonconformists, Roman Catholic or Protestant, and his violation of the Triple Alliance, was unpopular with the nation and violently resented by Halifax. When the decidedly Anglican Commons reared up, Halifax and other opponents of the king were—as a sop to gain their support—admitted to the Privy Council. Halifax was also sent to France to congratulate Louis XIV on the birth of an illegitimate son, and perhaps sound out the king about a peace settlement with Holland;

but on reaching Louis at Utrecht, Halifax found that two other English envoys, though sent later than he was to negotiate, had got first to the king. Having been opposed to the terms of his mission, which prevented any possible peace, Halifax was saved from agreeing to them, and probably also from public censure. A widower by now, in this same year he remarried.

Charles's Declaration of Indulgence, so far as it might ease Catholics, raised great Parliamentary opposition, Halifax's included. On this and other grounds, such as his acute criticism of Charles's famous Cabal, Halifax won the king's strong dislike. But, time passing, Halifax gained considerable influence in the House of Lords; refused, according to Bishop Burnet, to be secretary of state; and was also spoken of for the vice-royalty of Ireland; and when Charles, under pressure, made Halifax a member of a new Council of Thirty, his urbane manners and his wit won over the king, who kept him often about him, put him on an important council committee, and raised him from viscount to earl.

If the shifting 1670's had brought Halifax into the political arena and in direct contact with kings and counsellors, the tumultuous 1680's were to set him among the leaders in prestige and influence and—almost as important—in enmities and conflicts. Though happy about the king, who was ailing, he was far from happy about the king's possible successors. Thus one of them, Charles's brother James, was a Roman Catholic and viciously pro-France, two things to which Halifax was extremely hostile; and another of them, Charles's illegitimate, much-loved son, the Duke of Monmouth, was a reckless Protestant extremist toward whom Halifax was more hostile still. The best hope for the future was Charles's nephew, William of Orange, who had married James's daughter Mary and who violently hated France, with which Charles was once again constantly conspiring. James's *hereditary* claim to succeed his brother was unquestionable, but an anti-Catholic Parliament was ready to exclude him from the succession. Indeed, the House of Commons voted to exclude him, and the House of Lords was decidedly of a mind to; but Halifax, feeling this was going too far and might inspire a French-financed rebellion, fought exclusion in a tremendous, prolonged, enormously eloquent combat with his Parliamentary enemy, Lord Shaftesbury, and finally got the Exclusion Bill defeated. "Old men," wrote Macaulay, "who lived to admire the eloquence of Pulteney in its meridian, and that of Pitt in its splendid dawn, still murmured that they had heard nothing like the great speech of Lord Halifax on the Exclusion Bill." A more contemporary and pro-Exclusion writer defined Halifax as "the King's favorite, and *hated* more than ever the Lord Treasurer was, and has really deserved it . . . for he has undone all." Halifax himself confessed that "I must . . . cast about for a new set of friends, for my old ones have . . . thought it as meritorious to persecute me as others believed it excusable to desert me."

Halifax's later efforts to restrict James's powers, should he come to the throne, could not atone for his defeating the bill, and in fact got him accused of popery. He went briefly into political retirement but returned, favored more than ever by the king and gaining more prestige among his fellows. He now tried to win James back to Protestantism, and to win over Monmouth, who was anything but well-disposed toward Halifax and had vaguely challenged him to a duel. But—a portent in the form of a prank—in February 1682 funeral tickets were distributed among the nobility, desiring them to send their coaches and six to "accompany the body of George, Earl of Halifax, out of town." And indeed, though that summer he was elevated to Marquis of Halifax, and that autumn was made Lord Privy Seal, then a very high office, his hold on power now became loosened, while that of James, who had returned from a Scottish exile, was much increased. Halifax sought to counter this by way of Monmouth, who was now in hiding, only for James to counter things in turn and leave Monmouth out in the cold. Halifax equally lost out across the Channel, in asking action against Louis XIV's seizure of Luxembourg and Strasbourg: France's answer was an attempted bribe. Unsuccessful on the Continent, Halifax now accused James's brother-in-law, Lord Rochester, of corruption at the Treasury. James saved Rochester by having him lifted out of an important post into a largely high-sounding one, about which Halifax coined a famous phrase that suggests the twentieth century, not the seventeenth: Rochester, he said, had been kicked upstairs.

Though outmaneuvered by James, Halifax was not out of favor with the king: during the next months Halifax circulated his famous "Character of a Trimmer," giving the word, not its later sense of expediently shuttling back and forth to the best advantage, but its nautical sense of keeping a boat on an even keel; this while aiming the publication's message —that Charles should shake himself free of his brother—at the king. Whatever Charles's reaction may have been, he agreed—following Halifax's new plan—to call back Monmouth from banishment and to banish James to Scotland. This, very possibly a high-water mark in both influence and advancement for Halifax, was overturned by the sudden illness and death of Charles, who took the Catholic sacrament on his deathbed, and whose crown passed to James. Indeed, fifteen minutes after Charles's death James met the Privy Council to be recognized as king.

Halifax was not turned out of doors; actually James told him that the past would be forgotten "except the service which you did me in the debate on the Exclusion Bill." But elsewhere James spoke of Halifax as one of his "most dangerous enemies," and the future was not inviting. Halifax himself was now kicked upstairs and, when he opposed the repeal of the Test Act (for disqualifying Catholics from office) and of the Habeas Corpus Act (whereby troublemakers could be left to languish in prison), he was kicked downstairs. Going into retirement at Rufford, he wrote, and published anonymously, his "Letter to a Dissenter," rather successfully warning Protestant nonconformists against accepting an indulgence intended for Catholics; and he now wrote encouragingly to William of Orange, saying that James, by his tactics and indulgences, must do himself in, and his daughter Mary—William's wife—must take over as next in the succession. As time went on, James asserted his Catholicism not least by giving Catholics all possible rights and offices— "he would be served by none," he let it be known, "but those that would be for the repeal of the Tests." With the help of the infamous Judge Jeffries, he took harsh measures against his opponents and prorogued a Parliament that would never sit again. William of Orange by now filled the minds of Protestant leaders and roused them to start making plans, with Dutch envoys falling into step. But, though sympathetic with much of this, Halifax curiously refused to commit himself, would have no commerce with the Dutch envoys, was opposed to the maturing invasion plan, and was indeed not one of the distinguished group of peers who, at the end of June 1688, signed a cool, dispassionate invitation asking William to intervene. Halifax's indecision, or dissenting decision, is the more uncharacteristic because William represented a *via media* to supplant James's bigoted extremism. Possibly a constitutional-minded Halifax was against *deposing* James, however much he favored divesting him of all power;

possibly he was fearful that what turned out to be a bloodless revolution might prove an extremely bloody one.

When William with his army was ready to sail, James tried to conciliate Halifax; and Halifax declared, the day before William landed in England, that he had had no part in the invitation William had been sent. Halifax was accordingly one of three statesmen whom James sent to see William, with a mind to working out a compromise (though James had already decided to decamp); and his running away, in the face of possible successful mediation by Halifax, virtually put an end to any feeling of obligation on Halifax's part. Indeed, when the fugitive James returned to London, Halifax was one of the three men who sternly confronted him and sharply refuted his remonstrances. And when, a few days later, William summoned England's peers, Halifax was chosen to be their chairman. James now fled, for good and all, to France, and at the ensuing Convention Parliament, Halifax was not only chosen speaker but successfully fought both a proposed regency and a giving James's daughter Mary the crown, in favor of offering it jointly to William and Mary (the only terms on which William would serve). It was Halifax, again, who at the Banqueting House in Whitehall proffered the crown to William and Mary. In view of all this, there is support for Macaulay's opinion that, so far as the Revolution of 1688 bore the character of a single mind, it bore the "large yet cautious" mind of Halifax.

The day after Halifax presented the crown, he was made Lord Privy Seal, and thereafter was on confidential terms with William. But, though he had his adherents and admirers, he was attacked on one ground or another by rival and hostile persons and parties, and hounded for past sins; and after a year's service he resigned the Privy Seal and was later thrown off the Privy Council on the score that he almost never attended it. Retiring to a newer country house nearer London, he published pamphlets, essays, and his anonymous "Maxims of State" (his larger *Political, Moral and Miscellaneous Thoughts and Reflexions* was not published till long after his death). He continued, however, to attend the House of Lords, voting, among other things, against renewing the censorship of the press, and being frequently in opposition, so that when dukedoms were being conferred on Administration supporters, he was left out. By then he was in failing health, with perhaps a certain falling off of intellectual power. He died, having taken the Anglican sacrament, at his house in St. James's Square in April 1695. He was buried in Westminster Abbey, which, asserts his biographer, was simply "the usual place of retirement for dwellers in St. James's Square."

Although it is impossible to read of any phase of late seventeenth-century English history without coming on references to Halifax or to his playing a significant role, he has not, as a statesman, survived in the public memory as have most of his equals, or some of his inferiors. In much the same way, though Halifax must figure in any list of accomplished English pamphleteers, and figure very prominently in any list of distinguished English aphorists, of such aphorists he is perhaps the least well-known—indeed, the only modern volume of his works has long been out of print. Yet Halifax's relative obscurity in both fields is not too hard to understand. Although in terms of *career* he was a principal actor in the political life of his time, he seldom spoke or acted, or advocated or achieved, in a way to intrigue or excite posterity. He was part of England's most treacherous and turbulent era, one not given to noble causes or heroic aims; and where he proved chiefly valuable—in opposition—he stood for virtues that rouse no one's imagination: for moderation and sanity, rather than for magnanimity and valor. Moreover, he was a shadowy rather than glittering figure, yet not quite shadowy enough to have a sinister or serpentine fascination. Nor, unlike another aristocratic and urbane worldling, Queen Victoria's Lord Melbourne, was Halifax allotted so winningly paternal and sagaciously political a role in relation to his sovereigns. Finally, what in part is his own doing, he has been too little-known through being too well-known as a "trimmer"—a rather fatal designation, having about it none of the aura of courage or the bravura of crime. As for Halifax as aphorist, though he certainly read and must have been influenced by La Rochefoucauld, he is less shocking and subversive, and less of a pioneer. La Rochefoucauld, for all his detachment, is a kind of dramatist of cynicism and self-love, where Halifax is a realistic man of the world whose aphorisms offer a course in practical wisdom—the pitfalls of high life, the perils of politics, with, added, a touch of Poor Richard and a taint of King Charles. When we come to know La Rochefoucauld's biography, we grasp the embittered disillusionment beneath the impersonality of his maxims; when we come to know Halifax's, we find a certain dovetailing of preachment and practice. Being an experienced participant and an acute observer, he is no probing psychologist; he nowhere looks forward to Freud but sometimes harks back to his favorite Montaigne. Compared to La Rochefoucauld, he displays fewer "insights"—the great chic word of our era; but more wisdom, *his* era's great need.

As we do not fully "understand" so shadowy a man, so we do not greatly identify with him, with either the great representative of a powerful aristocracy or the great but not always resolute member of the opposition. His apologia for the Trimmer is an assertion of the middle way, a repudiation of extremism and excess, indeed a somewhat wishful vision of a sane and sound England. He argues that "our climate is a trimmer, between that part of the world where men are roasted, and the other where they are frozen"; that "our Church is a trimmer between the phrenzy of platonick visions and the lethargic ignorance of Popish dreams"; that "our laws are trimmers, between the excess of unbounded power and the extravagance of liberty not enough restrained." He argues that "true virtue hath ever been thought a trimmer, and to have its dwelling in the middle between two extremes"; that even "God Almighty himself is divided between his two great attributes, his mercy and his justice." This, if purely visionary as fact, is with Halifax temperamentally fundamental, indeed temperamentally insistent. Moreover, it had decided timeliness in an age when extremism and fanaticism assumed treacherous, ruthless, venomous shapes—an age when the Popish Plot let a vile Titus Oates merely accuse—to see condemned—all manner of Papist "suspects"; and when, after the Rye House Plot, matters were reversed and notable Protestants like Lord Russell and Algernon Sidney were beheaded. In politics and elsewhere, Halifax doubtless favored enlightened or temperate compromise over intransigent or unwieldy principles, and on occasion he doubtless sided with his ambitions as well as his temperament. He had, in any case, "fought the Whigs against perjured testimony for the life of Stafford, and . . . the Crown and the Tories against packed juries for the lives of Russell and Sidney"; and was no kin to the Vicar of Bray, no quick-change adherent of those in power. The belief in moderation which underlay his view of things aroused, in an age of bigots and careerists, extremely immoderate hostility: he was an often feared and an often hated man. In temperament he seems born out of his time; he would seem far more to fit the coming century which bespoke reason, an urbane worldliness, and a middle way. But in that century's emblematic Lord Chesterfield, Halifax did have a surrogate, for Lord Chesterfield was his grandson. Chesterfield, however, shows more enamel than Halifax and less iron; and where Halifax once gave good if prolonged advice to his daughter, Lord Chesterfield gave unending, indeed nagging and occasionally nonsensical, advice to his son.

As a born skeptical worldling, Halifax writes much less out of disenchantment than out of ripe understanding and educative experience. He knows the way of the world and he instructs his daughter, in his *The Lady's New-Year's-Gift*, how to bend before it, fall in line with it, guard against it: all this is much more to save her from harm than to assure her of happiness. Here and there he may seem too cynical, or in his comment on such matters as having a "Drunken Husband" seem rather comic, or now and then he may go in for all-too-familiar sermonizing. But his is good advice so far as it treats of a not very good world, and even better advice so far as it treats, *in* such a world, of women. Thus, among many injunctions: "A wife is to thank God her husband hath faults . . . a husband without faults is a dangerous observer." But the mentor softens into a father, affectionate and a little bereft, when he writes in anticipation of his daughter's marriage:

The tenderness we have had for you, my dear, is of another nature, peculiar to kind parents, and differing from that which you will meet with first in any family into which you shall be transplanted; and yet they may be very kind too, and afford no justifiable reason to you to complain. You must not be frightened with the first appearances of a differing scene; for when you are used to it, you may like the house you go to, better than that you left, and your husband's kindness will have so much advantage of ours that we shall

*yield up all competition, and as well as we love you, be very well
contented to surrender to such a rival.*

Halifax, in knowing the way of the world, knows the temper of any particular situation and the risks and stakes of every
worldly enterprise. He knows men, men in great place, or
seeking it, and not least, men in the highest place of all. His
"Character" of Charles II—which needs to be read entire—
is a small masterpiece, equally as portraiture born of observation and insight and as prose:

*One great objection made to him was the concealing himself and
disguising his thoughts. In this there ought a latitude to be given
. . . No King can be so little inclined to dissemble but he must
needs learn it from his subjects, who every day give him such lessons of it . . . Men given to dissembling are like rooks at play,
they will cheat for shillings, they are so used to it . . . His face
was as little a blab as most men's, yet though it could not be called
a prattling face, it would sometimes tell tales to a good observer.
When he thought fit to be angry he had a very peevish memory
. . . the whole inventory came out, there was not a slip omitted
. . . It may be said that his inclinations to love were the effects of
health and a good constitution, with as little mixture of the
seraphic part as ever man had . . . The King did always by his
councils as he did sometimes by his meals; he sat down out of form
with the Queen, but he supped below stairs . . . He had as little
eagerness to oblige as he had to hurt men . . . He would slide
from an asking face, and could guess very well.*

As against the largely social worldliness and domestic wisdom—a kind of negative guidebook on how not to antagonize
people, how not to lose reputation or make oneself "cheap"—
we have, in the admonitions and animadversions of *The Politi-*

cal, the Moral, the Miscellaneous Thoughts and Reflexions, a
Halifax writing out of a less than stainless experience, out of
a career not untarnished by contrivance; a Halifax who looks
out, and back, upon a world composed, in one sense, of men
contesting for power and scrambling for place—stunted
giants and corrupted genius, some of them; and composed,
in a more sardonic sense, chiefly of knaves and fools. This is a
Halifax who sets down in a sentence, or flings forth in a
phrase, the small truths, the swift touchés that proclaim the
superior aphorist. Though this is a wisdom made up of brief
statements, it opens into a panoramic view of court life and
political life. Though the subject matter does not much differ
from that in La Rochefoucauld, and the judgments on mankind are hardly more reassuring, Halifax takes a broader view
of man's motivations and gives self-interest a less ubiquitous
chief role. Halifax had diluted his somewhat Machiavellian
hardness with "the book in the world I am best entertained
with," Montaigne's *Essays*: indeed, he received the dedication of Charles Cotton's famous translation of Montaigne.
The dilution let him, in writing to his daughter, convert the
most worldly desires and ambitions into something very attractive: "Though nothing is so vain as the eager pursuit of
empty applause, yet to be well thought of, and to be kindly
used by the world, is like a glory about a woman's head; 'tis a
perfume she cometh* about with her, and leaveth wherever
she goeth; 'tis a charm against ill-will. Malice may empty her
quiver, but cannot wound; the dirt will not stick, the jests will
not take." From malice—prying and mendacious malice—in
that age there was constant cause for obloquy, and Halifax's
injunctions are prudential as well as moral.

* Halifax was among the last writers who used the old high-styled *-eth* with
the third person singular.

THE MARQUIS OF HALIFAX

Of the court, which he describes as "a company of wellbred fashionable beggars," he writes with aphoristic insight and perhaps a few grains of hindsight, and he starts at the very start: "A man who will rise at court must begin by creeping upon all fours: a place at court, like a place in heaven, is to be got by being much upon one's knees." As for its temptations: "Some places [i.e., appointments] lie so fair to entertain corruption that it looketh like renouncing a due perquisite not to go into it." As for the court's sincerity: "Men must brag of kind letters from court, at the same time that they do not believe one word of them." As for the courtier's sincerity: "There are hardly two creatures of a more differing species than the same man, when he is pretending to a place, and when he is in possession of it." And of courtiers' cleverness: "Men at court think so much of their own cunning that they forget other men's." As for *plus ça change* . . .: "After a revolution, you see the same men in the drawing room; and, within a week, the same flatterers."

About "Princes," or monarchs, and those who serve them, the portrait painter of Charles II is by no means uninformed: a king's conscience, says Halifax, "may without scandal be made of stretching leather, but it must be drawn by a steady hand"—this a matter of tactics; this, with more modern overtones: "A prince used to war getteth a military logic that is not very well suited to the civil administration." Nor is this at all un-modern: "When a Prince giveth any man a very extravagant reward, it looketh as if it was rather for an ill thing than a good one." As for the Prince's privileged self: "The first ground of prerogative was to enable the Prince to do good, not to do everything." And, wisely, for the Prince's judgment: "It is safer for a Prince to judge of men by what they do to one another than what they do to him."

THE LAST WORD

In the realm of politics, Halifax's own spotted but superior record was memorably summed up by Dryden in *Absalom and Achitophel*:

> *Jotham of piercing wit and pregnant thought,*
> *Endowed by nature and by learning taught*
> *To move assemblies, who but only tried*
> *The worse a while, then chose the better side;*
> *Nor chose alone, but turned the balance too:*
> *So much the weight of one brave man can do.*

"Jotham" was indeed sufficiently good and upright, but in politics sufficiently tempted, and just sufficiently tarnished, to have observed all its stratagems and absorbed all its lessons. He was certainly familiar with its euphemistic jargon: "*Fundamental*," he wrote, "is a word used by the laity, as the word *sacred* is by the clergy, to fix everything to themselves they have a mind to keep, that nobody else may touch it." (As for the clergy and religion: "The several sorts of religion in the world are little more than so many spiritual monopolies.") As for party government, which in the modern sense began in the late seventeenth century—Halifax, indeed, had just reached mid-career when one party was contemptuously called Whigs, after the covenanters in Scotland, and the other party nicknamed Tories, after rebellious outlaws in Ireland—it is perhaps enough that Halifax's very first comment is that "the best party is but a kind of conspiracy against the rest of the nation," and that his next comment is that party members "value themselves upon their principles, so as to neglect practice, ability, industry," and the like. On the law, he could sound a slightly cynical and a rather modern note: "There is more learning now required to explain a law . . . than went to the making of it"; and he could speak rather sharply: "The law has so many contradictions and varyings from itself that the law may not improperly be called a lawbreaker"—and become "little less a mystery than the Gospel." And of parliaments, ministers, lawmaking, the whole structure of governing, his summing up is a blunt warning: "State business is a cruel trade; good nature is a bungler in it."

It is in these, and many other, aphoristic reflections and admonitions that Halifax serves as a master of political realism, and sometimes of political wisdom. And, commingled with out-of-date comments and rather odd arguments, there are sensible and satirical ones in Halifax's pamphlet-essay, "Some Cautions offered to the Consideration of those who are to choose members to serve for the Ensuing Parliament." For members, Halifax rejects such candidates as "superfine gentlemen, carpet knights whose heads may be said to be only appurtenances to their perukes"; he rejects "men that have a tinsel wit" as inferior to the right kind of wit "as a fiddler at a wake is to the lofty sound of an organ"; he rejects "great drinkers . . . nothing is more frail than a man too far engaged in wet popularity." He rejects the very young, indeed he thought no one under thirty should be a member of either House: as for Parliament being "the best school for young men," it should be like a school only as youngsters "deserve to be whipped in it." He rejects "excessive spenders and unreasonable savers," both of whom suffer from infectious diseases; he rejects "men tied to a party, whose heads are squeezed as small as, in the Indies, are children's feet that they may stay at that size after they are grown." On subjects they have in common, Halifax's humor stands out against La Rochefoucauld's total lack, or suppression, of it.

But in writing more generally of the frailties and faults of mankind, Halifax comes closer to La Rochefoucauld, though in penetration he falls a bit short. Familiar with La Rochefoucauld's *Maxims*, he now and then echoes and even virtually repeats them, as with "Hope is generally a wrong guide, though it is very good company." But there is for the most part something more downright, concrete, graphically metaphorical about Halifax, as in "A man that should call everything by its right name would hardly pass the streets without being knocked down as a common enemy." As I have suggested, Halifax can sometimes be, in phrasing as in philosophy, kin to Benjamin Franklin, or as a giver of advice or trumpeter of warnings, in the tradition of practical moralists. Yet, as his place in history has been rather lost sight of, so has his place in prose literature which, lacking neither the suavity nor the breeding of the Augustans, provides the smack and pungency of the Restoration satirists and comedy writers.

Aphorisms

Anger raiseth invention but it overheateth the oven.

Men are so proud of Princes' secrets that they will not see the dangers of them.

When the people contend for their liberty they seldom get anything by their victory but new masters.

There is an accumulative cruelty in a number [i.e., group] of men, though none in particular are ill natured.

THE MARQUIS OF HALIFAX

Were it not for bunglers in the manner of doing it, hardly any man would ever find out he was laughed at.

Popularity is a crime from the moment it is sought: it is only a virtue when men have it whether they will or no.

It is less dangerous for a Prince to mind too much what the people say, than too little.

Most men's anger about religion is as if two men should quarrel for a lady they neither of them care for.

Folly is often more cruel in the consequence than malice can be in the intent.

By the time men are fit for company, they see the objections to it.

Love is presently out of breath when it is to go up hill, from the children to the parents.

Men are so unwilling to displease a Prince that it is as dangerous to inform him right as to serve him wrong.

The enquiry into a dream is another dream.

Men are not hanged for stealing horses, but that horses may not be stolen.

THE LAST WORD

Those friends who are above interest are seldom above jealousy.

Men are commanded not to covet because when they do, they are very apt to take.

A Prince who will not undergo the difficulty of understanding must undergo the danger of trusting.

Friendship cannot live with ceremony nor without civility.

III

Dr. Johnson

DR. SAMUEL JOHNSON stands forth—thanks almost as much to his biographer's genius as to his own—the greatest social talker that there is record of. He is also, I think, the most unmistakable one: as perhaps nobody talked better than he did, so nobody talked like him. And in a certain sense no great talker ever had Johnson's range or his readiness, which is to say his ability to speak instantly, vividly, aphoristically on so many subjects; to be in so many ways witty, if not always wise; memorable, if not always fair-minded; and undaunted, if by no means always right. He was also, at his best, a notable writer, and very pithy and impressive comments abound in his writings; but it is to his recorded speech that Johnson as an aphorist owes his fame.

He was born in Lichfield in 1709, the son of an unsuccessful bookseller who suffered from a "vile melancholy" which his son inherited. As a very small child, Samuel was a victim of scrofula, which disfigured and half blinded him, and for which he was ineffectually "touched" by Queen Anne, whom he recalled as "a lady in diamonds and a long black hood." He was sometimes carried to school by his school fellows and, being unfitted for games, he read romances. His schooling was irregular, his reading extensive but desultory, and in due course, despite strained family resources, he was entered, in 1728, at Pembroke College, Oxford. At Oxford he was "miserably poor," he was "mad and violent," now flouting authority, now suffering from hypochondria; but at Oxford he became deeply religious for life. His father died soon after when close to bankrupt, and Samuel, himself virtually penniless, now had his way to make. This he did for some years by tutoring and as a schoolteacher; by translating and as a writer of sorts. In July 1735 he married Elizabeth Porter, a widow in somewhat better circumstances than he was and twenty years older. She was hardly more attractive, but he described their union as "a love marriage on both sides" and in a peculiar way it seems to have proved not unhappy. They bought a house which they used unsuccessfully as a boys' school, having had very few pupils, though David Garrick was one of them. When in 1737 the school failed, Johnson set out for London, his wife staying behind and Garrick traveling with him. In London he made some beginnings as a writer; went back to Lichfield, where he finished his play *Irene*, then returned to London, this time accompanied by Tetty, as he called his wife. *Irene* went unproduced—Garrick would produce and act in it, with more success than the dreary play deserved, a dozen years later; but Johnson did become a regular contributor to *The Gentleman's Magazine* and later took down, and in some cases distorted and made up, Parliamentary debates. He by then had written "London," an imitation of one of Juvenal's satires and Johnson's first work of any value: Alexander Pope, then the great autocrat of poetry, said of the unknown author: "He will soon be *déterré*."

But, though he got to be better known, Johnson had many years of struggle ahead of him—years during which he took on odd jobs and hack work; years, thereafter, during which he fades completely out of sight, but during which he began planning a new edition of Shakespeare and announced his plans for a dictionary. During this hand-to-mouth period he actually wrote and published perhaps the most entertaining and flavorsome of his writings, the story of a writer who was also a rascal, and of a rascal who had also been his friend—the *Life* of Richard Savage. The work on the Dictionary, of which Johnson sold the copyright for £1,575, was toilsome and arduous despite the half-dozen copyists that Johnson hired; and dragged along for some eight years. Its publication was made noteworthy by Lord Chesterfield's belated puff of the book in hopes of receiving the dedication; and receiving instead Johnson's shattering blast of independence, Johnson's great blow at highborn patronage. Seven years had passed, he wrote to Chesterfield,

since I waited in your outward rooms, or was repulsed from your door; during which time I have been pushing on my work . . . and have brought it, at last, to the verge of publication without one act of assistance, one word of encouragement, or one smile of favor. Such treatment I did not expect, for I never had a Patron before . . . Is not a Patron, my Lord, one who looks with unconcern on a man struggling for life in the water and when he has reached ground, encumbers him with help? The notice which you have been pleased to take of my labours . . . has been delayed till I am indifferent, and cannot enjoy it; till I am solitary and cannot impart it; till I am known and do not want it.

The Dictionary itself was a remarkable work for its day— this despite the fact that Johnson was a very inadequate philologist and had scant knowledge of the early history of his own language. But the Dictionary's definitions and illustrative citations were generally admirable and, where least sound, were very often most striking. Several of these are justly well known: *network* is defined as "anything reticulated or decussated, at equal distances, with interstices between the intersections"; *oats* as "a grain which in England is generally given to horses, but in Scotland supports the people"; *lexicographer* as "a writer of dictionaries, a harmless drudge"; and *pension* as "in England . . . generally understood to mean given to a state hireling for treason to his country." Johnson's conclusion to the Dictionary's preface, one of the most melancholy of valedictories, is also a piece of magnificent prose.

In 1749, while in the midst of his work on the Dictionary, Johnson, with his gloomy moods matching his pessimistic sense of life, published the finest of his poems and the most unassailable of his writings, "The Vanity of Human Wishes." Here, freely rendering another satire of Juvenal's, Johnson is the sagelike moralist he will more and more become. He is also palpably didactic, but he endows his theme, set forth in his title, with a certain didactic grandeur; and steeps his poem in the bitter herbs and hemlock of experience. The couplets toll their burden:

> *There mark what ills the scholar's life assail—*
> *Toil, envy, want, the patron, and the jail;*
>
> *Yet hope not life from grief or danger free,*
> *Nor think the doom of life reversed for thee.*

The most famous lines, on Charles XII of Sweden, drive in one more harsh nail:

> *His fall was destin'd to a barren strand,*
> *A petty fortress and a dubious hand:*
> *He left the name at which the world grew pale*
> *To point a moral, or adorn a tale.*

During the Dictionary years there were two additional events in Johnson's life: in 1750 he began publishing *The Rambler*, periodical papers in the tradition of *The Tatler* and *The Spectator*, which, though containing much good sense and many well-put sentiments, was verbally top-heavy: its sale was small during its two-year life span, but the papers, when collected in book form, were esteemed and sold well. The second event was the death of Johnson's wife in 1752, a genuinely great loss to him despite undoubted vicissitudes of marriage. His friend Dr. Taylor, to whom he wrote a letter immediately after Tetty's death, said it "expressed grief in the strongest manner he had ever read"; and certainly there is poignancy in Johnson's reply to the school friend who doubted his having had a wife: "Sir, I have known what it was to have a wife, and I have known what it was to *lose a wife*. . . . It had almost broke my heart."

The publication of the Dictionary may be said to have put an end to Johnson's long struggle for adequate recognition and to his acrid experience of Grub Street; a stupefying project, it brought him—what would henceforth grow much greater—prestige. Though it was not till eight years afterward that he met Boswell, the Boswellian Johnson was by now taking shape, and by now Johnson *had* met many people of interest and consequence. For being now a widower, he would lead a somewhat different life, and even more so as a leading man of letters and a talker of note. Hereafter he would live in a house peopled by indigent, afflicted, and incapacitated women and men, not people whose company he craved, but whose needs he responded to; not those who would sweeten life for him, but who incessantly squabbled with one another. "[Miss] Williams," he remarked, "hates everybody; Levett hates Des Moulins and does not like Williams; Des Moulins hates them both: Poll loves none of them." Hereafter Johnson would frequent clubs, and help found, indeed, the most famous club in literary history. As early as 1749 he formed a club at "a famous beefsteak house" —this signalizing how much his food, as well as his friendships, mattered to him. Already well-acquainted with Garrick, Johnson through the *Life of Mr. Richard Savage* inspired Joshua Reynolds to want to meet him, just as *The Rambler* inspired the future famous musician, Dr. Burney, as well as two young aristocrats, Bennet Langton and, through him, Topham Beauclerk. These last two—we shall say more of Johnson's respect for the wellborn—became his very good friends.

In 1756 Johnson became editor of *The Literary Magazine*, for which he wrote frequently; when he ceased writing for it, the magazine also ceased. In 1758 *The Idler*, an inferior *Rambler*, appeared and ran until 1760. By then Johnson had published something of considerably greater importance: his only novel, if it can be called one. *Rasselas*, written in the evenings of one week to meet the expenses of his ninety-year-old mother's funeral, tells of a young prince and an old philosopher who escape from a happy, isolated valley to explore the world. Their exploration is really an exemplification of Johnson's pessimistic view of life, rich in sententious wisdom but lacking in all fictional rewards. Something of its tone is caught in such a sentiment as "I live in the crowd of jollity, not so much to enjoy company as to shun myself." Published in the same year as Voltaire's *Candide*, and following something of the same plan, it is as majestically slow-paced as *Candide* is marvelously headlong. *Rasselas* suffers a little on Johnsonian terms because, though often fine in its way, in that very way "The Vanity of Human Wishes" is finer.

Official recognition of merit, and relief from worry, came to Johnson in 1762, when he was granted a pension of three hundred pounds a year by the new-to-the-throne George III. Johnson felt a certain hesitation in accepting it, in view of his Dictionary definition, and was concerned that he might have political obligations to discharge. But after consulting with Joshua Reynolds, he accepted it, and on accepting it, he was assured by the prime minister, Lord Bute, that "it is not given you for anything you are to do, but for what you have done." As a confirmed Tory, Johnson was actually not at odds with either the king or his ministers, as later pamphleteering performances of his bore out. Perhaps the best-known and least-respected of these pamphlets, "Taxation No Tyranny," was written on the eve of the American Revolution and breathes equally Johnson's fierce dislike of America itself and blinkered opposition to American demands.

The pension gave Johnson—by now a man of great reputation who, thanks to Oxford, would become Dr. Johnson—the one thing further to make living easy: financial independence. He now could write, or not, as he chose; and could live, as indeed he proceeded to, as he chose. "The happiest part of a man's life," he said, glorifying his indolence, "is what he passes lying awake in bed of a morning"—a remark that must be bracketed with one of his most arbitrary generalizations: "Whoever thinks of going to bed before twelve o'clock is a scoundrel." The pension permitted him to spend many of *his* nights at taverns, which he judged the best of places to be:

As soon as I enter the door of a tavern, I experience an oblivion of care, and a freedom from solicitude: when I am seated, I find the master courteous, and the servants obsequious to my call, anxious to know and ready to supply my wants: wine there exhilarates my spirits, and prompts me to free conversation with those whom I most love: I dogmatize and am contradicted, and in this conflict of opinions and sentiments I find delight.

It was also at taverns that some of the clubs Johnson belonged to met, particularly The Club—as it was always called, though

47

officially named The Literary Club at Garrick's funeral. Founded soon after Johnson got his pension, it boasted such charter members, besides himself, as Reynolds, Oliver Goldsmith, and Edmund Burke, and acquired such others as Gibbon, Garrick, Boswell, Adam Smith, Sheridan—and Charles James Fox, whom Johnson so intimidated that, although the greatest of Parliamentary debaters, Fox seldom opened his mouth. The Club, at least in its early years, was one of the places where Johnson had the opportunity to expound, contradict, and elucidate for both immediate victory and the gratification of posterity. His greatest link with posterity, however, came a little before the founding of The Club, when on May 16, 1763, he met a twenty-two-year-old Boswell, whose genius for writing down, or writing up, what Johnson said, or Johnson shouted, or thundered, or audibly mumbled to himself, went farthest toward creating the greatest literary biography in the language.

The two men, however, did not nearly so much intertwine in life as they do in Boswell's *Life*—indeed, in the twenty-one years remaining to Johnson, they saw each other relatively little, for one reason because Boswell *lived* in Scotland. Actually Johnson saw a great deal more of other people; and many other people became part of his social life, preeminently the Thrales—Henry Thrale, a rich and not very alluring brewer or very faithful husband, Hester Thrale, a bright, busy, amusing, sharp-tongued society hostess who, for first-hand anecdotal information, ranks next after Boswell. The hospitality and solicitude of the Thrales gave Johnson, as a constant visitor, the sense of home he had always craved; and from them he for many years got regard and devotion. In the same years Johnson—now the greatest, if fiercest and on occasion the most offensive, of literary lions—met almost all the important writers and many of the scholars, as well as many

people in society, of his time. He dined out, he traveled about
—to his native Lichfield and to the Oxford he was fond of; to
Wales and to Paris—his only trip abroad—and to the Heb-
rides, during their longest spell together, with Boswell. Both
he and Boswell published accounts of the tour, Johnson's
being often markedly Johnsonian and, as it has been called,
"the most ceremonious of diaries"; Boswell's being superbly
animated and bright, thanks in part for having Johnson as a
central figure.

In later years Johnson published two important works.
One of these is the preface to the *Shakespeare* he edited, a
publication that took longer to appear than the Dictionary,
thus drawing from the satirist Charles Churchill the jibe:

> *He for subscribers baits his hook*
> *And takes your cash; but where's the book?*

The *Shakespeare* also drew an admission from Johnson when
asked why he did not print a list of the subscribers: "Sir, I
have two very cogent reasons for not printing any list of
subscribers: one, that I have lost all the names; the other,
that I have spent all the money." The book's *preface*, however,
is Johnson's solidest piece of criticism, and though not everywhere tenable or sound—Johnson, for example, astonishingly
ranks Shakespeare's comedy higher than his tragedy—is full
of sane, bold, perceptive comment. So are some of the notes
to the *Shakespeare*, such as this on *Macbeth*: "He that peruses
Shakespeare looks round alarmed and starts to find himself
alone." The second work, the *Lives of the Poets*, is all in all
Johnson's most attractive and rewarding one. The *Lives*
perfectly suit his talents, those of a distinguished man of
letters, rather than a specifically distinguished biographer, or
scholar, or critic. Johnson's endowment, rather, combines
something of all three, and in the *Lives* that combination is

most effectively displayed. The *Lives* are also the better for having been written in an untaxing mood, when Johnson had achieved great fame, and had no fears about money; and if not written with scholarly care, they exhibit, to their advantage, a superb sense of confidence.

Johnson's last years were, despite his fame and easy circumstances, marred by failing health (he died of a complication of diseases) and at the very end by a bitter cessation of friendship. Henry Thrale having died, his widow saw less of Johnson and in due course chose to marry a respectable Italian musician named Piozzi. On hearing of this, the aged, ailing, lonely Johnson erupted in words of great and insulting anger; Mrs. Piozzi's strong but respectful reply he answered civilly, and with touching gratitude for her kindness "which soothed twenty years of a life radically wretched"; but the two never met again. A deeply religious man, Johnson faced death with fighting courage: "I will be conquered," he said on his deathbed, "I will not capitulate." He died in December 1784 as he had lived—a man of tremendous character who, despite glaring faults, yet showed notable benevolence and compassion.

Dr. Johnson is one of a few English writers whose names are applied to their age, and none of these is oftener heard than the Age of Johnson. In gaining this title, Johnson had, to be sure, no great rival among his literary contemporaries, whether for authorship, personality, or prestige. (Fielding died too early and Gibbon arrived too late.) As an author, today, Johnson occupies a secure but specialized place: the often ponderous style by which he is tagged can make difficult reading and can be matched by an outworn or too moralistic substance. A good deal of Dr. Johnson, however, is splendid in its kind. The best of his prose has decided distinction; the best of his verse has power and grandeur; and even where his touch is heavy his perceptiveness, his robust humor, and his metaphorical and aphoristic way with language can make him very rewarding. It is all the greater tribute to people's constantly referring to the Age of Johnson in that he had none of the urbanity or the elegance that helped make the age distinguished; as it is, his writing style, in everything but sentence structure, harks back to the seventeenth century and is far closer to Sir Thomas Browne than to Laurence Sterne. Indeed, in the Age of Johnson there is no one else among the great who, far from prizing elegance, had no interest in cleanliness; who, far from being an epicure, could be a repulsive glutton; who, far from displaying urbanity, could be not only boorish but brutal; who, far from being courtly, could be crushingly blunt; and who, in an age that gives its name to Reason as well as to Johnson, could be so intemperate and autocratic in what he said. No one could glare more fiercely, nor more high-handedly pronounce judgment, or by the sheer impact of language so annihilate an opponent. "There is no arguing with Johnson," said Oliver Goldsmith, "for if his pistol misses fire, he knocks you down with the butt end of it." For much of this there was little or no excuse; but for much, also, there was a kind of explanation. All his life Johnson was scarred and ailing and neurotically depressed. Disfigured in infancy by scrofula, and in middle life alluded to as Polyphemus and Caliban, he could, in addition, neither see nor hear well; he suffered from dropsy, emphysema, and gout, and from tormenting stretches of sleeplessness. Hence, handicapped in appearance and racked by ill health, he used his gifts—his command of words, his powerful mind, his overpowering personality—as weapons. His poor sight and hearing, moreover, left him in ignorance of how terrifyingly he glared and how rumblingly he thundered. Time and again he was irascible, despotic, and, by drawing-room standards, outrageous. But he was never malicious or rancorous or fundamentally ill-natured.

Johnson's faults have become part of his heritage and play a conspicuous role in his famous biography. But, as opposed to them, Johnson's great qualities of character, and his talents for vigorously defining and discriminating, for wittily replying and retorting, go even further toward making him one of the supreme characters in not just literary, but in human, history. And this is not least true because, despite his bodily ills and disturbed and melancholy mind, he possessed enormous gusto, he truly *loved* life. He functioned at the very center of it in London with its great range of interests, its great variety of companions, its clubs and taverns, and above all its hubbub and excitement. "Whoever," he said, "is tired of London is tired of life." He knew his London well, its mean streets and miserable slums no less than its Parliament and palaces. No one spoke more compassionately about the poor, or more angrily, or more memorably. "Sir, all the arguments which are brought to represent poverty as no evil show it to be evidently a great evil. You never find people laboring to convince you that you may live happily upon a plentiful fortune." He, who had taken street walkers into his house to be nursed back to health, and in his more prosperous years gave most of his money away, was no prating moralist, but someone who could understand and forgive human frailties. Consider his comment on drunkenness: "He who makes a *beast* of himself gets rid of the pain of being a man."

And stanch, not to say benighted, Tory though he was—with a belief in inequality and a formal show of deference to rank—he never kowtowed to the nobly born or deferred to their opinions; indeed—obstreperous a thousand times sooner than obsequious—he often incurred their disfavor. "Great lords and ladies," he remarked, "don't like to have their mouths stopped." True, Johnson stopped their mouths uncouthly; and late in life was no mellow sage but often an intolerably overbearing pontificator, unwelcome in a good many drawing rooms. As against his asperity, and his unscrupulous tactics to avoid being beaten in an argument, Johnson had a very engaging downrightness about him, as when Boswell asked him whether he would write a preface to the work of a dunce: "Yes, sir, and *say* he was a dunce." Again: "Mrs Montagu has dropped me. Now, Sir, there are people whom one should like very well to drop, but not wish to be dropped by." Or, when asked to account for an absurd definition in his Dictionary: "Ignorance, madam, pure ignorance." And when writing his "life" of Congreve, he said of an early work he praised: "I would rather praise than read it." He had downrightness of mind as well as of language; when asked about his famous meeting with George III, he said: "I found his Majesty wished I should talk, and I made it my business to talk." And he had humor as well as ill humor. Half his antipathy to Scotland and the Scots was the fun he could have at their, and in particular Boswell's, expense —remarks like "The noblest prospect which a Scotchman ever sees is the highway that leads him to England." And when Johnson told an admirer of Scotland that it was "a very vile country" and was answered, "Well, sir, God made it," Johnson answered in turn: "Certainly He did; but we must always remember that He made it for Scotchmen; and comparisons are odious, Mr. S—, but God made Hell." Indeed Johnson in conversation lets fly, now picturesquely, now sharply, at almost any convenient target: "Being in a ship," he said, "is being in a jail with the chance of being drowned." "If," he remarked of an acquaintance, "he does really think there is no distinction between virtue and vice, why, sir, when he leaves our houses let us count our spoons." Or: "To marry a second time represents the triumph of hope over experience"; or: "This was a good enough dinner, to be sure, but it was not a dinner to *ask* a man to." And there is the answer when asked "Is not the Giant's Causeway [in Ireland] worth seeing?" "Worth seeing? yes; but not worth going to see."

It is the vibrance and pungency of his talk, the darting electricity in the air, that formidably sets him off, that indeed characterizes him. No one could speak on occasion with sounder sense or a stronger effectiveness; but no one, by virtue of his character, could on occasion be more delightfully wrongheaded. What could draw laughter better than Johnson's priceless "defense" of his friend Sir John Hawkins: "I believe him to be an honest man at bottom; but, to be sure, he is penurious, and he is mean, and it must be owned he has a degree of brutality, and a tendency to savageness, that cannot easily be defended." And in an age when boat riders on the Thames played a game of shouting insults at one another, Dr. Johnson, when shouted at, roared magnificently back: "Sir, your wife, *under pretense of keeping a bawdy house*, is a receiver of stolen goods."

In earnest he could be as crushing as in fun, as with Lord Chesterfield and even more with James Macpherson, the "translator" of Ossian, to whom Johnson wrote:

I received your foolish and impudent letter. Any violence offered me I shall do my best to repel; and what I cannot do for myself, the law shall do for me. I hope I shall never be deterred from detecting what I think a cheat, by the menaces of a ruffian.

What would you have me retract? I thought your book an imposture; I think it an imposture still. For this opinion I have given my reasons to the publick, which I here dare you to refute.

DR. JOHNSON

Your rage I defy . . . and what I hear of your morals inclines me to pay regard not to what you shall say, but to what you shall prove. You may print this if you will.

Johnson's fearlessness proved, in fact, fearsome, and was backed up by his physical strength, which, when "necessary," he visited upon offenders. What fear he had was a theological one for the fate of his soul and for his habitation in the after-world. He was—one might say he had to be—a strict believer, from having a strong tendency toward disbelief; he was also a deeply disturbed believer, from questioning his own moral virtue. He feared God, not loved him; and from his Anglican faith got small comfort and great perturbation. Asked what he meant by his fear of being damned, he thundered: "Sent to Hell, sir, and punished everlastingly." His was a gloomy pessimism indeed, in respect of the afterlife as well as this one, and his verdict on this one is among the most lugubrious of his aphorisms: "Human life is everywhere a state in which much is to be endured and little to be enjoyed."

Human life for him, however gratifying it might become in terms of eminence and esteem, was at bottom very lonely. Being lonely, he longed to be loved, to be remembered, to be included; being odd, he longed to seem normal. His marriage, however unusual a one, at least gave him the sense of normal living; his physical prowess and midnight carouses gave him the sense of normal enjoyments; his being named one of Thrale's executors gave him the sense, as he self-importantly bustled about, of a normal man of business. In these ways he found compensation for what isolated and set him apart, equally in genius and grotesqueness, in eminence and oddity. If there is something pathetic about the effort, there is something close to heroic about the achievement. He refused, though sick, to be an invalid; he refused, though pious, to be a puritan; and weighted down with melancholy, he refused no one compassion.

Johnson's compassion did not tolerate sentimentality; nor his piety, lip service. Of all his admonitions perhaps the most famous is "Clear your mind of cant." "When a butcher," he said, "tells you that his heart bleeds for his country, he has in fact no uneasy feeling"; and when Mrs. Thrale lamented the loss of a cousin killed in America, he bade her "have done with canting; how would the world be worse . . . if all your relatives were at once spitted like larks and roasted for Presto's [the Thrales' dog] supper?" This last suggests something doctrinaire in Johnson rather than insincere in Mrs. Thrale, and he himself sometimes canted on the subject of cant, and even made a weapon of the word to legitimize his prejudices; but at other times, from his knowledge of the world, he detected, or deprecated, false sentiment and fictitious virtue in others. This might be about something light, as in Garrick's song, "I'd smile with the simple and feed with the poor": "This will never do," said Johnson. "Let me smile with the wise and feed with the rich." Or it might treat seriously, if a little cynically, of something: "Very feeling people," he said, "are not very ready to do you good. They *pay* you with *feeling*."

For his great biographer Johnson had much affection and regard, if also an ever-ready tendency to contradict, rebuff, and flare up at him. Johnson and Boswell were much different in many ways—in age, to begin with, Johnson being twenty-one years older. Johnson also—morally if not conversationally—displayed great self-control; he gave up drinking—"Abstinence is as easy to me as temperance would be difficult"—where Boswell was constantly drunk. Again, where Johnson said to Garrick, "I'll come no more behind your scenes, David; for the white bubbies and silk stockings of your actresses excite my genitals," Boswell "sallied forth like a roaring lion after girls" and constantly caught "the venereal disorder." And where Johnson had a kind of rough dignity and great self-respect, Boswell was totally uninhibited; forever banged on strangers' doors, and asked impertinent questions; and went to great trouble, it might be said, to make a fool of himself. But the two men had much in common also. They were alike in their politics and in their piety; in their enjoyment of society and their love of talk; in their tremendous gusto and—though Johnson's ran deeper—in their melancholy. Vain, egotistical, exhibitionistic, Boswell had, where it mattered, the disinterestedness of the true artist and a rare ability to tell the truth—not just in setting himself down as the butt of an anecdote but, when writing about himself, in confessing to his motives and his mistakes. On occasion Boswell's stratagems could give us Johnson at his most delightful, as in Johnson's meeting with John Wilkes, whom he deeply disapproved of—a meeting which Boswell had skillfully contrived and which wound up with the inflexible Tory moralist and the libertine politician hitting it off and, with their joint scorn for Scotland, having at Boswell, who reports:

Johnson: *You must know, Sir, I lately took my friend Boswell and showed him genuine civilized life in an English town . . . for you know he lives among savages in Scotland, and among rakes in London.* Wilkes: *Except when he is with grave, sober, decent people like you and me.* Johnson (*smiling*): *And we ashamed of him.*

Here we encounter a very engaging quality in Johnson, his playfulness.

The wonder is that Johnson, so odd in his habits, so set in his beliefs, so stubborn in his prejudices, and moving so decidedly against the cultural and political current—he strongly disapproved of Voltaire, Rousseau, and Hume; he had no interest in painting or music; and he opposed, unlike almost every other great Englishman of his day, both Wilkes's claims in the Middlesex elections and the grievances of the American colonists—the wonder is that he could also be so many-sided in his interests, and so sane and sharp in his comments and observations. To be sure, some of his extreme Tory tenets make sense when understood: his insistence, for example, that all men are created unequal is incontrovertible if judged, as Johnson meant it to be, by how greatly men differ in social or financial status, in looks, in health, mind, body, personality, opportunities. In much the same way, though he might refuse the people the power of governing, he would make those who governed strictly responsible for the people's welfare. "A decent provision for the poor," he said, "is the true test of civilization." The more one comes to know him, the more one sets him apart, not as a "character" but as a man of character. Yet, early and late, one returns to him as the greatest of all masters of conversation in the course of which all sorts of comments and contradictions, retorts and rebukes, observations and comparisons tumble about, and all sorts of aphorisms accumulate. A great many are philosophic, metaphorical, witty, pungent, audacious; surprisingly many are in one way or another prudent, perceptive, and wise.

Aphorisms

A man should be careful never to tell tales of himself to his own disadvantage. People may be amused and laugh at the time, but they will be remembered and brought forth against him upon some subsequent occasion.

The law against usury is for the protection of creditors as well as debtors; for if there were no such check, they would be apt, from the temptation of great interest, to lend to desperate persons by whom they would lose their money.

No man is a hypocrite in his pleasures.

Solitude is dangerous to reason without being favorable to virtue.

Marriage has many pains, but celibacy has no pleasures.

It is as unreasonable for a man to go into a Carthusian convent for fear of being immoral, as for a man to cut off his hands for fear he should steal.

For my part I mind my belly very studiously . . . for I look upon it, that he who does not mind his belly will hardly mind anything else.

THE LAST WORD

Nothing is more hopeless than a scheme of merriment.

Some cunning men choose fools for their wives, thinking to manage them, but they always fail.

Hell is paved with good intentions.

Courage is a quality so necessary for maintaining virtue that it is always respected, even when it is associated with vice.

If I accustom a servant to tell a lie for me, have I not reason to apprehend that he will tell many lies for himself?

Were it not for imagination, sir, a man would be as happy in the arms of a chambermaid as of a duchess.

Patriotism is the last refuge of a scoundrel.

So much are the modes of excellence settled by time and place, that men may be heard boasting in one street of that which they would anxiously conceal in another.

If a man could say nothing against a character but what he can prove, history could not be written.

In lapidary inscriptions a man is not upon oath.

IV

Chamfort

SEBASTIEN ROCH NICOLAS DE CHAMFORT returns us to France during a distinguished age boasting Voltaire, Rousseau, and the Encyclopedists, and a destructive age produced by the French Revolution. Unlike earlier aphorists, Chamfort was no aristocrat by birth, was indeed a nobody. He gained admittance, however, to the world of grandees, brightening their lives with his often insolent wit while he himself cut a figure in the literary life of the time and became a friend of its most notable writers. It was not, however, till the French Revolution, and his passionate support of it, that he opened the eyes of the highborn to his real feelings, as the Revolution would open his own eyes to the excesses of revolutionaries. As brilliant at his best as any French aphorist who would claim to stand second only to La Rochefoucauld, Chamfort in addition circulated insulting witticisms and explosive epigrams, coined vivid phrases, and collected telltale anecdotes.

About his birth, which was most probably illegitimate, there is a great deal of supposition and speculation. His father is thought to have been a canon, perhaps at the Sainte-Chapelle; his mother, a governess or, possibly, Thérèse Croiset, the woman who brought him up and whom he greatly cared for and spoke of as his mother—though she would have been past forty when he was born. His birth date has been set at 1740, 1742, and most likely 1741; his birth-

61

place near Clermont-Ferrand in the Auvergne; and the only name that he would seem to have any right to is his baptismal one of Nicolas. The disparities about his origins are all the more tangled—and become somewhat the more "significant" —by his own additions to them: a certain shame for his birth and for his early background having led him at times to strip himself naked and at other times to dress himself up ostentatiously; just what is fact and what is fiction would be hard to prove.

By the time Nicolas was five he was at a famous school for poor children in Paris, the Collège des Grassins. Being there on a scholarship, he was expected, as he grew older, to excel —expected, indeed, to win first prize in whatever he studied; and having one year been a disappointment for gaining all but one of the prizes, he took all five the next. In due course he was made an abbé but rejected an ecclesiastical career: he cared too much, he said, for quiet, honor, and woman, and too little for bickering, honors, and money. His sharp wit and good looks very early won him a place—often both bed and board— in society, one of his conquests remarking of him that beneath the Adonis there existed a Hercules. It was a famous and largely frivolous aristocratic society that he gained access to, one that dabbled in culture and delighted in wit, that considered marriage no sacrament and jealousy decidedly bourgeois. (When Fragonard spoke of love for a week to a limelighted dancer, she said, "A week! Why, that's as bad as a marriage.") Though accepted and admired, Nicolas had yet his way to make, and made it variously—by writing sermons for a louis each, by tutoring a stingy nobleman's nephew, by hack journalism, by writing a poem that won a prize, and by writing a play that was produced very successfully at the Comédie Française and then given a command performance at Versailles, and praised by Voltaire. All this had its value, but when Chamfort quitted the salons and the boudoirs, he went home to a garret; his health was anything but good and he may already have contracted the syphilis he was known to have a few years later; he also suffered from mental depressions and would seek out a kind of solitude. All his life he was to repudiate society, only, all his life, to go back to it; to be drawn, like so many other writers, by its glitter and elegance and sophistication, and then be repelled by its frivolousness and callousness and caprice. And almost from the beginning he could be insolent in his witticisms, becoming, in the guise of society's delightful jester, its relentless judge.

Prizes continued to come his way: one for a poem at the Académie de Rouen, another for a poem at the Académie de Marseille, a more important one, for prose, at the same Académie; and most important, an Académie Française prize from an *Eloge de Molière*. But again and again he was reduced to near or actual poverty, being eventually helped when a young admirer passed on to him his annual pension. A few years later—in 1774—an Académie de Marseille prize on the subject of La Fontaine, certain to go to the critic and poet La Harpe, was awarded to Chamfort. Greatly admiring both Molière and La Fontaine, Chamfort gave a higher place to La Fontaine because, where Molière treated of passing absurdities and foibles, La Fontaine exposed permanent vices; and where Molière made Chamfort worry about how the public might judge, La Fontaine brought him face to face with his own conscience.

By now Chamfort was established in the literary as well as the social world; but in spite of the assistance of *grands seigneurs* like the Duc de Choiseul, and of visits to châteaux and fashionable watering places, he was periodically broke and quite often in ill health. Then influential friends helped to get a new tragedy of his, *Mustapha and Zéangir*, performed at Fontainebleau, Chamfort having previously read it to Louis XVI and Marie Antoinette—who admired it—at Versailles. When it was produced, the king wept and after the performance the queen bestowed a pension on Chamfort; though presumably of small merit, *Mustapha* was also reasonably successful when produced at the Comédie Française.

On the heels of Marie Antoinette's pension, Chamfort was offered an excellent post by the powerful Prince de Condé: as *secrétaire des commandements*, he would receive a hundred louis a month and quarters at the Palais-Bourbon. But in accepting it, Chamfort found it meant taking care of a rather vast correspondence and turning up at a great variety of official functions—duties that would badly cramp him as a writer. When, in a letter to the prince, he tried to beg off, Condé told him to forget about the duties of the job but to keep the title; and to keep or give up, as he chose, his apartments at the Palais-Bourbon. He stayed on for a while to avoid offending so sympathetic a benefactor, but eventually, and on amicable terms, he bowed out—his withdrawal signalizing a more extensive withdrawal from the social and the literary world alike. Once again his health was poor; his attacks of nerves and his depressions once again were frequent; his pessimistic view of life had grown darker; and despite an offer to be a drama critic, he stopped writing. What he did persevere at was winning admittance to the Académie Française and, after a number of attempts, he was elected in 1781, when he was roughly forty.

In turning so considerably away from the world, Chamfort removed to Auteuil, where his great friend the widow of Helvétius lived and entertained, and where she assigned Chamfort a pavilion. Here he met, among others, Benjamin Franklin; and elsewhere he met a widow, Madame Buffon, to whom he became greatly attracted. She had been attached to the household of the Duchesse du Maine at Sceaux, and though some years older than Chamfort, was still much admired, as well as witty. At the height of their ardent liaison at Auteuil, he insisted that love had no part in it, but they in due course moved to a house of Madame Buffon's in the country, where they kept to themselves and where, he confessed, he was very happy. But some two years after they had met— it was now the summer of 1783—she was taken ill and did not recover. The union in which love played no part was clearly the happiest episode of Chamfort's life, a life fashionably libertine; and only the efforts of his friend, the Comte de Vaudreuil, ultimately drew him out of the house that had secluded him with Madame Buffon, and brought him back to "the clamorous desert" of Paris. There, despite a continuing propensity for retirement that smacked of pose as well, he went about, and saw people; indeed went on a journey with Vaudreuil, and two other members of the nobility, to Holland.

After his return, he received a rather special appointment— that of secretary to Elizabeth of France, the king's sister; an appointment brought about, as Chamfort acknowledged, with the help of his friends and one that definitely gave him position, a number of prerogatives and two thousand francs a year. He could scarcely have sought anything better, whether as a means of enjoying a life of aristocratic pleasures or as an opportunity for tweaking the noses of aristocrats. The tweaking was regarded—so noted was he in society for his brilliant conversation—as a talent rather than a taunt: "He said things," Powys Mather remarked, "which made all future friendship impossible—and hosts of friends sprang up about him." His being made Elizabeth's secretary came in the same year that his friend Beaumarchais's *Marriage of Figaro* came on the boards; and Chamfort, as a far more privileged servant, must often have let drop in palace circles much that resembled what the public heard at the playhouse. By now Beaumarchais was just one of Chamfort's gifted literary friends, with Vaudreuil—whom he greatly valued—simply the closest of his patrician ones: by now Chamfort was also on easy terms with Talleyrand and getting to be on intimate ones with Mirabeau. Almost ten years older than Mirabeau, Chamfort became very much his literary master, the future moderate Revolution statesman consulting him about his writings and hailing him as a Tacitus for genius, a Lucian for wit, and a Voltaire for high spirits. Mirabeau, when he was writing, would say to himself: "This would make Chamfort frown; we mustn't do *this*, we mustn't write *that*." Their friendship persisted through the 1780's, though they were not too much *en rapport* in the year that ended the decade. As that memorable year approached, Chamfort detected, far more than did his aristocratic friends, the explosive realities in the pre-Revolution rumblings. The situation, Chamfort told Vaudreuil, was much too grave for him to follow Vaudreuil's suggestion that he write a satire on the moblike outcries of the time, at a moment when "democracy" was merely a word, and over twenty million people were ready to do far more than grumble about their plight. And, however cultivated and sympathetic Vaudreuil may have been, in July 1789 he was one of the earliest émigrés to England; with Chamfort, by then, very differently occupied.

When the Estates General convened, Chamfort played no official or politically active role, but he began, and continued, to do a good deal of writing for the press. He had a hand in the speeches of his friends, among them Talleyrand; he helped found the Club of 1789, which he later withdrew from; and he is thought to have been present at the storming of the Bastille and one of the first to enter it. He, indeed, wrote an article on the event for quick propagandist circulation—an article, with its militant tone and highly colored details, not unlike many other broadsides. It pictured the governor of the Bastille begging for powder to blow himself up with; the mob rushing into the fortress and often killing their own friends; the prisoners who had thought the clamor they heard meant death, and found it meant liberation; the appalling weight of the chains, the sight of the hideous instruments of torture, the touches of pathos and tragedy. The verbal lunges he had made with fashionable buttoned foils in the drawing room were now seen for what they had signalized, as was he seen for where he stood. As time passed, Chamfort got Mirabeau to found a new, far-from-extremist club called the Jacobins; but as time continued to pass, Robespierre gained ascendancy over the club and Chamfort seldom went to it. The Revolution had put an end to Chamfort's royal pension, and he moved into very modest quarters, all the time carrying on his journalistic writing while often not being well. When in August 1792 the monarchy fell, he wrote to a friend that he had been going the rounds of the overturned statues of kings, which his doctor prescribed as "very salubrious exercise." Under the new régime he was made director of the Bibliothèque Nationale, where he also lived. As the Revolution darkened and Girondist power waned, he spoke out with his usual boldness, got into Danton's black books by refusing to write against the freedom of the press, and into Marat's for having attended a gathering where Marat was ill-treated and then thrown bodily out. In May 1793, when twenty-two Girondists were rounded up and later guillotined, Chamfort was arrested but soon released. Then a contemptuous remark he had made was blown up by a subordinate at the Bibliothèque who wanted Chamfort's post, and he was once again arrested, and taken to the Madelonettes prison to be, after a short time, released; but the experience so horrified him that he vowed he would rather die than go to prison again. His release this time put him under a kind of house arrest, only for the police officer after a while to tell Chamfort and others who were confined to pack their bags before going to a house of detention. Thinking this meant Les Madelonettes, Chamfort used the time allotted for getting his bags packed, by going to his study, misfiring a pistol that wounded his face and right eye, wielding a razor that bloodied him without successfully cutting his throat, and then, with no greater success, slashing his wrists and opening his veins. A hideously bloody sight—and indeed close to dying—he was put to bed while doctors were sent for and while he himself dictated a statement that he would rather die free than live a slave. (While he was lying near to death, surrounded by officials, doctors, police spies, and friends, a writer who had heard of what Chamfort had attempted, outdoing any satiric invention of Chamfort's, pushed into his room and announced that "Monsieur de Chamfort has apparently not read my discourse against suicide! The work has been very successful. I prove my case *primo*, I prove it *secundo*.")

Although a constantly ill man who had all but murdered himself, Chamfort recovered and was able to get about again. He had resigned from the Bibliothèque but had plans for writing. Then a fever brought on by a walk on a cold day led to various complications in his maimed body, and in April 1794 he died. His obituary in the newspapers was a purely factual one, his standing in Terrorist eyes a decidedly wobbly one, his burial a very small one; but, says his rewarding translator and biographer W. S. Merwin, "most of those who were invited came."

A somewhat prolific writer, Chamfort survives for the briefest things he wrote, or spoke, or collected: for his aphorisms, epigrams, and repartees, and for the anecdotes he amassed. These were brought together in an unfinished work to be called, ironically, *Products of the Perfected Civilization*, the book's contents being exposures of various forms of folly, corruption, and vice. What Chamfort had done over a considerable period of time was to jot down on small squares of paper various anecdotes, repartees, and aphoristic thoughts, and thrust them into portfolios. But many of these vanished after his death, and the larger intentions of the *Products*, which might have made for a work of real stature, diminished into the Maxims and Considerations, and the Characters and Anecdotes, as we have them.

A mélange of genres in their very titles, they are of uneven value but considerable range—at their best, the brilliant reflections of someone critical by nature and embittered by life; the flings and retorts of someone of acid and insolent wit; the lightning flashes of a protesting social critic, and the high-society anecdotes and salon witticisms Chamfort had systematically collected, many of them from several generations back. As it is not hard to infer from his life, Chamfort derogated the milieu he was insistently drawn to: a nobody by birth, he could not but be elated by the friendship of the high-born, as he could not but profit by the opportunities they found for him. But the luxurious living and elegant pleasure of the *haut monde* were for this prickly man not pleasure enough: he had to make impudent witticisms at the *haut monde*'s expense; he had to offer his thanks in the form of insults. This is not at all unusual: many good writers—necessarily witty ones—who have longed for a place in exalted society have ruthlessly satirized it; we need only mention Swift, Pope, Wilde, Proust, and Evelyn Waugh. In Chamfort's case, however, no sooner was his vanity stroked and put to sleep than his pride would be awakened: his insults were destined to show, above all, his lack of servility. But something else, something better, was present—his were a mind and a heart full of protest against the life they saw about them; but they were a pessimism as well, which eventually dulled the protest, seeing no better solution in revolutionary procedures than in the *ancien régime's*. If perhaps Chamfort's most stinging witticism concerns the *ancien régime*—"The nobility, say its members, is the intermediary between the King and the people . . . Indeed yes, just as the hounds are the intermediary between the hunter and the hare"—this is pretty well matched by Chamfort's slogan for the revolutionaries: "Be my brother, or I will kill you."

Yet Chamfort's life, however unfulfilled, was a full one in terms of personal experience. It constantly ran to extremes: often, at the same time that Chamfort dined with a prince, he lived as a pauper; though he ran the whole gamut of journalism, he enjoyed a high place in the literary world; great ladies were both his hostesses and his mistresses, *grands seigneurs* both his patrons and his pupils; above all, his emotions were as various as his employments, toppling him from elation to dejection, from admiration to contempt. His reacting to so much about life in extremely short sentences—with his longer writings of little worth—helps to characterize, as well as in a small way to immortalize, him. He had a kind of brilliance that fits into the drawing room, however much it may be directed against it; he had a kind of audacity that is a chief element in a successful man of wit, and indeed he wielded his brilliance like a rapier and wore his audacity like so much lace. His pessimism was at least as personal as it was philosophical, as was much else about him. He writes his maxims in the very midst of life, often with an immediacy far different from the impersonal, clinical assessments of La Rochefoucauld. What wisdom he has is not lucid or serene, but near neighbor to indignation and half brother of irony. Chamfort's career was in many respects a decided success story, from the prizes he won as a schoolboy to the places he gained as a man. Yet he could never for long find satisfaction, let alone happiness; he had to greet aristocratic pleasure with disdain or choke in protest. He was a self-dramatizer with no taste for happy endings, and in the very moment of fulfillment he felt, or contrived to feel, frustrated. Though he might say, at the outbreak of the Revolution, *"Guerre aux châteaux, paix aux chaumières,"* he was in no sense revolutionary, but a humanitarian and a species of angry man; and inevitably the excesses of the Revolution would alienate and repel him. George Saintsbury has lightly bracketed Chamfort with Swift; and in small ways—a love of puns and plays on words—as in large ways—a burning indignation and a blistering irony—the two had a good deal in common. Thus, both men delighted to live among the great; thus, Swift in Ireland raged over oppression, as Chamfort did in France. Swift's taking leave of life—his tombstone inscription with its *saeva indignatio* and its *cor laceratum*—finds kinship in Chamfort's departing a world *"où il faut que le coeur se brise ou se bronze."* Chamfort's thus departing the world—and even more his living so embitteredly in it—clearly owed something to how he had entered it, illegitimate and ill provided for; just as with Swift, something so rankled from straitened early days as to mar or mishandle the rest of them. Just so, however much what Chamfort said might glitter, even more frequently must it sting.

Though Chamfort's anecdotes and witticisms are on the whole very good, some of them suffer from our knowing too little about the people they pillory or about the world they portray. Others fall short of true wit, or are the ancestors of jokes and repartees that have grown stale. Thus we find the patina rather thin on the man who was appointed royal dentist to the king on the same day that the king lost his last tooth; and there is nothing very original in the man who said "If it weren't for the Government, there'd be nothing left in France to laugh at." Though most of the anecdotes, in step with Chamfort's own *mots* and maxims, proclaim the faults and follies of the great world, some of them concern the plight of the far from great: thus, an indigent author of a book excoriating the government cried, "Heavens, they haven't sent me to the Bastille—and my rent's almost due!" Among the rather gossipy or malicious tales of real people, there is that of a cardinal's sister who complimented an archbishop on his success with women, and particularly for a child of his by Madame de Mazarin. The archbishop, denying the whole thing, said: "Scandal hasn't spared *you*, Madame, either. There's no more truth to the story about me and Madame de Mazarin than to the one linking you and your brother." "Well," said the lady, "if that's the case, then the child *is* yours." Perhaps the funniest of such stories tells of the Marquise de Saint Pierre, who was present at a party where someone said that a certain nobleman had had a great many women without having loved a single one of them. "That is easily said," broke in the marquise, "but I just happen to know a woman whom he traveled three hundred leagues to be reunited with. And as soon as he got back to her, he flung the woman on her bed with tremendous passion—and we were there for three days!" And here is one of the better anecdotal snubs. One day a Vicomte de S. approached a Monsieur de Vaines and asked him: "Is it true, monsieur, that at a house where they were kind enough to say that I had wit, you said that I hadn't?" "My dear sir," was the answer, "there's not one word of truth in it. I was never at a house where anybody said you *had* wit, and *I* never said that you hadn't." For a final, and fittingly Chamfortesque, anecdote, a witty man said of a cold-blooded, calculating companion who had come back to him when, after ups and downs, he became very prosperous: "Monsieur X not only wants his friends to be successful; he insists that they be."

As a society wit and raconteur, Chamfort spun his own anecdotes—the one, for example, about a pedantic academician who came home to find a man in bed with his wife. The man, caught out, turned to the lady and said: "*Je vous disais, madame, qu'il était temps que je m'en aille!*" To which the academician husband replied: "*Que je m'en allasse, monsieur.*" Indeed, Chamfort, however pleased to be a member of the Academy—we know what efforts he had made to become one —delighted in making fun of it and its members, one of whom is pictured as proposing "that not more than four persons be allowed to speak at once." Of another, and extremely stingy, member who is thought not to have made a certain called-for contribution, the collector says indulgently: "I believe he did, though I didn't see him do it," whereupon the celebrated Fontenelle interposes: "*I* saw him do it, but I don't believe he did."

As a coiner and collector of such things, Chamfort has us in his debt, and he belongs among the notable aphorists, with Dr. Johnson and Oscar Wilde, as also a great wit whose best remarks smack of conversation, of impromptu, of the instantaneous retort. He shares with them too a gift of metaphor, of lighting up his sentiment with a picture rather than a precept. Thus the sentiment itself is less important than what it is compared to in "A fool who shows a sudden flash of wit both astonishes and shocks us, like cab horses at a gallop." This is again true, but more searching as well as shocking, in Chamfort's "A man who, behind an appearance and acknowledgment of friendship, conceals tyranny, patronage, or alms reminds me of that infamous priest who did his poisoning with holy wafers." And nothing could be more graphic than "Divorce is so completely natural a thing that, in many houses, it sleeps every night between husband and wife."

With Chamfort we look back upon an age which he helps illuminate by metaphor, and even more by concrete details of its manners and morals. Thus, as an anecdotist, he is something of a social and cultural historian, and as an aphorist, something more of a social and cultural critic; and this, served up as it often is with a scathing wit, can even today have a certain shock value. But we oftener feel more like spectators than participants, like people who witness the beatings rather than feel the whip. Our own faults and vices are rather different ones. Chamfort doesn't make us frequently wince, as La Rochefoucauld does; and in much the same way, he doesn't make us wiser. But as a social critic he has a second and greater value: he attacks society, not in the limited sense of the weaknesses of the wellborn, but in the opprobrious sense of the inequalities of mankind; of the oppression and exploitation, of the deprived and the poor. On this head, Chamfort might be called one of the greatest of short-sentence pamphleteers, whose sayings are sometimes militant slogans and at other times ironic jibes. He tells of a man who "said innocently" to a friend: "We condemned three men to death this morning. Two of them clearly deserved it." "The poor," Chamfort said memorably, "are the Negroes of Europe." "There are seven million men in France asking for alms," he remarks elsewhere, "and there are twelve million men unable to give them any."

The pessimist in him could somewhat defeat the pamphleteer, the man of the world impede the man of action. Chamfort came to have an intense dissatisfaction with life itself, which led him to distrust, not to say reject, all programs and solutions; his protest spoke for the humanitarian in him, but gave no sustained help to the reformer. Again and again certain of Chamfort's anecdotes about other people would seem to bear out an attitude in him. There is the man who said that for life to be bearable, men would have to destroy hell and reorder heaven. There is the greatly gifted man who, when Chamfort asked why he played no part in the Revolution of 1789, said that, having for twenty years found men malevolent individually and in private life, he could look for little in them collectively and in public. And there is the famous remark that one must swallow a toad every morning if, in going about among people, one is to find nothing more disgusting the rest of the day.

Chamfort's aphorisms often strike a similar note; whether or not heaven needed reordering, there was in Chamfort's view little hope for harmony on earth; and though he might for a time be an embattled pamphleteer, he was too embittered to remain one long. Neither was he a distinguished psychologist or philosopher, qualifications for most eminent aphorists. Yet his aphorisms rank very high: Saintsbury said that "they hardly admit a rival"; Schopenhauer and Nietzsche have also been among his admirers, and in our day, Camus. Never a true man of action, he verbally fired innumerable pistol shots; and these, unlike his attempt upon his life, were masterfully aimed and swiftly found their mark.

Aphorisms

Whoever is not a misanthrope at forty can never have loved mankind.

THE LAST WORD

Knaves have always a certain need of their honor, somewhat as police spies are paid less when they move in less good company.

Once love is purged of vanity it is like a feeble convalescent, hardly capable of dragging itself around.

We must be just before we are generous; we need shirts before ruffles.

Sperone Speroni explains very well why a writer's form of expression may seem quite clear to him yet obscure to the reader: the reader is advancing from language to thought, the writer from thought to language.

One must do more, think less, and not watch oneself live.

Most books today seem to have been written overnight from books read the day before.

In France we threaten the man who rings the alarm bell and leave in peace the man who starts the fire.

In a country where everybody strives for attention, it is better to be bankrupt than to be nothing.

Poverty sets a reduced price on crime.

CHAMFORT

Love, as it exists in society, is only the exchange of two fantasies and the contact of two skins.

Of what matter whether Titus or Tiberius occupies the throne, when every minister is a Sejanus?

Vice would fail to be total vice if it did not hate virtue.

It is easier to make certain things legal than to make them legitimate.

All passions exaggerate: it is because they exaggerate that they are passions.

V

Lichtenberg

GEORG CHRISTOPH LICHTENBERG is one of the most attractive and individual of aphorists, and in the face of his profession—a professor of physics—perhaps one of the least foreseeable. Still, a hundred years after the professor of physics flourished, a professor of mathematics would be writing *The Hunting of the Snark* and *Alice in Wonderland*. Lichtenberg's scientific attainments still cling to his reputation but no longer affect it, and the reputation itself still falls short, outside of Lichtenberg's native Germany, of its due. But, with the publication in English some years ago of his aphorisms, Lichtenberg gained a very responsive and often enthusiastic readership which has continued to grow; on the strength of the aphorisms, Lichtenberg's letters have come to be known, and half a dozen years ago his brilliant and remarkable *Commentaries on Hogarth's Engravings*—published in America as *The World of Hogarth*—won him a niche in the art world and in cultural studies of eighteenth-century England. Lichtenberg's life, though it yields very little that is dramatic or eventful, communicates much that has flavor, that has character, that has substance, and that in its way has importance—has intellectual activity, imaginative liveliness and force, scientific observation, self-observation, much playful wisdom and some that is profound.

Lichtenberg was born in 1742 in Oberranstadt, a village

near Darmstadt; his father was the village pastor, and Georg Christoph was the eighteenth child. When very young he became a victim of his nurse's negligence by suffering a fall that had very unfortunate consequences. When he was eight years old his spine began to curve; very short of build, he became a hunchback and for the rest of his life was plagued with ill health. Apparently his mother, who was at once lively and sympathetic, helped him to surmount his physical handicaps; his father, a quite learned theologian who became the most important church dignitary of the region—general superintendent at Darmstadt—had scientific interests which crept into his sermons and even more into his son. When in 1751 his father died, the nine-year-old Georg went to the Gymnasium at Darmstadt, where his scientific gifts were quickly recognized: in due course he received a grant of four hundred florins from a neighboring Landgraf, which made possible his studying astronomy, mathematics, and physics at the University of Göttingen, then one of the most renowned universities in Europe. Georg's most distinguished professor there, A. G. Kästner, was not only a major figure in physics but gained a considerable reputation for his epigrams.

By the time Lichtenberg was twenty-five he was invited to be professor of mathematics at the University of Giessen in Hesse but, presumably from having ambitions to teach at Göttingen, he turned down the offer. Three years later he became professor *extraordinarius* in physics at Göttingen, and five years later he was named professor *ordinarius*—a position he would hold for the remainder of his life. His lectures were extremely popular, thanks partly to their wit; and his influence on students was great, thanks considerably to his knowledge and kindliness. He had early in life learned English, and read and admired a great many eighteenth-century English novelists and poets—Swift, Pope, Fielding—his admiration of them all the greater because of the overblown, *langweilig* work of contemporary German writers. The pleasure Lichtenberg got from England's literature fired him with a great desire to know something of its life; and in 1770 he made the first of two long visits there. In Germany, before this, he had served as the tutor of two young English students, the sons of Lord Boston; and Lord Boston's friendship and hospitality, coupled with Lichtenberg's professional standing in Göttingen, gave the visitor the entrée to English society, not to speak of a genuine friendship that developed with George III and Queen Charlotte. The Hanoverian king and the Hessian professor had their German blood—one has difficulty in imaging what else—in common.

Lichtenberg found London extremely stimulating but somewhat confusing. It was a mélange, he wrote to a fellow professor at Göttingen, of sights and sounds—from the king with his crown on in Parliament to a multitudinous shouting in the streets of the king's bogey, "Wilkes and Liberty," and with the streets so jammed with traffic that you either arrived very late at your destination or never got there at all. Moreover, you had to dress, as you had often to dine, twice a day and, wherever you dined, be part of "a large company." Lichtenberg found having to accustom himself to such elegant living—which he would soon be forced to abandon and which in any case had come too late in life—all in all unattractive and he wanted no more of it. He seems less romantic than satiric about what he experiences, and on the whole less responsive than observant. About English food he writes: "You find few complicated dishes" but "a host of simple things." "They eat," he continues, "at midday and then they drink at midday, two completely different things. At the latter occasion the women are no longer present"—so that they can't pilfer secrets of state from the men, or the men gather secrets from them. "In the evening, or in plain German, at night, it's no better—I mean about eating and drinking; about the secrets, it is definitely worse."

A second visit to England a few years later, lasting for a year and a half, produced much the same animated interest in London's animated scene, and provided, in a letter to a Göttingen colleague, a very animated account:

Scarcely do you stop than crash! a porter runs you down crying "By your leave" when you are lying on the ground. In the middle of the street roll chaises, carriages and drays in an unending stream. Above this din, and the hum and clatter from church towers, are the bells of the postmen, the organs, fiddles, hurdy-gurdies and tambourines of English mountebanks, and the cries of those who sell hot and cold viands in the open at the street corners. Then you will see a bonfire of shavings flaring up as high as the upper floors of the houses in a circle of merrily shouting beggar boys, sailors and rogues. Suddenly a man whose handkerchief has been stolen will cry "Stop thief!" and every one will begin pushing and shoving—many of them not with any desire of catching the thief but of prigging for themselves, perhaps, a watch or purse . . . That is Cheapside and Fleet Street on a December evening.

No one could have been much more observant, and nothing could be more Hogarthian. We shall come back to Hogarth's work—the painter himself having died in 1764; but there was still living an Englishman for whom Lichtenberg showed an almost equal admiration and interest—David Garrick. The admiration had grown out of Lichtenberg's response to the English theater, and out of Garrick's acting in Shakespeare, whose greatness Lichtenberg had long saluted. He saw every detail of a Garrick performance, and every detail of Garrick's physical self—"the flick of his eye; the way he takes snuff, wears his hat, or carries his cane." But Lichtenberg also saw into Garrick, lending perceptiveness to portraiture. Garrick, he wrote, had observed and studied mankind

from the cultured and artificial denizens of the salons of St James's to the savage creatures in the eating houses of St Giles. He . . . did not wait to be inspired, but worked hard (for in England all is not left to genius as in Germany) . . . in London . . . a man with such talent for observation can learn as much by experience in a year as in a whole lifetime spent in some little town.

Lichtenberg's career at Göttingen continued to flourish and in 1777, after he had made a striking discovery in electricity, he was given a chair—the first in Germany—of experimental physics. The discovery, still known as "Lichtenberg's figures," was that the discharge of an electric spark produces, on the surface of certain materials, starlike figures; and, though the figures themselves had been noticed earlier, the fact that Lichtenberg perceived their regular formation and orderly arrangement has been cited as proof of his powers of observation—a gift that would dominate his study of Hogarth in the last years of his life. By then Lichtenberg would have been elected a member of the Royal Society and of the Academy of Science at St. Petersburg, and have turned down an invitation to teach at Leyden, then the center of studies in physics. By then also he would have written a number of essays and pamphlets, some of them scientific, some satiric. Though marred by ill health, his personal life seems to have been, for most of his life, in no real way unhappy: he won esteem for his work, praise for his wit, friendship for his kind, likable nature, and, to add to the enjoyments of existence, there were a number of mistresses and eventually a wife. A curious and touching relationship concerns a twelve-year-old flower seller he had met in 1777, had taken into his house as a maid, and, when she was fifteen, had begun to live with as man and wife. When she was seventeen he wrote of her to a friend: "Two hours after my excellent girl had been carried away, the little Dietrich girl [her father was Lichtenberg's best friend] died. Every hour they asked about each other's health, and their graves are close to each other." He was very much affected by this loss, and wrote later to another friend: "The machine is moving again; for how long, only He who was pleased to ruin its movement, knows."

In 1794 he writes to yet another friend:

I don't know whether you had heard that at the very time . . . the revolution broke out in France, a most remarkable one broke out . . . in my domestic life. I got married, and that is the fine side of the upheaval; I was attacked by a convulsive asthma which threatened me with suffocation . . . that's the ugly side. On the first part . . . I live most happily and pleasantly, and have four children running about me . . . I look back . . . on when I could have been married but was not, as on a half-savage state.

During these years Lichtenberg also gained a reputation as a writer, his *Letters from England* having been published in the late 1770's; his editorship, during the 1780's, of the *Göttenisches Magazin der Wissenshaften und Literatur*, which he founded, having exerted a considerable influence, as did his writing and editing for the *Göttingen Taschen Kalender*. The two things, however, for which in America Lichtenberg is best known today—the *Hogarth* and the aphorisms—appeared, respectively, not till the end of his life (the least happy period) and long after his death (at the beginning of the twentieth century).

Lichtenberg's *Commentaries on Hogarth's Engravings* has a value and sharpness not unrelated to the aphorist in him—his close observation of a purveyor of humanity so remarkable as

THE LAST WORD

Hogarth seems but a step or two removed from Lichtenberg's own keen study of mankind. His commentary on the *Hogarth* is so close and detailed as to lend itself far better to our reading his book than to our quoting copiously—as any adequate account demands—from it. In either case, moreover, it would be pointless if we failed to have the engravings at our side. Yet Lichtenberg can describe or comment on the engravings with as much humor, and as much accuracy, as Hogarth can visually portray them. To take a well-known, indeed a memorable, example, Hogarth's *Strolling Actresses Dressing in a Barn*—a masterpiece of everything that is makeshift, congested, disheveled—Lichtenberg begins by questioning the title of the engraving: male figures, he points out, are quite visible, so that he wonders, can they be females in disguise? Next he spots the playbills—two of them "lying there on the bed, directly behind the grill, close to the broken eggs, the chamber pot and the empty pair of trousers"; then he salutes Juno, the queen of heaven: while she is studying her part, "she stretches out her immortal leg . . . and lets the Goddess of the Night . . . darn her eternal stockings." As for the *déshabillée* Diana, "she who among the ancients was the chaste and unapproachable one, stands here almost without fortification." And we watch Lichtenberg pick up, scrutinize, and, often in a double sense, put down the hundred and one things that Hogarth has so carefully, so cunningly, so exhaustively found room for. Turn to an engraving even more famous than the *Strolling Actresses*, and as hideously grim as the *Actresses* is comically messy—the final plate of *A Rake's Progress*, where Lord Rakehell, in Bedlam, is put in chains; and Lichtenberg's descriptions are equally valid. Not the least valuable merit of Lichtenberg's *Hogarth* is how much he points out and points up, which the reader would almost certainly not notice, or at any rate, would not sufficiently appreciate.

Lichtenberg must, during much of his life, have written aphorisms—often, I have no doubt, when he did not particularly mean to. This, very likely, is to some extent true of most aphorists, naturally endowed as they are with a gift of concise, pointed expression and with a certain instinct for a striking analogy or antithesis. Lacking this gift, no matter how sharp or original their insights, they somehow fall short of the terseness and trenchancy that come close to defining the aphorism. At times Lichtenberg himself exhibits a Germanic tendency to overexpand his definitions or overextend his original idea; but he is for the most part refreshingly un-German, belonging to that small galaxy of bright and witty writers in German that includes Heine, Karl Kraus, and on one side of him, Nietzsche. Neither much wit nor much humor is, need I say, a common German virtue, the first from Germans' being solemn and ponderous, the second from their being pompous and self-important. But Lichtenberg had a great deal of wit and humor, had that acute sense of lighting on resemblances which is a fundamental of wit, and that acute sense of noting incongruities which is a great flavorer of humor. His humor can be amusingly earthy and show a touch of wit as well, as in: "It rained so hard that all the pigs got clean and all the people dirty." His wit, in turning satiric, can be also just sufficiently subtle: "If, as I once read, no one dies before having done one sensible thing, then M— begot a son who is immortal." In both of these talents we cannot fail to notice an uncommon imaginativeness, ranging all the way from the merely playful to the genuinely perceptive. There is, as we all know, a touch of melancholy in much of the best humor; with Lichtenberg, as with Hamlet, we feel a touch of humor in the melancholy; and there is a good deal of self-ridicule in Lichtenberg's citation of his plights. We find also a good deal of rewarding speculation in his scrutiny of his neurotic fears and anxieties, and we are fortunate in encountering, in so brilliant an aphorist, a striking, and not merely unconscious, autobiographer of sorts. Although Lichtenberg failed to write an autobiography, he wrote down—as material for one—many reminiscences and observations, confessions and comments, and he proved at times as subjectively relentless an observer as he could be an objectively amused or amusing one.

His imagination, he correctly reported, was his most faithful companion; and it seems to have companioned him not least during his late-in-life afflictions and neuroses. Thus he confesses that when, according to the best doctors, his only ailment was abdominal cramps, he proceeded to think he had thirteen other ailments, among them diabetes, arteriosclerosis, incipient dropsy, convulsive asthma, a tumor on his liver, and water in the head—this last, he conceded, the only one an outsider would think had any foundation. Lichtenberg called himself a "pathological egotist": at one stage, he spent a year and a half in bed, to get out of bed much less lighthearted and life-loving that he had been—indeed, he saw himself, before he had reached fifty, as an aging man. Moreover, during the last years of his life—he died in 1799—he had a secret love affair which was altogether lacking in love and altogether lacking in gaiety—enough to fill him with guilt and sentence him to suffering.

But in happier times—his journal jottings go back to his student days—there were small insights, humorous comments, and jokes about himself (Goethe remarked of Lichtenberg generally that inside every joke of his a problem was hidden). Lichtenberg spoke of having few friends, despite the fact that his friendly manner made many people think him their friend. He had loved, he said, just once happily, and once not unhappily. He had been, since a boy, a freethinker who could yet pray with fervor; but after he was sixteen he could not make himself believe that Christ was the Son of God, and he wished that Christ had written down "more information" about Joseph of Arimathea. Lichtenberg records that he felt he could spot most people's weaknesses in a reasonably short time, adding aphoristically that "no dissembling helps against a personal relationship of three weeks." He also records having asked himself how he had liked a party, his answer being "Fine; almost as much as being alone in my room." Neither his crooked body, he felt, nor his manner of clothing it, was usually good enough for formal parties; indeed, he enjoyed dinners of no more than three courses with wine, but with at the least potatoes, apples, wine, and bread. He felt that he hung suspended in the world "between philosophy and the cunning of housemaids"; and certainly he himself was capable of all sorts of imaginative extremes—whether it was giving each of his bedroom slippers a name or dreaming that he was to be burned at the stake. About dreams he was rather prophetic: "If people," he wrote, "would recount their dreams truthfully, one might define character more correctly from dreams than from faces." And again: "It is one of man's claims to superiority that he dreams and *knows it*. We have hardly made the right use of this yet." And, most strikingly, he said of someone: "I cannot say that I was his enemy, but neither was I his friend. I never dreamt of him." So remarkably keen is Lichtenberg about the fanciful as well as the factual, the odd as well as the familiar, that one wonders whether he did not, together with so much else, *dream* aphorisms.

In any case, the aphorist in Lichtenberg shows a good deal

of diversity and range. He could detect very graphically a human *type* in this or that particular person: thus, of someone: "He moved as slowly as an hour hand amidst a crowd of second hands"; and of someone else: "When he was expected to use his mind, he felt like a right-handed person who has to do something with his left." He adds one more satiric reversal to the list of assaults on human complacency: "as foolish as it must look to a crab when it sees a man walking forward." He could catch, in a phrase, the good and bad side of parochialism: "A little town where each face rhymes with every other." He could reinterpret what seems like a bold gesture: "To do just the opposite is also a form of imitation." And he could provide us with a very concise bit of intellectual biography: "One man begets a thought, the second baptizes it, the third sires children on it, the fourth visits it on its deathbed, and the fifth buries it."

Lichtenberg can also be witty or whimsical at almost every turn: he speaks of someone with "an Amen face"; he tells of someone who "received warm, not to say burnt, thanks"; and he disposes of a good many of his fellow men as "*Non cogitant, ergo non sunt.*" The outright satirist in Lichtenberg frequently joins hands with the aphorist: "He who is in love with himself has at least this advantage: he won't encounter many rivals in his love." He has a good deal to say, with a good deal of tartness, about—or against—readers, writers, and professors. Thus: "The critics instruct us to stay close to nature, and authors read this advice; but they always think it safer to stay close to authors who have stayed close to nature." Or: "We acquire professors . . . we acquire books; [we] read, excerpt and argue ourselves white, yellow, consumptive—and frigid and impotent." Again: "A book is a mirror: when a monkey peers into it, no apostle can look out." Once more: "I would often rather read what a famous author has cut out of a work than what he has left in it." And finally: "He was a busy writer, and a very diligent reader of his own articles in the learned periodicals." Let us hear Lichtenberg on marriage: "One of the main conveniences of marriage is to be able to pass on to one's wife a visitor one can't stand the sight of." And: "Nowadays beautiful women are counted among the talents of their husbands." Here the satire is playful: "A donkey appears to me like a horse translated into Dutch." Here, it is about himself: "A worry meter . . . my face is one." And here he exhibits us as the slaves of particular custom, familiarity, sensibility: "How much depends on the way things are presented in this world can be seen from the very fact that coffee drunk out of wineglasses is really miserable stuff, as is meat cut at the table with a pair of scissors. Worst of all, as I once actually saw, is butter spread on a piece of bread with an old but very clean razor." Apropos of razors, Lichtenberg remarks of someone: "He kept continually polishing himself and finally became dull before he became sharp."

In addition to writing aphorisms, Lichtenberg commented on the writing of them; and on how to go at it. By studying one's own ideas and sensations, he says, and giving sharp, individualistic expression to them, "one can in a short time build up a store of observations that can be put to good use in many ways—we come to know ourselves; to add to our observations; and to strengthen our ability to observe." He wishes he could see the notebooks that "immortal works" grew out of; but, failing this, one must learn through oneself to see into others. And he continues to set limits to the value of reading: "One cannot easily think too much, but one can easily read too much"; he himself, in reading, "spread myself without strengthening myself." As for the nature of an aphorism, a witty thought, to be striking, must be apposite—

but more than apposite; other people must wonder why something so evident had not occurred to them. And an aphorism, like all good writing, must not betray the labor that went into shaping it. In such precepts of Lichtenberg's there is no wit and no particular originality, but there is a certain amount of acquired wisdom. As for Lichtenberg's own insight and original thought, his able translators and editors, Franz Mautner and Henry Hatfield, tell us that in "waste-books," discovered after his death, he anticipated twentieth-century depth psychology, linguistic analysis, and theories of knowledge. It is no wonder that, along with Lichtenberg's *literary* admirers, there have been some of the greatest and most revolutionary of scientists, psychologists, and philosophers—Herschel, Volta, Kant, Nietzsche, Kierkegaard, Freud, and Wittgenstein. Lichtenberg was not only a man whose sanity and perspicacity begot much that was valuable; he was also one whose ailments and neuroses begot very little less. That as either of these things he could be so pithy and picturesque in manner is his special gift, and his reader's very special gain.

Aphorisms

We must make people feel obliged to us in accordance with what they are, not we.

Strength without bigness is never laughable, but bigness without strength almost always is.

LICHTENBERG

If an angel were to tell us about his philosophy, I believe many of his statements might well sound like 2 × 2 = 13.

Man loves company, be it only that of a small burning candle.

To many people virtue consists chiefly in repenting faults, not in avoiding them.

When men watch them, nursemaids kiss and rock children with vigor; when only women are looking on, they handle children very quietly.

As soon as people learn that someone is blind, they think they can tell it from behind him.

The fly that doesn't want to be swatted is most secure when it lights on the fly swatter.

In courteous towns it is impossible to acquire any knowledge of the world; every one is so courteously honest, so courteously rude, so courteously deceitful.

He swallowed a lot of wisdom, but it seemed as if all of it had gone down the wrong way.

THE LAST WORD

There are people who think everything one does with a serious face is sensible.

Nothing can contribute more to peace of mind than having no opinion at all.

One must judge men not by their opinions but by what their opinions have made of them.

People who have read a great deal seldom make great discoveries.

To totally block a given effect requires a force equal to that which it cost. To send it in a different direction, a trifle will often suffice.

A man really never knows whether he may not be sitting in a madhouse.

I am convinced that a person doesn't only love himself in others; he also hates himself in others.

VI

Goethe

JOHANN WOLFGANG VON GOETHE, the greatest and most famous of German writers, ranks also among the greatest of aphorists—this from sometimes having purposefully composed them, or having at other times struck them off in his treatment of a subject or in his general text. One of the few European writers who have commanded great attention from not only their own country but from all of Europe and beyond, Goethe was also among the few who wrote successfully in many forms—as poet, novelist, dramatist, autobiographer, student of science and philosophy—and who in one sense was an innovator and in a different sense a spokesman for the traditional and the established. For just such reasons, his particular importance has tended to rise and fall; but, however bruised or dented, or in one way or another subject to dispute, his stature has undoubtedly survived.

Goethe was born in Frankfurt in 1749, the grandson of a prosperous innkeeper and the son of a student of law who, denied an official government post in Frankfurt, withdrew into rather affluent private life, becoming an imperial councilor and marrying, at the age of thirty-eight, the seventeen-year-old daughter of a Frankfurt Bürgermeister. Johann, the eldest son of the marriage, was the only one to survive childhood. His very young, and lively and extremely imaginative, mother proved both a congenial companion to him as a child and the source of some of his genius. If she contributed to Johann's temperament, his stern, schoolmasterish father proved of influence in shaping his character; but thanks to the trophies of his father's rather extensive travels, the boy grew up in a house filled with books, pictures, and various objects of art. When still very young, Johann had a "love affair" with a girl named Gretchen, which had an unhappy ending; he then took to writing a novel that had to do with the biblical Joseph, and a number of religious poems.

At sixteen he was packed off to the University of Leipzig, where he was not inspired by the professors he had or in the poems he wrote. He was strongly drawn, however, to a young Leipzig girl named Anna Katharina Schönkopf, the Annette after whom a collection of lyrics was named; and he was strongly drawn also to the study of art. His stay in Leipzig was terminated by a sudden and serious hemorrhage from which, back in Frankfurt, he recovered slowly, doing a great deal of reading, which included books on astrology and the occult. In due course his father sent him to finish his legal studies in Strassburg; there he also made some studies in medicine; there he encountered and was much impressed by Gothic architecture; there he met and was influenced by the not much older German critic and poet Herder; and there he became impassioned of a country parson's daughter, Frederike Brion. But she was someone too obscure for him to marry; their love affair ended unhappily, with Goethe lashing himself for it, a few years later, in a play called *Clavigo*. But most important for the future during Goethe's Strassburg days was a draft of *Götz von Berlichingen*, a drama about a rapacious sixteenth-century robber knight whom Goethe endowed with finer qualities than he had possessed in real life; but which, when produced, had considerable dramatic vigor and a considerable success.

In 1771, on receiving his law degree, Goethe returned to Frankfurt, where his legal activities, which very little interested him, did not come to much; but where, once again, romance beckoned and his writing bore fruit. He fell passionately in love with a girl named Charlotte Buff, but also once again matters moved toward an unhappy ending, with Goethe in so black a mood that for many nights he kept a dagger near him. He then fell in love with another girl, a banker's daughter named Anna Elizabeth Schönemann, whom he became engaged to; but finding her life too superficial and frivolous, he backed out of the marriage. He would write, soon after, a play called *Stella*, which in its first version created a great deal of hubbub by having the hero, who was in love with two women, live with both of them under the same roof. But what was most important during these Frankfurt years was Goethe's writing the novel that commemorated his love for Charlotte Buff, *The Sorrows of Young Werther*, which, steeped in sentiment and concluding in suicide, drew tears from all Europe and set going the reign of *Sturm und Drang* (the famous phrase derived from the title of a "wildly exotic" play by Maximilian Klinger). The nerve-shattering emotionalism of *Werther* made it, as Thomas Mann says, "the horror and detestation of the moralists," something that "evoked a storm of applause which went beyond all bounds and fairly intoxicated the world with an ecstasy for death. It ran like a fever and a frenzy over the populated earth . . . An audience already existed for the book before its appearance . . . it was as though the public in every country had been secretly and unconsciously waiting for this very work." Long afterward, Thackeray provided satiric amusement to *Werther*'s tearful finale:

THE LAST WORD

Charlotte, having seen his body
Borne before her on a shutter
Like a well conducted person
Went on cutting bread and butter.

Werther brought great fame to Goethe in his mid-twenties, and led to a change of scene and change of status in his life that would dominate the more than half-century which remained of it. The young prince Karl Augustus, soon to become Duke of Weimar—"a small but independent state," to quote André Maurois, "with a castle, a court, a cathedral and the University of Jena"—in 1775 invited Goethe, who was eight years his senior, to come to Weimar for a long visit. Although Goethe's father disliked the idea, Goethe accepted; and though the duke's carriage that was to bring Goethe to the duke failed to come for him on the day set, all was soon well; indeed Weimar became his home. Though, out of jealousy, the established courtiers looked askance at Goethe, the liberal-minded young duke loaded him with honors, sent him on missions, made him a privy councilor, and gave him ministerial duties which he very ably executed and which led to new and more important ones. These involved agricultural and scientific studies which Goethe mastered—indeed, he was to discover an affinity between the human jawbone and a bone in apes; as he was also to make discoveries in plant life, and to challenge Newton's theory of colors. In Weimar, it will be no surprise, Goethe found romance—this time with the wife of an official, Charlotte von Stein, a superior woman older than Goethe was, and of all his women perhaps culturally the one most suited to him. Their relationship lasted for a number of years, during which Goethe wrote some of his very best short poems, but no large work of importance, other than his getting started with

Wilhelm Meister as a "theater" novel which included Mignon —the Mignon of Ambroise Thomas's opera—as its heroine, and contained what, lyrically and operatically, is the most famous of his songs, *"Kennst du das Land"*:

> *Know you the land where the lemon trees bloom?*
> *In the dark foliage the gold oranges glow . . .*

In 1786 Goethe went on his first and long-awaited visit to Italy, which was in its way—like the removal some ten years before to Weimar—a crucial event in his life. He remained in Italy for something like a year and a half, centering himself in Rome but going as far afield as Sicily. Italy bespoke a classical tradition very different from the romantic, not to say sentimental, atmosphere of Goethe's Germany—though it was less Italian works of art than the Greek and Roman works of antiquity that detained Goethe and inspired him. In Italy he, among other things, made a new version of his *Iphigenia in Tauris*, which has been called "the most perfect post-Grecian work on a Grecian theme," and he finished his *Egmont*, a drama about the famous Low Countries patriot who, having been elevated by Spain for his victories against France, was, for opposing Spain's autocratic rule, to be executed for high treason.

The years that followed were to lack a certain stability: there were new travels, among them a disillusioning one—so much had Goethe cherished Italy—to Venice; and one in 1792 in the suite of the Duke of Weimar when he was campaigning against France. (Goethe felt, and wrote, disapprovingly about the French Revolution.) As a kind of compensation for these disappointments, Goethe had been elevated to director of the theater at Weimar, a position he would hold for twenty-two years. And during the 1790's he resumed work on his novel, now called *Wilhelm Meisters Lehrjahre* (Apprenticeship), and expanded it to become a young man's initiation into life. *Wilhelm Meister* would eventually include a *Wanderjahre* as well, this added during the last years of Goethe's life. *Wilhelm Meister*, taken as a whole, is a large and various work bearing no "classical" finality or form. Nevertheless it became, as it remained, the most influential of Goethe's books, both as a work of "education" and as a work of fiction.

As the eighteenth century expired Goethe was just past fifty, the great man of Weimar and the great literary figure of Germany. Only two years earlier he had published another major work, *Hermann und Dorothea*, a "simple story of village life" set forth in verse; and these were years when Goethe was given to writing poetry. Also, after a long period during which he and his greatest contemporary had noticeably kept their distance, Goethe and Schiller now entered into a very friendly relationship, with, indeed, Schiller and his wife settling in Weimar. In any very personal sense the two men still kept their distance—"we found the strongest band of union in our common efforts," said Goethe, "and had no need of what is commonly called friendship." Schiller, the lesser writer but the far more gifted playwright, and the lesser, but far more accessible and human, man, served Goethe as both consultant and stimulant; it had been Schiller who urged him to turn to the kind of poetic work that resulted in *Hermann und Dorothea*, and the writing of poetry generally.

Not just Schiller, but many notable people, and many in the literary world, came to Weimar—or came and went: indeed, Goethe repeated the saying that Weimar was a small place with ten thousand poets and a few inhabitants; while, thanks to the duke's enlightened attitude and to Goethe's great prestige, Weimar had become one of the great artists' capitals of Europe. Goethe enjoyed a prominence only com-

parable to that, half a century earlier, of a very dissimilar
Voltaire. Just so, Goethe was an august, indeed an awesome,
figure, as he has largely remained—"schoolboys," Thomas
Mann remarked, "learn his love affairs by heart." The love
affairs, in their multitudinousness and their rather theatrical
emotionalism, can seem today more than a little comic,
though they are at the same time the least exalted and the
most human of Goethe's postures. It was not until 1806, when
he was fifty-seven years old, that Goethe married: moreover,
his wife, Christiane Vulpius, had previously been for many
years his housekeeper and mistress; and had, early in their
relationship, borne him a son. She was quite lacking in
personality, and also in social position—nor was she, after
marrying him, allotted any. But as a well-functioning
Hausfrau, and as a pillow to fall back upon, she made Goethe
the kind of wife he would find most to his liking.

Goethe's marriage followed, doubtless not altogether by
accident, Schiller's death. For with the other, for the most
part much younger, poets of his time Goethe could prove in
varying ways difficult. Consider three poets of real talent:
Novalis called him "the governor [Statthalter] of poetry on
earth"—surely not entirely a compliment, and there isn't a
trace of a compliment in his "Goethe has done for German
poetry what Wedgwood has done for English art." Hölderlin's way of being received by Goethe was to watch the
master thumb through one of Hölderlin's books without so
much as once glancing at him. Of Kleist's work Goethe remarked that he could never think of it "without shuddering."
To a lesser poet, who had sent Goethe his poems, he replied:
"I have glanced through your little book. But since one must,
right at the start, protect oneself against an epidemic of
cholera, I have laid it aside." The *régisseur* of the Weimar

Court Theatre said that where Schiller would "walk through
the crowd with head bent, replying in a friendly manner to
anyone who saluted him," Goethe "strode among these same
people . . . proud as a king" while receiving tributes
(which Schiller found embarrassing) as no more than his
due. Schiller himself said, before their rapprochement: "To
see Goethe very often would make one a very unhappy man.
Even with his closest friends he never lets himself go . . . I
detest him thoroughly even though I love his intellect with
all my heart." Actually, the two men first managed to get
together through meeting at a conference where, it seems,
they argued their way, to Goethe's annoyance, into a meeting
of minds.

In any case, Schiller's death in 1805 ended an era in Goethe's life; but in the twenty-seven years that remained to
him there was a good deal of both activity and achievement.
Several major works would appear—in 1808, the first part of
Faust (which, begun in the 1770's, Goethe spent sixty years
writing and rewriting); much later appeared the second
part; in 1809, Goethe's *Wahlverwandtschaften* [*The Elective
Affinities*]; in 1819, The West-Eastern Divan poems; and
the first three volumes of Goethe's autobiography, *Dichtung
und Wahrheit* [*Poetry and Truth*], the last part being published the year after his death. (The actual autobiography
runs only to 1775, just before Goethe left for Weimar.)
Faust remains the most famous of Goethe's writings, taking
its place indeed with the masterworks of European literature.
Part I, at least, still ranks among the great stage dramas; in
Part II the play becomes considerably symbolic, philosophic,
allegorical—an unwieldy work which, except for certain
scenes, is not very well suited to the stage. This is less to
deny its virtues than to indicate their particularity. Of the
whole of *Faust* Santayana has said it "is like human life: it

has a beginning, it has an end, but it has no totality, it is not one whole."

The Elective Affinities, which Mann called "the most daring and trenchant novel of adultery that the moral culture of the Occident ever produced," is a psychological study of four persons in a free-wheeling relationship indicated by the title, which is yet a kind of plea for respecting marriage, and which Goethe consolingly winds up, after the death of his reunited lovers, by saying: "How happy a moment it will be when, at some time in the future, they awake together." Though, today, very far from required reading, *The Elective Affinities* had an unforeseeable place in the elderly Goethe's development and an inevitable influence on German fiction. Goethe's *Italian Journeys*, on the other hand, remains thoroughly accessible; and the later poems are contributions to German and, in a certain sense, world literature. Almost everyone knows, along with *"Kennst du das Land,"* the Erlkönig (*"In seinen Armen das Kind war tot"*), the Wanderer's Night Song (*"Über allen Gipfeln/Ist Ruh"*), "Who ne'er his bread in sorrow ate" from *Wilhelm Meister*, as well as such phrases as *"Vorweile doch ..."* and—the last line of *Faust—"Das Ewig-Weibliche."* Of all Goethe's writings, perhaps his lyrics, though weakened in translation; his aphorisms; and a well-produced *Faust*, Part I, are the most "living" introduction to him. One thing more, however, must unquestionably be included— a notable work, not by Goethe but about him, the *Conversations with Eckermann*. This, it so happens, is laden with aphorisms—open the book at random and quite possibly you will find one, and then another, staring out at you, as I have just done—now Goethe's "Hate injures nobody; it is contempt that casts men down"; and now his "People always fancy that we must become old to become wise; but in truth, as years advance, it is hard to keep ourselves as wise as we were." Johann Peter Eckermann (1792–1854) came as a young man to Weimar, fired with admiration for Goethe; won his approval and served as his secretarial Boswell—in merit, a very comparable Boswell. As Boswell, to quote his own words, refused to turn his tiger into a cat, so we might say that Eckermann never quite turned his savant into a statue. In setting down his conversations with Goethe, which extend from 1823 to 1831, he produced an invaluable work which Nietzsche was pleased to call "the best German book there is." Goethe—though even with Eckermann he never let himself go; there are no "confidences" in the book—would not permit its being published during his lifetime, and neither alive nor dead paid sufficient tribute to his "collaborator." The collaborator, though immensely admiring, was not fatuous about Goethe; indeed there are moments in the book where Goethe becomes fatuous. The *Conversations* is a remarkable portrait of the man and a great revelation of his mind—reflections, opinions, commentaries, many of them bespeaking the man of letters; many others, the man of the world; still others, the sage (in contradistinction to the poet, the sage is what T. S. Eliot praised Goethe for).

In his later years—and married ones—Goethe was still roused by women, two of whom had a place in his life and have a place, or niche, in literature—Bettina von Arnim, whom he met in 1807 and who, after his death, wrote, perhaps exaggeratedly, of their relationship; and Minna Herzlieb, who seems to have mattered more to him than Bettina did. As for his relations with mankind, they would seem to have remained aloof, measured, magisterial, equally arousing devotion and dissent, and sometimes strong opposition as well as reverence. "Amid hostilities from high and low, cultured and crude, covert and overt, accompanied too by the veneration of lofty minds, his authority grew with his years, solely by virtue of his age and the ever-increasing weight of his personality." So speaks Mann, who very noticeably tended to identify with Goethe; and who adds: "The hatred he had to endure was essentially political, it had to do with his coldly obstinate and repellent attitude toward the two main tendencies of his century, the nationalistic and the democratic." Goethe was indeed an intellectual aristocrat who cut a great figure at the court, where he very possibly became the most celebrated and saluted *éminence grise* in history. Old age, all the more for being coupled with his high-seated role, brought with it a certain high-altitude loneliness and, we may imagine, a certain stiff and ceremonious gravity. He felt, in respect of the world about him, somewhat isolated as well as exalted. "Why should I not confess to myself," he said, "that I belong more and more to the people *in* whom one may gladly live, but *with* whom it is not so pleasant to live"—an avowal, apropos great men and minds, that has the validity of an aphorism. It would seem— which could be mere human fright, but could also smack of grandiose fantasy—that Goethe thought it possible, as the work of a young political hothead who thought him a reactionary, that he would be assassinated. The greatest homage he received came from people of other countries: the prospect of meeting him was part of many distinguished foreigners' travels, and the reactions to meeting him came oftenest in the form of tributes. Among his fellow countrymen he seemed, perhaps, more like a renowned fossil, "an honor yet something of a burden" for Germany to have.

Goethe's greatness is perhaps most challenged, not by his egotism or his olympianism—"However he may condescend, he is always a great man," said a friend of Eckermann's—

but rather by his slightly comic and more than slightly
pompous German-ness; and a good deal more, by his pettiness. Here is an instance of the *echt-Deutsch* Goethe:

*"Young [Englishmen] do well to come to us," he tells Ecker-
mann, "and learn our language . . . he who now knows German can well dispense with many other languages—Greek,
Latin, Italian, Spanish; we can read the best works of those
nations in such excellent German translations that . . . we
need not spend much time upon the toilsome study of those languages."*

Much more damagingly, the exalted Goethe could be extremely vain and touchy, and indeed jealous and envious.
When, in the years before Goethe and Schiller came together,
Schiller, in reviewing *Egmont*, praised but also found fault
with it, Goethe thought the nonreverential tone of the review an "impertinence." Equally, when Goethe, having
written an undistinguished play called *The Natural Daughter*,
encountered Herder's wisecrack, "I prefer your natural son,"
he terminated a long-standing friendship. Like less olympian
writers, Goethe as he got older not only resented criticism
but stood more and more in need of praise; this at a time when
his own "harshness"—as Kleist named it—toward younger
poets was all too apparent. And when Goethe did not snub,
he tended to preach or to prophesy: "The incredible arrogance in which the young are growing up will result in a few
years in the greatest follies." "The young," he said again,
"will not listen any more"—this, we may suppose, not just a
manner of speaking, but the comment of someone who very
decidedly expected to be listened to. The tremendously
admiring Eckermann is not only Goethe's great chronicler
and our invaluable informant; he must have been a comfort as

so deferential a companion. "I have never had much respect," the master tells Eckermann in one of their conversations, "for mere princely rank as such . . . I felt so satisfied with myself that had I been made a prince I should not have thought the change so very remarkable."

Perhaps more than any other very great writer, and in part perhaps from his being so German a one, Goethe has come to seem imbued, outside Germany, with a certain stiff-necked, stuffed-shirt complacency, not enough to imperil his classic eminence but enough to smile at it. The brilliantly malicious monkey in Voltaire and the bellowing bull in Dr. Johnson have, even where they repel us, a sufficient humanity about them. If there is anyone to compare Goethe with, it may be Gibbon; for as he was said to mistake himself for the Roman Empire, Goethe may be thought to see himself crowned and enthroned on Mount Olympus. "He compared himself," André Maurois tells us, "with the Titans." And adds: "He hated Zeus."

Yet one must turn to him in the end as not very much mistaken about himself, and as a commanding figure in the life and culture of his times. Emerson—in places a smaller-sized Goethe with a sense of humor—called Shakespeare the greatest of poets but Goethe the greatest writer; and such men as Carlyle and Matthew Arnold gave him very high rank. There is furthermore Napoleon's comment after their famous meeting in Weimar: *"Voilà un homme!"* In any case, no one during Goethe's lifetime, or after it, left so much of an achievement in such a number of ways—not just in virtually all forms of literature but in the field of science and of philosophy, and as a tremendous public figure. Perhaps one reason why not too many people read him in bulk is their awareness of how much bulk, and how many books, and what diversity of subject matter, he entails. It is thus something of a blessing that, besides his lengthier claims to distinction, there is the splendid brevity of the lyrics and of the aphorisms.

As an aphorist—because as a man—Goethe was very often a teacher. Though he himself acknowledged that nothing new could be said about man as a moral being, he had "an inclination toward educating others, and [toward] moralizing," and indeed attempted to serve as a mentor. Eckermann, the prime recipient in the flesh of Goethe's wisdom, is much less a great man's writer-disciple than his intelligent *pupil*; and who will much less learn how to write from the master than what to think. It is only fair to say that Eckermann not only waited for Goethe's counsel but solicited it; and the moralist-as-aphorist sometimes responded quite tritely: "If I had not busied myself so much with stories," said Goethe, "but had spent my time on something better, I might have won the finest ornament of diamonds." Again, one need not be a Goethe to proclaim that "whoever works joyfully and rejoices in what he has accomplished is happy." Nor to deliver this: "We have sufficient cause each day to clarify our experience and to cleanse our mind and spirit." Goethe can also speak what seems less an aphorism than a commonplace proverb: "To realize that the sky is everywhere one need not travel all over the world."

But such injunctions and counsels as I have quoted are sprinkled through the texts of many distinguished aphorists; and Goethe is not alone in having much of his didacticism swallowed up in his egoism, in his using his virtue rather than his vulnerability in the way of examples. At times, however, he has been unfairly accused of excessive rectitude and loftiness, as with his famous "last words," where his request to have the shutters opened to brighten the room is transformed into a characteristically didactic "More light." He had in his way a good deal of humanity, and was not without humor. If his light touch doesn't approach his "More light" touch, it can prove enjoyable: "We mustn't spoil pretty women too much," he said. "They are so ready to get out of bounds. Even at Elba, Napoleon was sent milliners' bills—and had to pay them." And there is the well-known tribute to Shakespeare: "Shakespeare gives us golden apples in silver dishes. By studying his works, we indeed gain the silver dishes, but alas! we have only potatoes to put in them." And there is a humorist, at least in the wording, in Goethe's comment on "Know thyself." "If I knew myself," he said, "I'd run away."

If the humorist in Goethe has distinct limitations, the aphorist, in spite of lapses into commonplace, is a very distinguished one. At his best he gives us the observations and insights that we look for in a great man, and that we sometimes do not expect of a Goethe. Thus we remember his saying that there is no crime committed by others that he could not imagine being guilty of himself; as we recall his saying "Only when we know little do we know anything at all, for as knowledge grows, so does doubt." Goethe, it would seem, was the man who first said "There is no patriotic art, and no patriotic science" and this, beyond its own value as a statement, testifies to Goethe's European rather than German, Goethe's cosmopolitan rather than native, outlook. He could deplore his compatriots' limitations:

The Germans are, certainly, strange people. By their deep thoughts and ideas, which they seek in everything . . . they make life much more burdensome than is necessary. ["What we Germans suffer from most," Goethe said elsewhere, "is philosophy."]

And again:

*We Germans are of yesterday. We have indeed been properly culti-
vated for a century, but a few centuries more must elapse before
. . . our people . . . will appreciate beauty like the Greeks . . .
before it will be said of them "It is a long time since they were
barbarians."*

And, in the very same breath, he could both accuse and acclaim himself:

*I have never met a more presumptuous man than I am. I never be-
lieved in trying to do anything. Whatever I set out to do I found
I had already accomplished.*

He thanked "very heartily" a contemporary English critic
who praised his "panoramic ability"; praise that he deserved.
And there is something rather panoramic, or at any rate diversified, about the nature of his aphorisms. Obviously he will
have much to say about literature and art, and on writers and
artists:

*If it were only the narrow-minded masses that persecuted noble
men! But no . . . Platen runs down Heine and Heine, Platen,
and each tries to make the other hateful. . . . Everyone possesses
an enemy in his own talent.*

Again: "Properly speaking, we only learn from books that
we're not competent to judge. If we *were* competent, the
author of the book would have to learn from us." Once more:
"The form must be absorbed as well as the subject matter,
and is the more difficult to absorb." And: "The man who does
not know the mechanical side of a craft cannot judge it."

But Goethe's eye observes much more than is found in
books, and it takes notice of not just the monuments and the
mountaintops of the world; his mind doesn't stop with the
philosophical, it can be very shrewd and sharp; and his experi-

ence has given him much worldly knowledge and understanding. "Excessive scruple," he says, "is simply hidden pride." "Confronted," he says, "by outstanding merit in someone else, there is no way of saving one's ego except by love." Again: "I can promise to be sincere, but not to be impartial." Here the comment is solid silver if also worn thin: "A vain man can never be completely ruthless; he wants to win applause and therefore inclines himself toward others." And here speaks the true man of the world: "We do not learn to know men through their coming to us. To find out what sort of people they are, we must go to them." And here there is humor, though possibly unconscious: "When one is polite in German, one lies."

The many-sided list continues: "Lawgivers or revolutionaries who promise equality and liberty at the same time, are either utopian dreamers or charlatans." Again: "He who cannot learn to love must learn to flatter." Here speaks the cosmopolite: "The patriotism of antiquity . . . developed naturally from the whole condition of a people . . . with us it is an awkward imitation. *Our* life requires not separation from other nations, but constant intercourse with them." And here speaks the man who knows not only others but himself: "People will allow their faults to be shown them; will let themselves be punished for them; will patiently endure many things because of them: they only become impatient when they have to lay them aside."

Goethe, as he might have said of himself, can only be summed up in a too clever sentence or at considerable length. His career, as the chronicling and itemizing of it reveals, spelled both success and achievement on many fronts, and even the briefest biographical sketch of him makes plain the towering role he played in the life of his time: his voice was heard, his counsel was heeded, in Weimar and all cultural

Europe alike. He cannot be said to have been lacking in hubris; but he was not struck down, he was raised up, by the gods; and of his aphorisms we may wonder whether they resulted from his achievements, or were the rules of conduct he went by in achieving them.

Aphorisms

Court life is like music, which everyone must keep time to.

The cruder minds are taken in by variety and exaggeration; the more educated ones by a sort of ceremoniousness.

Man must strive and, in striving, must go wrong.

In every artist there is a touch of audacity without which no talent is conceivable.

It is a mistake for a taciturn, serious-minded woman to marry a jovial man, but not for a serious-minded man to marry a light-hearted woman.

Everybody wants to be somebody; nobody wants to grow.

GOETHE

We must not take the faults of our youth into our old age, for old age brings with it its own defects.

If I blunder, everyone can notice it; not so, if I lie.

Superstition is rooted in a much deeper and more sensitive layer of the psyche than skepticism.

The epoch as such never promoted science and knowledge; always particular men did. It was the epoch that made Socrates drink poison and burned Huss at the stake.

What we do not understand we do not possess.

Art is art because it is not nature.

There is strong shadow where there is much light.

Certain defects are necessary for the existence of individuality.

Viewed from the summit of reason, all life looks like a malignant disease and the world like a madhouse.

It is unpleasant to miss even the most trifling thing that we have become accustomed to.

THE LAST WORD

The artist . . . alone sees spirits. But after he has told of their appearing to him, everybody sees them.

The intelligent man finds almost everything ridiculous, the sensible man hardly anything.

Microscopes and telescopes really confuse a man's clear sense of sight.

We cannot beware sufficiently of two things: of obstinacy if we limit ourselves to our field; of incompetency if we leave it.

There is nothing more dreadful than imagination without taste.

VII

Hazlitt

WILLIAM HAZLITT has an unquestioned place in any list of important English literary critics, being indeed part of a notable age of criticism that also includes Coleridge and Charles Lamb. Like Dr. Johnson, he was a wide-ranging man of letters, and someone for whom writing, often as a journalist, was a matter of livelihood. Like Lamb, Hazlitt was a very distinguished essayist, and an essayist on many subjects, ranging from prize fights to old books, from dreams to sundials. Unlike Johnson and Lamb, Hazlitt, though in his own way admirable, has—as a talker—no reputation for either aphorisms or witticisms; and though he published anonymously a small book called *Characteristics*—a bundle of maxims suggested by La Rochefoucauld—it is much less in these than in his general writings, and in his compact, pointed style, that Hazlitt excels as an aphorist.

He was born at Maidstone on April 10, 1778, the son of a dissenter in religion also named William, who became first a Unitarian, and eventually a Unitarian minister. Though admiring and fond of his father, the son was in temperament sufficiently unlike him to say later that he "began life with the French Revolution." Before he formed this connection with France, however, young William was to visit other regions, for after a church quarrel, his father took his family to Ireland and later moved them to America. They arrived in the ship that brought the news to America that the Revolutionary War was officially concluded, with the Hazlitts hoping for a perfect land where "no tyrants were to rule, no bigots to hate and persecute their brethren." The years in America were spent first in Philadelphia, where William's father—though offered a college presidency—could only, from his refusal to submit to religious orthodoxy, become an itinerant preacher; and then, in or near Boston, where his father is said to have founded the first Unitarian church. But, making small progress and once again a wandering preacher, the father sailed in October 1786 for England, the rest of the family returning there some months later. Hazlitt's only recollection, in his writings, of his American years is of still having "the taste in his mouth of barberries." But in a letter to his father, at the age of eight and a half, he says of America that "it would have been a great deal better if the white people [in the face of the Indians] had not found it out."

On their return, the Hazlitts, after a few months in London, went to Wem in Shropshire, where William's father was given a small congregation and would stay for some twenty-five years, and where William would stay for the better part of twelve. He was a precocious schoolboy with many interests; writing, at ten, to an older brother, he calls himself a "busybody" who "can jump four yards" and who "drew eyes and noses till about a fortnight ago," who wants "to know all the Latin and Greek" he can, and doesn't want his brother's old clothes. He was also, as a child, described as "one of the most entertaining and prepossessing children ever seen," yet, when he "thought himself slighted, he became sullen, and this sullenness continued." His father, it appears, hoped that this bright son of his might go into the ministry—"he would far sooner," said the son, "I had preached a good sermon than painted a Rembrandt." But though Hazlitt would later write eloquently of the virtue of dissenting ministers, he early showed the greatest distaste for being one himself. All the same his father sent him to an unorthodox theological college, which chiefly produced dejection and disappointments. Like his older brother John, who studied under Sir Joshua Reynolds, William had thoughts of being a painter; yet, during the eight years after he left the seminary, he lived at home in Wem, without an occupation. There, reading, thinking, taking long walks, and looking at pictures, he began to form himself.

When he was twenty, something important happened: he met Coleridge, having gone ten miles to hear him preach. Soon after, Coleridge came to the Hazlitts' home, where, as he put it, he conversed—so tongue-tied was William—"with William Hazlitt's forehead." But they soon became better acquainted and William paid Coleridge a longish visit that was full of talk about literature and was finished off with a jaunt down the Bristol Channel. When William came back home, however, he found it impossible to write and definitely decided to become a painter. By going from Wem to London and his brother John, he got to know a number of well-known "liberals"—Godwins, Wollstonecrafts, Burneys; and, most important, he got to know Lamb. He worked enough at his painting to be commissioned by a Mr. Railton of Manchester to go to Paris and make five copies, at the Louvre, from its Old Masters. His four months in Paris brought freezing weather and very pinched means, but were exhilarating, inside the Louvre and out. While inside, he wrote in a letter, "I saw Bonaparte"—his life hero; and later, "I have not yet seen Bonaparte near." In 1803 he made a second visit to the Lakes, which started off well but soon led to differences. Coleridge, though commenting that Hazlitt "says things that are his own, in a way of his own," spoke of his "singularly repulsive manners, and of his being jealous, gloomy, and of an irritable pride." Hazlitt painted Coleridge, whom he made, it was said, resemble "a horse stealer on trial and looking guilty"; and Wordsworth, whom he made to look like a "gallows' bird." He was also, for a while, an itinerant painter, at five guineas a portrait; but, aware of his limitations, he gave up painting as a profession in 1806.

A year earlier he had published his first book, called *Essay in Defense of the Natural Disinterestedness of the Human Mind* and treating of metaphysics. But though it would be reprinted thirty-one years later, on neither occasion did it arouse interest, even among metaphysicians. The following year Hazlitt published a political pamphlet, attacking, among other things, the younger Pitt, Hazlitt in turn being attacked in the Tory *Quarterly Review* for "slime and filth." Some time after appeared, first, a volume of excerpts from notable Parliamentary speakers, with character sketches by Hazlitt; and, second, his anonymous rebuttal of Malthus's *Essay on Population*, a work which Coleridge had characterized as "a quarto volume to prove that man could not live without eating." In 1808 Hazlitt married Sarah Stoddard, of a very respectable family, and a good friend of Charles and Mary Lamb, as by now Hazlitt himself was. The marriage had its interest because earlier the slovenly, rather graceless Hazlitt had been anything but a favorite with ladylike women. Henry Crabb Robinson, the greatest diarist of the period in respect of the literary world, who is also in his sometimes priggish way our best informant about Hazlitt, said that "in company the girls made game of him" and that "like other gross sensualists, he had a horror of the society of ladies." Hazlitt's wife had an annual income of £120 and a sensible personality, and took William to live in a cottage she owned near Salisbury. He commenced married life by writing a *New and Improved Grammar of the Eng-*

lish Tongue, which was slow in finding a publisher and even slower in finding a public. He still painted as a hobby, he still was close to the Lambs; Mary Lamb spoke of him as "most brilliant, most ornamental" at their Wednesday evening parties. A second child—the first having died—was born in 1811, and Charles Lamb wrote that he hoped the boy would be "like his father, with something of a better temper and a smoother head of hair." Soon after the child's birth the Hazlitts moved to London.

The need of a better temper was true enough, particularly in a London where Hazlitt came upon all kinds of people. In makeup he was far from calm, or courtly, or warmhearted, indeed he was hotheaded and rather selfish. In politics, if hardly a radical, he was violently opposed to kings, reactionaries, and turncoats. He took offense quickly and was inclined to be quarrelsome. "I have quarreled with all my old friends," he said late in life, in an essay called "The Pleasures of Hating"; he even quarreled with someone as benign as Lamb. In addition, soon after moving back to London, he took to drink, but swore off, since this aggravated his splenetic side, and thereafter drank nothing more potent than the blackest and strongest of tea. During his early years in London he lived in Westminster in a house where John Milton had once lived and where his landlord was Jeremy Bentham; Bentham in due course put an execution for rent into the house, with the excuse—when he was remonstrated with—that he knew nothing of Hazlitt except as a tenant. Despite his wife's income, Hazlitt's financial state was seldom reassuring—Crabb Robinson in 1814 said it was "painful to witness [Hazlitt's] painful exertions for a livelihood." One exertion was in giving a series of ten lectures on the Rise and Progress of Modern Philosophy, his object being to abuse modern philosophy and combat it; thus, in one antithesis of the new and the old,

"Dr. Priestley's whole aim," he said, "seems to be to evade the difficulties of his subject and [Jonathan] Edwards', to answer them." He next became, as once Dr. Johnson had been, a Parliamentary reporter, and like Johnson, no very accurate one. But beyond being paid four guineas a week for his labors, he was greatly interested in watching the life of the House of Commons and in listening to its speechmakers, all of which later served as material for his essay-writing. He can turn aphoristic about oratory: "An orator can hardly get beyond *commonplaces*; if he does, he gets beyond his hearers"; and again, for an orator "to give a reason for anything is to breed a doubt of it." Hazlitt can wax sarcastic about Parliamentary leaders: "The excitement of leading the House of Commons must act upon the brain like brandy or laudanum. . . . That any one accustomed all his life to the tributary roar of applause . . . should think of dieting himself with the prospect of posthumous fame . . . is like offering a confirmed dram-drinker a glass of . . . water."

From reporting speeches Hazlitt went on to reviewing plays, becoming drama critic first for the *Morning Chronicle* and later for Leigh Hunt's *Examiner* while also writing on politics and literature. As a drama critic, Hazlitt subordinated theater to literature, having a greater interest in language than in stage business, and a far greater interest in the classics than in contemporary plays. Shakespeare, however, he thought too great for the stage, as—among other things— too profound to absorb in performance; nevertheless, his greatest admiration among actors was Edmund Kean in Shakespearean roles. Of Kean he wrote so glowingly that he was unjustly rumored to have been paid, by Drury Lane, £1500 for puffing him. Hazlitt was equally ecstatic about Mrs. Siddons, writing that "it is pride and happiness enough for us to have lived at the same time with her." Of a quite different type of performer Hazlitt could write quite differently: for example, "Mr Young ought never to condescend to play comedy, nor aspire to play tragedy."

Writing during these years for the *Examiner*, Hazlitt contributed a great many pieces to a feature called The Round Table. These contributions were indicative of what, as a writer, Hazlitt would most effectively become, and would most engagingly remain: an essayist on many subjects and a stylist with a fine touch for writing them. On several heads, Hazlitt is linked with Lamb—beyond their personal relationship and their being almost exact contemporaries, they had a kindred gift for both critical writing and "familiar" and autobiographical essays. As critics, they also shared a notable gift for what today, under the dictatorship of academic criticism, is looked upon with scorn: appreciation. Already in the two volumes of *The Round Table*, published in 1817, Hazlitt included such well-known essays as "On Posthumous Fame," "On Gusto," "On Actors and Acting," "On Mr Kean's Iago," "On Modern Comedy," and "On Hazlitt's Marriage a la Mode." And in *Characters of Shakespeare's Plays*, published a year after *The Round Table*, and the first of Hazlitt's books to win immediate success, he wrote some of his most enduring criticism. In *The Round Table* aphoristic observation clearly begins to emerge, and in *Characters* the aphorism itself: "Men of genius do not excel in any profession because they labor in it . . . they labor in it because they excel."

As Hazlitt got going in London, he was also moving about a great deal and meeting a number of the best-known people in the arts. Some of these appear in Hazlitt's best-known essays: his famous tribute to Lamb is, in addition, an example of his own vivacious prose:

THE LAST WORD

*There [at the Lamb parties] was Lamb himself, the most delight-
ful, the most provoking, the most witty and sensible of men. He
always made the best pun and the best remark in the course of the
evening. No one ever stammered out such fine, piquant, deep,
eloquent things in half-a-dozen half sentences as he does. His jests
scald like tears and he proves a question with a play upon words.
What a . . . vein of home-felt truth! How often did we cut into
the haunch of letters while we discussed the haunch of mutton on
the table! How we skimmed the cream of criticism! How we got
into the heart of controversy! How we picked out the marrow of
authors!*

Hazlitt could talk well too: Bryan Waller Procter said that,
though Lamb said the most pithy and brilliant things and
Leigh Hunt displayed the most ingenuity, Hazlitt "was the
best talker of the three." The parties at the Lambs', however,
were one thing; for parties in general Hazlitt did not care
much, they were too genteel for his downright personality—
and for his liberal politics; and too insipid for his lively and
probing mind. He liked odd people—at any rate his painter's
eye or his sense of humor did; he made friends with a poul-
terer and saw a good deal of a hard-drinking solicitor whose
mind "can be neither wheedled or browbeat," and who "if he
has nothing to say . . . drinks your health." Though no
keen party-goer, Hazlitt was anything but a homebody: for
one reason, his marriage was not a happy—though both husband and wife kept it from being a hateful—one. They had
serious shortcomings, she being untidy and no homemaker,
he unreliable and no peacemaker, and both of them selfish.
But they seem to have avoided dangerous scenes and show-
downs and kept on friendly terms; and they shared, and were
solaced by, their small son. Nor were money matters a great
help, for though Hazlitt now was never in want, he was also

never in clover, £500 or £600 a year being the most he could earn; and his wife's housekeeping made it seem less. His steadiest source of income came from the most famous periodical he wrote for, the *Edinburgh Review*, to which he was a contributor for the last sixteen years of his life. Writing for such a great Whig quarterly enabled him to combat, among other things, the onslaughts of the Tory *Quarterly Review*, whose editor, William Gifford, attacked him systematically and venomously.

Hazlitt was to write drama criticism once more—for the London *Times*, which he later praised as an excellent employer. And by way of a *Times* editor, he was asked in 1818 to give a series of lectures on the English Poets, these being followed in the next two years by lectures on the English Comic Writers and on the Dramatic Literature of the Age of Elizabeth. His friend, Mr. Justice Talfourd, wrote pungently of Hazlitt's audiences

with whom he had but "an imperfect sympathy." They consisted chiefly of Dissenters, who agreed with him in his hatred of Lord Castlereagh, but who "loved no plays"; of Quakers who approved of him as the opponent of slavery and capital punishment, but who "heard no music"; of citizens . . . who had a hankering after "the improvement of the mind" but to whom his [conception of the mind] was a riddle; of a few enemies, who came to sneer; and a few friends who were eager to learn and to admire . . . When he [favorably compared an English cottager] with Voltaire, they broke into a joyous shout of self-gratulation that they were so much wiser than a wicked Frenchman.

Among these hearers, however, was John Keats, who greatly praised Hazlitt on Swift, Voltaire, and Rabelais but was "disappointed in his treatment of Chatterton." The lectures, to a considerable degree put together from reading specifically for the occasion, remain among Hazlitt's best-read work, for one reason for their still living subject matter, for another, for their personally enjoyable and appreciative approach, and not least for how well they are written. Poetry for Hazlitt was something that gave great pleasure, not something that called for total dedication—"a very fine thing but there are other things besides": yet in one of the aphorisms that dot the lectures, he also said, "Poetry is not a branch of authorship; it is the stuff of which our life is made." It has been said that the poetry he hadn't read "would fill many volumes," as it has been said that in later life Hazlitt, like Dr. Johnson, almost never read a book through. If both accusations, whether true or not, tend to coincide with his temperament, neither of them does damage to his talents. The last of the English Poets lectures concerned the Living Poets, and was far from everywhere complimentary; thus the well-known banker-poet Samuel Rogers was said to write poetry merely "because no line or syllable of his reads like prose"; Hazlitt's comments on the then famous Thomas Campbell "made an enemy for life," and, concerning Wordsworth, Hazlitt remarked that "he does not like even to share his reputation with his *subject*, for he would have it *all* to proceed from his own power and originality of mind."

Gifford, when the *Lectures on the English Poets* was published, once more had at Hazlitt, and this time his enraged victim decided to hit directly back, in the form of *A Letter to William Gifford Esq.*, wherein Gifford is described as "a receptacle for the scum and sediment of all the prejudice, bigotry, ill-will, ignorance and rancor afloat in the Kingdom." The *Letter* delighted Keats, who in one of his own letters says, "The force and innate power with which it yeasts and works itself up . . . is in a style of genius. He hath a demon, as he himself says of Lord Byron."

HAZLITT

The early 1820's brought family changes: Hazlitt's father died, and by then his relations with his wife had reached a crisis—in addition to her own shortcomings, she failed to show, to her husband's mind, great enough interest in his work (though he had written in an essay that he did not "care a fig for any woman that knows even what *an author* means"). They separated, Hazlitt often staying at an inn between London and Salisbury, and later finding London quarters in Chancery Lane. Here he became passionately involved with his landlady's daughter, Sarah Walker, and, wishing to marry her, sought a divorce from his wife. Foiled of divorce by English law, "Hazlitt and his wife," Crabb Robinson states on the authority of Mary Lamb, "are gone to Scotland for the express purpose of obtaining divorce by the commission of adultery by Hazlitt . . . and this though she must swear that there is no collusion." Back in London, Hazlitt discovered that Sarah had deceived him for a younger lover, and in place of marriage banns, there emerged, in due course, a book, *Liber Amoris*, in which Hazlitt wrote harshly of Sarah, and for which he got £100 from a publisher. The whole thing, however shoddy the cause of it, was very little to his credit.

In 1824, a year after the publication of *Liber Amoris*, Hazlitt married a Mrs. Bridgewater—in England a marriage that for Hazlitt was bigamous. His bride was a colonel's widow with an annual income of £300, a substantial addition to her new husband's means; and the two of them soon after set forth on travels in France and Italy, which Hazlitt afterward turned into a book. With his interest in art, the tour was something that Hazlitt greatly desired, and on arriving in Paris, the first thing he did was rush to the Louvre; the second was to run into his previous wife. About France he wrote, whether of its people or its pictures, in a somewhat hostile way; he also compared French things with English, in a somewhat insular one. "Paris," he wrote, had "greasy holes for shop windows" and a "pile of tall and dirty alleys"; nor were its charms equal to London's West End or Primrose Hill. Hazlitt on Rome smacks of Gifford on Hazlitt: "tawdry, fulsome *commonplaces*," "vulgar-looking streets . . . [smelling] of garlic"; "a putrid trattoria." In Florence, Hazlitt met a distinguished contemporary, more hotheaded and irascible than himself, Walter Savage Landor; but the two of them got on very well. It was long supposed that, after these travels on the Continent, Hazlitt went back to England in 1825 without his wife, and without ever seeing her again; but it appears that the breakup happened at the end of a visit to the Continent in 1827, when Hazlitt was in Paris working on his biography of Napoleon—the reason for his wife's parting from him being the "ill conduct of his son," whatever that may mean, but might well mean the son's loyalty to his divorced mother. (One of the shadowiest of figures, the second Mrs. Hazlitt survived her husband by almost forty years.) A series of portraits of contemporaries, which Hazlitt had worked on while abroad in 1824–25, appeared in book form thereafter: called *The Spirit of the Age*, the book is one of his best and, in its asperities, one of his most benevolent.

We have reached by now Hazlitt's last years, which were busy ones, with his, even then, writing for a living in a number of periodicals and newspapers and on a number of subjects. Two further volumes of superior essays, called *The Plain Speaker*, enhance his permanent stature; there also appeared in magazines what would emerge as his *Conversations of James Northcote*, in which Northcote, a well-known and aged painter, and Hazlitt talk back and forth about art and other matters, in a sometimes vivacious but only sometimes verbatim style. Hazlitt's last large—indeed, largest—effort was the *Life* of his great hero, Napoleon, concerning whom he was somehow never disillusioned. After Waterloo, the painter Benjamin Haydon, very possibly exaggerating, said that Hazlitt "seemed prostrated in mind and body, he walked about unwashed, unshaved, hardly sober by day and always intoxicated by night . . . for weeks." Undoubtedly, though to Crabb Robinson he did not deny Napoleon's bad side, Hazlitt so strongly hated kings and despotisms that he did not see how little their punisher, and how much their imitator, Napoleon had become. The first two volumes of the *Life* won scant notice; the last two, published in the year that Hazlitt died, completed a failure; and a financial failure of his publishers left Hazlitt unremunerated. His health had for some time been growing worse and his means more straitened. By then Lamb had said, "I wish he would not quarrel with the world at the rate he does," and Hazlitt himself had asked, "Why does everybody dislike me?" But tributes to his abilities and (though less so) to his personal qualities were never wanting; and when he died, in September 1830, the last words he is said to have spoken are among the most cheerful he ever spoke: "Well, I've had a happy life."

Hazlitt is a great essayist by dint of his variety and vivacity, of his having something to say and a splendid style to say it in, where Dr. Johnson—with whom he had things in common —whatever the merits of his essays, is limited in range, didactic in tone, and inclined to be ponderous in style. A fair number of Johnson's best aphorisms turn up in his periodical pieces, but the vast number of them spring out of his talk. The aphorist in Hazlitt, on the other hand, lives inside the essayist, adding point to vivacity; and to pungency, succinctness. His aphorisms fall neatly into place rather than becoming didactically obtrusive; and have, many of them, to do with what is faulty and mismanaged in our lives, perverse in our reactions, and vulnerable in ourselves. Though Hazlitt ranks with, or just a short step below, the greatest aphorists, conceivably his having a lesser reputation than a number of his peers in the field lies in his having a greater reputation elsewhere; having it, indeed, twice elsewhere—as an essayist and as a critic. Speak of essayists and one says "Hazlitt" as of aphorists one says "La Rochefoucauld" or of novelists, "Dickens." But no one can in any way be criticized for saying "Hazlitt" apropos of aphorisms, and in one respect—the diversity of his insights and observations—he stands very high indeed. He rides no aphoristic hobby, like La Rochefoucauld; he shows no touch of formula, like Oscar Wilde; he is not, like Chamfort, all bite and brilliance. But he can be as terse, indeed lapidary, as any aphorist, whether with "Death cancels everything but truth" or with "We are not hypocrites in our sleep." And in the second of these two examples, he emerges far closer to truth than is a far more famous aphorism on a similar theme, Dr. Johnson's "Nobody is a hypocrite in his pleasures." For where Hazlitt is, with few exceptions, right, Johnson much oftener is not. Many people are hypocrites in their pleasures: think of all those who, while suffering infinite boredom, pretend—so as to be accounted highbrow or superior—to love music or art or the ballet; and think, too, of those who, to be thought one of the boys, drink or gamble or go in for sports far more than they actually want to.

As with most aphorists, there is an autobiographical element in many of Hazlitt's reflections, an element that is also colored by Hazlitt's surroundings, and by his *profession*. If it is really true that he "boasted of never changing an opinion after he was sixteen," then it is clear that his trumpeted love of truth must have been riddled with error, and his integrity been in large part mere obstinacy. It is certainly true that he could be testy and irascible, that he had very nonconformist manners, no tact, and many prejudices. At the same time, however, he was part of a literary and journalistic world that, if very notable for its writers, is equally notorious for its wrangling. Of several of his contemporaries it would be difficult to say which was greater, their gifts or their egos; or whether Wordsworth and Coleridge took offense more than Hazlitt gave it. Hazlitt's quarrelsomeness is not to be justified because his was an age of quarrelsome writers, but they *were* quarrelsome—in a long-term feuding form and, with politics a major element, in a decidedly public way. The Whig *Edinburgh Review* and, worse, the Tory *Quarterly Review* uniformly championed their literary partisans and denounced their literary opponents, often in the latter case, viciously. Hazlitt, as a literary critic, never deliberately chawed writers for nonliterary reasons, though he certainly *was* outraged and hostile with a once "liberal" Wordsworth and Southey for their becoming political turncoats. Add to all this the constant malicious literary gossip, the clash of temperament, the revenges of hurt vanity, and no wonder that even Wordsworth and Coleridge could quarrel, let alone Wordsworth and Hazlitt! And no wonder that—despite his having "had a happy life"—Hazlitt should sum up the world he lived in as "We grow tired of everything but turning others into ridicule, and congratulating ourselves on their defects." Yet, all in all, Hazlitt doubtless *had* a happy life, quarreling. Even had he not changed *half* of his opinions after he was sixteen, he must have proved too unyielding not to be personally difficult and too intolerant not to be heatedly challenged. So strong a dissenter should at times have dissented from himself. He could hardly have excluded himself from one of his most famous aphorisms: "Those who are fond of setting things to right have no great objection to seeing them wrong," and certainly he would have included himself in his "When a thing ceases to be a subject of controversy, it ceases to be a subject of interest." And we may wonder how autobiographical an element may be encountered in "The falling of teacups puts us out of temper for the day; and a quarrel that commenced about the pattern of a gown may end only with our lives."

Yet this dissenter, this controversialist, this decided *individual* inhabited a larger and more varied world than most of his fellow writers; and though he was personally never close to the Byron–Shelley circle, he was often close to them in political and humanitarian feeling, and had something of the same unconventional and bohemian tastes. He had also—it is the making of many of his best essays—a very human and downright side: no sports writer has ever excelled Hazlitt's classic of boxing, *The Fight*, or written a grander obituary than Hazlitt's of the fives champion, James Cavanagh:

It is not likely that any one will now see the game of fives played in its perfection for many years to come, for Cavanagh is dead and has not left his peer behind him. It may be said that there are things of more importance than striking a ball against a wall. There are things indeed which make more noise and do as little good, such as making war and peace, making speeches and answering them, making verses and blotting them, making money and throwing it away . . . [Cavanagh's] eye was certain, his hand fatal, his presence of mind complete . . . He did his work with the greatest ease, never took more pains than was necessary; and while others were fagging themselves to death, was as cool and collected as if he had just entered the court. His style of play was as remarkable as his power of execution. He had no affectation, no trifling. He was a fine, sensible, manly player who did what he could, but that was more than any one else could even affect to do.

HAZLITT

There follows a touch of Hazlittitis:

His blows were not . . . lumbering, like Mr Wordsworth's epic poetry, nor wavering like Mr Coleridge's lyric prose, nor short of the mark like Mr Brougham's speeches, nor wide of it like Mr Canning's wit, nor foul like the Quarterly, *nor* let *balls like the* Edinburgh Review. *He was the best* uphill *player in the world.*

Fives, as a matter of fact, was the great pleasure of Hazlitt's life:

The game of fives is what no one despises who has ever played at it. It is the finest exercise for the body, and the best relaxation for the mind . . . He who takes to playing at fives is twice young . . . Debts, taxes, "domestic treason, foreign levy, nothing can touch him further."

A handful of Hazlitt's aphorisms can serve as a trayful of his succulent *hors d'oeuvres variés*: "There is a division of labor, even in vice. Some persons addict themselves to the speculation only, others to the practice." And: "It is better to be able neither to read nor write than to be able to do nothing else." Again: "It is a sign that real religion is in a state of decay where passages in compliment of it are applauded at the theatre." And once more: "The more ideas a man has of other things, the less he is taken up with the idea of himself."

Like many superior men, Hazlitt was a good deal wiser about others than about himself and, as is not unusual, more severe. But oftener than not he lost his temper over the right subjects for indignation; and if, in doing so, he sometimes lost his friends, it was more from his being hard to put up with than easy to prove wrong. One might, at any rate, have perhaps suffered less in "social" conversation from Hazlitt than from Dr. Johnson. Hazlitt, it is true, was very fond and admiring of Dr. Johnson; but one can wonder just what might have happened had they been contemporaries who, meeting in their prime, took to discussing politics.

Aphorisms

If a person has no delicacy, he has you in his power.

The rule for traveling abroad is to take our common sense with us, and leave our prejudices behind.

There is a pleasure in madness, which none but madmen know.

It is provoking to hear people at their ease talking reason to others in a state of violent suffering.

Fashion is gentility running away from vulgarity, and afraid of being overtaken.

Man is the only animal that laughs and weeps, for he is the only animal that is struck with the difference between what things are, and what they ought to be.

I only hate halfway houses in religion or politics that take from us all the benefits of ignorance and superstition, and give us none of the advantages of liberty or philosophy in return.

HAZLITT

I like a friend the better for having faults that one can talk about.

Barbarism and rusticity may perhaps be instructed, but false refinement is incorrigible.

The most silent people are generally those who think most highly of themselves.

Landscape painting is the obvious resource of misanthropy.

The conversation of authors is not so good as might be imagined but, such as it is . . . it is better than any other.

He who is not in some way a pedant, though he may be a wise, cannot be a happy, man.

We are not satisfied to be right unless we can prove others to be quite wrong.

Violent antipathies are always suspicious, and betray a secret affinity.

Those who are at war with others are not at peace with themselves.

There is an unseemly exposure of the mind as well as of the body.

VIII

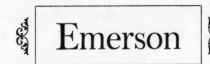

Emerson

RALPH WALDO EMERSON might have supplemented Alexander Pope's "I lisped in numbers" with "I lisped in aphorisms." They, or kindred short utterances, are decidedly the salt of his writings—indeed something more than the salt, something that comes very close to the substance. His beliefs and his "philosophy" had a considerable influence on American thought, and are doubtless what came first with him; but perhaps no other man has so often achieved, with a short sentence or even half of one, the effect of exhortatory prose, the conciseness of lapidary inscriptions. Such conciseness, and often concreteness, of language is what most compensates for the metaphysics and abstractness of Emerson's thinking; and the pungent metaphorical variousness of his short sayings— rather often homely and domestic, humorous and downright —makes wonderfully accessible a man who, with many of us, is far less inviting in large doses, or not always gratifying on large themes. But in short heats he can be extremely quotable as well as impressive.

Emerson was the first-born member of that notable generation of New England writers, once widely picture-framed as New England worthies—Hawthorne, Longfellow, Whittier, Lowell, Oliver Wendell Holmes, Thoreau; and, more than any of the others, the chief resident and Representative Man of Concord. Born in Boston in 1803 of mercantile people on his mother's side, he had, for ancestors on his father's, seven New England ministers, one of them an evangelist who hunted down sinners even into alehouses; another, a scholar who every night prayed that none of his descendants might ever be rich. Emerson's father was the literary-minded Unitarian preacher of Boston's First Church. Perhaps the most important influence on Emerson's early years—all the more, as his father died, far from affluent, when the boy was eight—was his father's sister, Mary Moody Emerson, a brilliant, dogmatic old maid who loved, and did much to form and educate, him, but with whose granitic religious orthodoxy he was to find himself at odds. His "formal" education, which included the famous Boston Latin School, culminated at Harvard, where he tutored and waited at table and began the journals that he would keep until very late in life. On graduating, as class poet, he was confronted, in the matter of livelihood, with familial and regional traditions—preaching, school teaching, writing—and consolidated them into an ambition to become a professor of elocution and rhetoric. But he began at a considerably lower level, teaching in, and later taking over, a girls' finishing school, which he found very unattractive; and though he had decided misgivings concerning the ministry as both a call and a career, he turned to it by entering the Divinity School in Cambridge.

He was now twenty-two, well read, and fired with literary ambitions, and comfortingly aware that as a minister he might also be an orator. He was burdened at the Divinity School, however, by having to do outside teaching and by suffering from ill health: the first of these obstacles left him somewhat deficient in theology; the second forced him—very soon after he was "approbated to teach"—to go to Florida, and later to Georgia, to fight off tuberculosis. Returning to Boston in better health, he preached there and in other New

England pulpits, becoming in March 1829 the minister of Boston's Second (Unitarian) Church. He married, soon after, Ellen Tucker, a Boston merchant's daughter whom he was much in love with and who died, a year and a half later, of consumption. As a preacher, Emerson was becoming successful and popular, his sermons already revealing his great gift of words, while also being simple and straightforward in content, and unbigoted and large-minded in theology. But in 1832, having decided that he could only celebrate the Lord's Supper by omitting the bread and wine, he calmly put forth his feelings in a sermon: the congregation split over it and, when he tendered his resignation, reluctantly accepted it. Earlier he had recorded in his journals that "in order to be a good minister, it would be necessary to leave the ministry," and though he would often preach thereafter, he never again had a church of his own.

His interests and ambitions having become larger and more literary, and his health once again not too good, Emerson, on Christmas Day 1832, sailed for the Mediterranean. In Italy he met Walter Savage Landor; in London, Coleridge, both of them men he much wished to see; and in Scotland, soon after, the man he most wished to see—Thomas Carlyle. Despite great differences of personality and taste, Emerson and Carlyle became great friends and were to conduct a celebrated correspondence; and each introduced into his own part of the world the other's early books. As Mark Van Doren has put it, "They filled hundreds of pages in explaining themselves to each other," yet shared a passion for capturing and communicating truth. Before sailing for home, Emerson met one more man whom he greatly admired and wanted to see—Wordsworth. Carlyle, Coleridge, and Wordsworth had all been attracted by German idealistic philosophy, which became a distinct factor in Emerson's thinking, as Goethe became an educative figure. These influences would in time help shape a New England movement which Emerson, officially, never associated himself with, but of which the outside world generally thought him the leader: Transcendentalism. Here as elsewhere he was chary of dogmas and certitudes, and held aloof from them—"I wish to say," he remarked, "what I feel and think today, with the proviso that tomorrow, perhaps, I shall contradict it all." In any case Emerson had, in his thinking, a number of intellectual ancestors, and came under a number of philosophical influences—his actual New England Unitarian forebears to begin with; but also Plato and the New Platonists; the religious writers of the East; Montaigne and Swedenborg. Much of his response to mysticism was countered by an element of skepticism; moreover, the physical world attracted Emerson no less than the metaphysical; and of the varied ingredients that went into his contradictory, reversible feelings, New England itself might act as a stirring spoon. Indeed, when he returned from abroad, Emerson went to live with his mother in that New England house of thought, Concord, Massachusetts, where indeed he would be anchored for the rest of his life.

In 1835, two years after settling in Concord, Emerson made a second marriage, with Lydia Jackson, and settled down with her in a house on the edge of the village. This indeed was very much of a settling down—as husband and father, as neighbor and villager, with mornings at the work table, with afternoons walking in Concord and in the woods, with evenings of talk with the family and of get-togethers with friends. Concord was an unmaterialistic and exalted— possibly a trifle *exalté*—community; a place "without crime," which the young Henry Adams would approach "as he would have entered a Gothic cathedral." Settling down in such a place was in one sense distinctly ironic, since Emerson was to spend a great part of his future life elsewhere, on lecture tours; but even they were more of an extended routine than of a different life; nor would two trips abroad in some thirty-five years very much unsettle things. Concord remained the hub of *his* universe; and Concord acquired, we may imagine, an atmosphere of his making.

Much of what spun around Concord, in new beliefs and behavior, in reforms and fashions, Emerson closely looked at, listened to, tasted, tested: he felt that much of the past, with its set traditions, was outworn and inadequate; but the new faiths, some of them mere fads, did not for the most part rouse him. Nor would he make an ideology of his idealism. He tried being a vegetarian and saw no benefits in it; he tried having the servants eat with the family and found the servants opposed to it. He listened, in 1840, to all the plans for starting the communal Brook Farm, but did no personal experimenting; he listened, a little later, but did nothing beyond that, to Bronson Alcott's similar plans for Fruitlands. It was projects like these, much identified with Transcendentalists like Alcott, Margaret Fuller, Orestes Brownson, Jones Very, and others, that kept Emerson from fully aligning himself with Transcendentalism, though he often spoke up for it, and employed the word itself. The Transcendentalists' "bowls of sunrise for breakfast"; their Alcott who "soared into the infinite and dived into the unfathomable, but never paid cash"; their mildly freakish extravagancies and nonconformities, had little meaning for Emerson. All the same, they were his friends and he was often their admirer; and having much in common with them, he was in some degree their mentor. His imperturbable calm, his constant if somewhat distant friendliness, his renowned and reassuring "angel face" must have counterbalanced the Transcendentalists' swirling emotions and enthusiasms, though they conceivably were a little chilled by his spoonfuls of high-mindedness for dinner.

During these years Emerson's own life was an active one, and his career was taking firmer shape. In 1836 he had published his first book, *Nature*, the title word being the fundamental fact in Emerson's search for a new culture and commonwealth: "There are new lands, new men, new thoughts. Let us demand our own works and laws and worship." This was followed up by his famous Phi Beta Kappa address at Harvard, "The American Scholar," in which Emerson argued for a cultural break with Europe; for our turning to our own potentialities for growth; and to the scholar's primary role and principal study: Nature. This speech, which Oliver Wendell Holmes called "our intellectual Declaration of Independence," had a rousing favorable effect; on the other hand, a speech a year later at the Harvard Divinity School in which Emerson declared that the church was moribund and impotent, and advocated self-reliance and self-study in place of traditional theology, created something of an uproar and a counterattack. Harvard, for example, would have nothing to do with Emerson for some thirty years.

The Divinity School speech did not, however, harm his public speaking; he was more and more in demand as a lecturer—indeed, lecturing became virtually his livelihood, and he went farther and farther afield. There was much to insure his success: he was impressive in appearance; he was magnetically eloquent in speech; his subjects were frequently among the major themes or grand truths of life; and his language could be by turns simple and homespun, chiseled and marmoreal. Furthermore, all this fitted into the pattern of the age, when the lecture platform spelled culture, when the lyceum was a species of theater, when life in many parts of the country needed outside stimulation. Emerson, despite his great success, was not altogether pleased with what led to it; and though *he* did not talk down, he felt the lecture platform dealt in something watered down—and all too popularized. That his own lectures showed little of this is best proved by their almost always deriving from reflections in his journals, and their being destined in turn to provide the substance of his essays. The first volume of essays appeared in 1841, the second in 1844, the titles of most of them being as succinct as the text, and often the key words for what he stood for and would become famous for: "Self-Reliance," "Compensation," "The Over-Soul," "The Past," "Character," "Nature." These volumes carried his "philosophy" and his fame much farther than his lectures had done; carried his teachings from America to Europe as well as from the lectern to the fireside. His was also more than a literary reputation: it was one of those mid-century voices that sounded new chants and faiths and undertakings, that revealed the pathfinder and the prophet.

A course of lectures in 1845 (which five years later would appear in book form) on Representative Men, and a volume of *Poems* soon after, strengthened Emerson's appeal; and when in 1847 he went abroad, he was a figure of some prominence. In England he lectured very successfully in London, Liverpool, Manchester; and no less so in Edinburgh. In England he saw Carlyle again and met such leading lights as De Quincey and Macaulay, Thackeray and Dickens. From England, before returning home, he went to Paris; from England he brought home many impressions of its life and culture, which he would turn into lectures and which were later turned into one of his most attractive books, *English Traits*. He had grown to respect and admire England, to enjoy much that it offered, and to praise much that it had achieved; but not that gross materialism which such Britons as Carlyle, Arnold, and Ruskin were also inveighing against.

Emerson was now, and for a considerable period would remain, at the height of his lecturing career: carrying him great distances, it brought him large fees and very small ones, enthusiastic audiences and bored ones—audiences in the sticks walked out on him because he "wasn't funny enough"; and lecturing, as he reached and at length exceeded middle age, could become burdensome and exhausting.* His lectures on so Emersonian a theme as the Conduct of Life were particularly successful, as, in due course, was the book that bore the same name. These years of winter lecture tours found Emerson more alert to the life around him, and more affected by it, than the earlier and less earthbound ones: he was led to reflect on social and political problems, social and political reforms. He characteristically never became heated about them, and about some he was also, so to speak, sympathetically lukewarm. Woman's rights failed to make him an advocate of conventions for woman suffrage; and though he disapproved of drunkenness, he would have no truck with rabid prohibitionists. Nor were rabid abolitionists much more to his liking—even as he became increasingly roused over

* An account of a late-in-life lecture in Boston, set down by a visiting minister, David McCrae, nas revealing details: "On the chairman asking what the subject of the lecture was to be, Emerson said he had brought two lectures with him and would take a look at the audience before deciding which to give . . . [He] took off his overcoat . . . and began to adjust his manuscript, which (made up of sheets and scraps of every size, age and hue) looked like a handful of invoices taken from a merchant's file . . . [He] stood waiting with . . . thoughtful eyes passing dreamily over the sea of faces, till there was perfect silence. Then he began, 'The first lesson of Nature is perpetual ascension.' [He] went on thus for an hour and a half . . . Insofar as he speaks to the audience, he is curt, aphoristic, oracular. There is no reasoning, no explaining . . . the giant hurls his steppingstones into the river bed and strides across, seldom looking back to see if you can follow. ['If you blow your nose,'] said one gentleman, 'you may lose him and never be able to pick him up again the whole night.' "

slavery; protested the Fugitive Slave law; wanted to help arm the antislavery people in Kansas, and supported John Brown when he came to Concord. "I think," said Emerson, "we must get rid of slavery, or we must get rid of freedom," and he went forth to make antislavery speeches, and at last show signs of heat when his speeches were hissed. When, at length, war was declared he said: "Sometimes gunpowder smells good."

As time passed, Emerson won increasing recognition as a poet and acquired something more of a literary life. What with many writers—Emerson, Hawthorne, Longfellow, Lowell, Holmes, Dana—living in or near Boston, the famous Saturday Club, with regular dinners and discussions, came into being. Harvard, by now, so far relented as to have Emerson deliver a Phi Beta Kappa address; as to confer on him an honorary degree, elect him to the Board of Overseers, and finally, in 1870, have him deliver a series of lectures on the Natural History of Intellect. He went about, socializing with considerable charm but never really fellowshipping: "My friends and I," he told his journals, "are fishes in our habit . . . As for taking Thoreau's arm, I should as soon take the arm of an elm tree." He did not find it altogether easy to talk, though he had a liking for conversation and an ability to listen to it. He remained a Concord man, in no social way a cosmopolitan; he disliked crowds, though his lectures might draw them; and was unhappy in cities, though certain aspects of them might prove attractive. In 1870 he published *Society and Solitude*, a very Emersonian antithesis, a very congenial theme.

Controlled, contemplative, serene, he was yet, as age came upon him, to be less bathed in intellectual sunlight than dimmed in mist and fog. He was a tired man when in 1871 friends took him in a private Pullman car to California, to which he quickly responded, but could make by now no full-blooded response. His memory was deserting him and his mind slowly falling away: he could not remember names or words, and had to act out the simplest statements to be understood. He still gave lectures, but now to no effect; and as late as 1876 he published a book of essays, *Letters and Social Aims;* but the manuscript had first to be worked over. And he went on a last visit abroad, seeing Carlyle and such celebrities as Ruskin and Browning, Turgenev and Taine, and going to Egypt and seeing the Valley of the Nile. Back in Concord, he pottered tranquilly about, even giving readings of sorts and helping to put together a book; but though he remained outwardly benign and dignified, senility was more and more apparent. At Longfellow's funeral he could not remember Longfellow's name. Scarcely more than a month later, on April 27, 1882, Emerson died of pneumonia.

A great voice in his own day, Emerson is a much lesser one in ours, but is still a great writer. As a voice, no one could offer more bracing and salubrious mottoes for calendars covering every day in the year. One has only to open his books, as I have done, at random to encounter such quotations —"Nothing interests us which is stark or bounded, but only what streams with life." "It is the ardor of the assailant that makes the vigor of the defender." "Difficulties exist to be surmounted." "Speak with the vulgar, think with the wise." "The Sahara must be crossed as well as the Nile." We turn from these sentiments with a feeling of how glibly inspirational, how smacking of Poor Richard they are; and if we knew nothing more than this of Emerson, we should associate him with Samuel Smiles and—correctly—set him down in the plump, flabby, yea-saying mid-nineteenth century. Emerson was an idealist whose stepping-stones were among the most exemplary and exalted of abstract nouns; an idealist, he was also an optimist who denounced all the devils in the community, or for that matter in the cosmos, yet always saw light breaking in on the darkness, and the dream lending hope to the reality. And this idealism, this optimism, sent forth in the resonant voice that Emerson commanded, proved a rousing element in the culture and morality of his time, and established itself afterward in the calendars on the wall, or the convocations of the pious, or the aspiring assemblies of the marketplace, and indeed the Stock Exchange. For it was a rousing element in our economy as well as our morality, a credo that could fall prey to evil designs and imbue with heroic significance robber-baron blood. In other words, such a credo could station idealism in the midst of our grossly materialistic ambitions; and optimism in the very face of our exploited and sweated poor, on whose starved dinner tables it set down such food as "Difficulties exist to be surmounted," and "The Sahara must be crossed as well as the Nile."

Such a contrast is not, of course, what Emerson meant, or is to be directly blamed for; but in his optimism there *was* a glaring distance between abstract nouns and concrete facts, and in his idealism, there was a withdrawal from most of life as the deprived and hungry live it. His purity of feeling required a corresponding purity of atmosphere: "Emerson," said Nietzsche, "is someone who lives instinctively on ambrosia—and leaves everything indigestible on his plate." Emerson himself, we might add, in bidding men hitch their wagon to a star, was, just so, leaving everything problematical in human "transportation" unresolved. And in this sense a good deal—and perhaps more since his own day—of his counsel, a good many of his injunctions, are anything but down to earth; and, worse, are facile preachments that work *against* the needs of humanity, and do so in poetry as well as prose:

> *In the mud and scum of things*
> *There alway, alway, something sings.*

But this is simply to say that Emerson's influence has often run counter to his principles and objectives; and that what was inspirational about him could prove very impracticable. He perhaps saw life steadily *because* he refused to see life whole. Nor did he wish to: his was in good part a mystical nature, and his self-reliance and serenity were nurtured by his looking inward, and upward, and out upon restorative landscapes; but not into dark smelly corners, or upon squalid sights and slums. To be sure, we must put this in proper perspective; must realize how much of the visionary poet there was in him, and recognize how true a sage he could be at his best. However misleading or unrealistic a guide for men's lives, Emerson—in his insights, his trenchancy, his wisdom—could notably illuminate and intensify many moments in our own.

He had also what might be called breadth of utterance, whether or not of interests. Against Emerson's abstract nouns might be set down his very pungent adjectives; and if he could deck out New England's virtues in poetic robes, he could also strip New England's eccentricities bare. Moreover, there is much of New England's benevolent humor in his way of writing, with none of the pinched New England-ness that can tighten its humor as well as its purse. Happily, too, his breadth of utterance is almost always accompanied by a conciseness of syntax, a more or less aphoristic syntax, whether in poetry:

THE LAST WORD

That memory may their deed redeem
When, like our sires, our sons are gone

or:

Things are in the saddle
And ride mankind

or in prose:

In Maine they have not a summer, but a thaw

or:

People say law, but they mean wealth.

It is perhaps such formal neatness that helps create a sense of
distance in Emerson, even at his most humorous and earthy.
his coarsest material, his very mud and scum, has somehow
been washed; his swamps have somehow been drained. But
though the sense of distance may provide an element of the
toga, Emerson does not wear a frock coat. His essays, to be
sure, are in almost every sense *not* "familiar essays,"—for if
Emerson speaks somewhere of "all zones and altitudes," he
himself makes use of very few. Actually he has said all this
first: "I prefer a tendency to stateliness," we read in his
journals, "to an excess of fellowship." This may seem the
more curious, as coming from his journals, the last place
where he need be ceremonious or stately. Yet it is under-
standable, since his journals *are* more concerned with truths
than facts, with perceptions than occasions, with the stuff of
epochs than the news in the paper—with particular zones and
occasionally frozen altitudes. A word that Emerson speaks
scornfully or disparagingly of is *appearances*; another is
surfaces—sometimes suitably, as that New York is all surfaces; but sometimes ineptly, as that Dickens is. Emerson

had, indeed, no great interest in novelists, possibly because theirs *are* the broadest interests, the "busiest" and most crowded zones, the most numerous of human activities. Emerson uses manners, though very well in his way, metaphorically and morally, rather than as things in themselves.

But, if opening him at random can yield much that is too optimistic and didactic, it can just as abundantly yield statements and comments that are acutely critical of society, and others that are stimulating, or penetrating, or wise. "If I should go out of church whenever I hear a false sentiment, I could never stay there five minutes"; "When believers and unbelievers live in the same manner, I distrust religion"—in many sentences like these Emerson would chide, not cheer us. He could be very critical of pedants and professors: "It is easy to read Plato, difficult to read his commentators"; "Scholars should not carry their memories to balls"; "I confess to some pleasure from . . . a rattling oath in the mouth of truckmen and teamsters. How laconic and brisk it is by the side of a page in the *North American Review!*" He could sting: "The word *liberty* in the mouth of Mr. Webster sounds like the word *love* in the mouth of a courtesan." He could become the more humorous for *being* stately: "I have heard with admiring submission the experience of the lady who declared that the sense of being perfectly well-dressed gives a feeling of inward tranquillity which religion is powerless to bestow." And in larger contexts we find many such pithy definitions as "The virtues of society are vices of the saint."

However restricted Emerson's interests in the arts, he could yet make striking comments: "Let not the author eat up the man, so that he shall be a balcony and no house." Or: "That which the droning world . . . will not allow the realist to say in his own words, it will suffer him to say in proverbs without contradiction" or "It is not metres, but a metre-making argument that makes a poem—a thought so passionate and alive that . . . it has an architecture of its own." For the most part, however, Emerson seems chiefly interested in language itself, in its vividness, its power, its individuality. Indeed, language—in a sense that goes beyond its being the tools and materials of every writer—is Emerson's forte and, with him, is notable for its freshness. H. W. Garrod called him a "word-watcher"—and a "word-catcher." Yet his is much less the work-table search for the *mot juste* than the self-bubbling instinct for the vibrant and operative word, something which attests the born aphorist as well as the born writer, and can call forth the humorist: "Yankees and dollars have such an inextricable association that the words ought to rhyme"; "Philanthropic and religious bodies do not commonly make their executive officers out of saints"; "A weed is a plant whose virtues have not been discovered." Or not too far from humor: "The secret of drunkenness is that it insulates us in thought whilst it unites us in feeling"; "You must hear the bird's song without attempting to render it into nouns and verbs"; "The chief mourner does not always attend the funeral." Such concrete, fanciful touches have a very saving quality; for Emerson, unlike most great aphorists, is chiefly affirmative and yea-saying (though he can ally himself with the nay-sayers). And the affirmativeness has indeed its goody-goody side: "What we seek we shall find, what we flee from, flees from us." It can enunciate a far too sanguine belief: "The people fancy they hate poetry, and they are all poets and mystics"; and it can slide into rank platitude: "The first wealth is health." And indeed Emerson can be poetically parochial and provincial; in other words, pastoral and rural, which enables a Santayana to say that Emerson's was "a fairyland of thoughts and fancies"; Hawthorne to say that Emerson was a "rejector of all that is, and seeking for he knows not what"; Melville to say that had Emerson been present at the Creation, "he might have offered some valuable suggestions"; and John Jay Chapman to say that "if an inhabitant of another planet should visit the earth, he would receive, on the whole, a truer notion of human life by attending an Italian opera than he would by reading Emerson's volumes. He would learn from the Italian opera that there were two sexes." Yet it enables Matthew Arnold, despite reservations about Emerson, to say that where Wordsworth had done "the most important [nineteenth-century] work" in English verse, Emerson had done "the most important work in English prose."

And if an often tiresome and rather too wholesome diet, Emerson can be magnificent with snacks and spoonfuls of imagination and insight. His was never the detailed inquest nor the broadly lighted scene; rather, the memorable epitome and the revealing flash: "We cannot forgive one another for not being ourselves"; " 'It is bad taste' is the most formidable word an Englishman can pronounce"; "In English only those sentences stand which are good both for the scholar and the cabman." Yet he was an observer as well as a visionary, indeed a keen and sharply critical one. If often his approach was actually withdrawal—from what was sordid, venomous, ruthless—and his distantness could lend astigmatism to the view, his consistent protest—to go no further —against an increasingly gross materialism was a proved prophecy and a reverberant if unheeded warning.

Aphorisms

Truth is beautiful. Without doubt, and so are lies.

A man in the wrong may more easily be convinced than one half right.

Solitude is impracticable, and society fatal.

Good manners are made up of petty sacrifices.

[Poetry] must be as new as foam and as old as the rock.

The louder he talked of his honor, the faster we counted our spoons.

There is a certain satisfaction in coming down to the lowest ground of politics, for we get rid of cant and hypocrisy.

There is always a certain meanness in the argument of conservatism, joined with a certain superiority in its fact.

Democracy becomes a government of bullies tempered by editors.

EMERSON

In every work of genius we recognize our rejected thoughts; they come back to us with a certain alienated majesty.

Few envy the consideration enjoyed by the eldest inhabitant.

Between cultivated minds, the first interview is the best.

Children are aliens and we treat them as such.

A man of genius is privileged only as far as he is a genius. His dullness is as insupportable as any other dullness.

Religion is as effectively destroyed by bigotry as by indifference.

I suppose you could never prove to the mind of the most ingenious mollusk that such a creature as a whale was possible.

It is a luxury to be understood.

In skating over thin ice our safety is in our speed.

IX

Samuel Butler

SAMUEL BUTLER was a writer with many ambitions and many attainments: his *Complete Works* in twenty stately volumes reveal a novelist, a satirist, an essayist, a scientist, a painter, a composer, a philosopher, a biographer, a quasi-autobiographer, a translator, a sheepherder, and—in the light of posterity's judgment, last but by no means least—an aphorist. A controversial Victorian figure who tilted at almost all forms of entrenched and obstructive Victorianism, Butler has a reputation today, as he had for other reasons a hundred years ago, which is not easy to evaluate, even though two or three of his lesser interests are virtually forgotten, and his speculative "scientific" side, once part of an embattled era, has been respectfully interred. But no one word—not even "man of letters"—can satisfactorily classify Butler, and no one person who acquires the hard-to-come-by *Complete Works* would have a strong interest in the contents of all twenty volumes. Two or three of Butler's books, however, still enjoy a virtually classical prestige, and two volumes of excerpts from his *Notebooks* give sustenance and enjoyment to a persisting body of readers. And no list of distinguished aphorists could leave out Butler's name.

The oldest son of the Reverend—later Canon—Thomas Butler, and the grandson and namesake of a headmaster of Shrewsbury School who was afterward Bishop of Lichfield

SAMUEL BUTLER

and Coventry, Butler was born in 1835 in his father's rectory in Nottinghamshire. His mother was the daughter of a sugar refiner, and his family background a solid one. When he was eight years old his parents took him on something of a grand tour—spending the winter in Rome and Naples—which seems to have left a great impression on him. His education, interrupted by a second trip to Italy, began at a school near Coventry, continued under his grandfather's successor at Shrewsbury, and was completed at Cambridge, where he graduated from the family college, St. John's, standing twelfth in the first class of the classical tripos of 1858. At Cambridge he was grounded in Greek; and, in *The Shield of Achilles*, wrote a clever undergraduate spoof of a Homeric "crib." On leaving Cambridge, he went to London, where, at his father's insistence, he was prepared, under one of the curates of a fashionable Piccadilly church, for ordination. This included "living among the poor and doing parish work"; this also invited, on Butler's part, doubts concerning the efficacy of infant baptism; and *this* resulted in Butler's refusal to be ordained. An angry exchange of letters with his father, who was supporting him, followed—"I think it right to tell you," said Canon Butler, "that not one sixpence will you receive from me after your Michaelmas payment till you come to your senses"—but Sam would not change his mind, nor would his family consent to his becoming a painter. The upshot of these altercations was that, with money from his father, Butler sailed in September 1859 for New Zealand, where in Canterbury Province he started sheep farming. Along with profitably tending his sheep, he did a good deal of writing for the press—notably in 1862, "Darwin on the Origin of Species: A Dialogue," and in 1863, "Darwin Among the Machines" (he seems to have taken easily to writing scientific prose). Also in 1863 Butler published his

151

first book, *A First Year in Canterbury Settlement*, mostly put together from his letters to his family in England, a good deal of it having the tart flavor that became a familiar part of him.

After five years in New Zealand he sold his sheep run, virtually doubling the money his father had given him, and returned to England with enough money to live modestly in London at 15 Clifford's Inn—his home for the rest of his life—and to get started, after long delay, as a student painter. Thereafter, for something like a decade, he would exhibit paintings at the Royal Academy and elsewhere, the best-known of his pictures being the satirically effective and amusing *Family Prayers*, and the highest destined of them, *Mr Heatherly's Holiday*, acquired by the Tate Gallery. By then, however, Butler was much involved in a number of other activities, not to say controversies, and in consequence the painter in him, though not the critic of painting, shut up shop. Soon after his return from New Zealand, Butler had published an anonymous fifty-odd page pamphlet he had written there, "The Evidence for the Resurrection of Jesus Christ as contained in the Four Evangelists critically examined," in which he concluded there was insufficient evidence that Christ rose from the dead. Religion, whether accepted or repudiated, was a subject of importance to him, and crops up, on various occasions, in his writing.

In 1872 Butler published anonymously *Erewhon*, the best-known of his books, and the one that had by far the greatest success during his unremunerative lifetime—3,842 copies by 1900, the runner-up, *Life and Habit*, published in 1877, having sold 640 copies. *Erewhon*—an anagram of Nowhere—is a strong satiric attack on Victorian living and thinking, habits and beliefs, hypocrisies and compromises, and though it has its modicum of "fun and naughtiness," it is on the whole a sweeping together of Butler's feelings and findings, prejudices and indignations. The narrator in *Erewhon*, coming upon a much-unexplored New Zealandish world, encounters many targets for the vivacious author to shoot at. At his best, Butler could hit the bull's-eye, as in the famous trial of a consumptive charged with "laboring under pulmonary consumption," with his counsel pleading that the defendant was "simulating consumption in order to defraud an insurance company from which he was about to buy an annuity," and hoped, for being so sick, to get it on easier terms. Instead, having already been convicted of "aggravated bronchitis," the defendant is found guilty of a "radically vicious constitution" and sent to prison at hard labor for the rest of his life. In such Erewhonian surroundings embezzlement, on the other hand, is no crime, simply a weakness that calls for therapy; other subjects treated are the educational system, ecclesiastical institutions, and despotic parents. The book's most "relevant" target today is the growth of machinery, which already in 1872 so much threatens to rule the population that it has to be abolished. Perhaps the greatest irony attending *Erewhon* was nothing in the actual contents of the book, but the public's wrong guess concerning who wrote it: the book sold well because it was thought to be the work of the highly respectable Lord Lytton; when Butler revealed himself, sales dropped by 90 percent.

Butler's next book, *The Fair Haven*, was, so to speak, all irony, pretending as it did to defend the "miraculous element in our Lord's ministry upon earth, both as against rationalistic impugners and certain orthodox defenders." It appeared under the name of a deceased author, John Packard Owen, with a memoir of Owen by his brother—the faked names being due in part to Butler's not wanting any further clashes with his father, and in part, by way of such names, to have the ultra-Protestant press take the spoof seriously. At this point Butler's investment of the money he had made in New Zealand had gone awry, with the result that he stopped writing. Part of his financial loss took him, without the ability to recoup when he got there, to Canada, though it was there that he started writing again, writing indeed *Life and Habit*, the first of his works that took issue with certain aspects of Darwinism, notably Darwin's "banishment of mind from the universe"—Butler insisting that certain habits can be hereditary. In Canada he also wrote "A Psalm of Montreal," whose uniform stanza ending has entered the language. Though Butler found Montreal agreeable, he found its inhabitants "too busy with commerce" to care greatly about masterpieces of Greek art; indeed he discovered that plaster casts of Antinous and the Discobulus had been banished from public view. On his asking why, an old custodian who was stuffing an owl told him: "They are rather vulgar." Butler thereupon wrote the "Psalm," a poem seven stanzas long, recording the (perhaps actual) conversation between the custodian and Butler. One stanza runs:

> *The Discobulus is put here because he is vulgar.*
> *He has neither vest nor pants with which to cover*
>   *his limbs;*
> *I, Sir, am a person of most respectable connexions:*
> *My brother-in-law is haberdasher to Mr Spurgeon*

to which Butler appends, here and six other times:

> *O God! O Montreal!*

The counter-Darwinian arguments, or perhaps the controversial scientific ideas, which began with *Life and Habit*, were continued, in either book or periodical form, between 1879 and 1890: *Evolution, Old and New; God the Known and*

SAMUEL BUTLER

God the Unknown; Unconscious Memory; Luck or Cunning?
and "The Deadlock in Darwinism." In these Butler would
seem to have discovered defects concerning natural selection,
having incidentally found that a Prague professor had a
theory much like his own, namely that "memory" had more
to do with evolutionary variations than mere chance did, and
that useful habits, stored in unconscious memory, can be
transmitted—in other words, that modifications are intrinsic,
not fortuitous. If all this, today, is part of the *pulvis et umbra*
of biological history, it was yet one of the chief intellectual
endeavors, and most challenged ones, of Butler's career.

During the many years when he was working at this, much
else was taking place. For one thing, Butler published in
1881 perhaps the most delightful, and very possibly one of
the most durable, of his works, *Alps and Sanctuaries*, a travel
book which deals with human activity and mountain scenery,
with digressions into comments of all sorts. For another
thing, having abandoned painting, Butler began in 1883 to
compose music, and to compose it "as nearly as he could" in
the style of the man whom of all men he most admired and
cherished: Handel. He insisted, however, that he and his
collaborator "do not think we are imitating Handel; we
think that we are working upon Handelian principles."
For a third thing, Butler in 1888 took up photography, and
in the same year published *Ex Voto*, concerned with the
Sacro Monte at Varallo-Sesia and the art of Gaudenzio
Ferrari and a Flemish sculptor known in Italy as Tabachetti
—an archaeological and aesthetic project of some substance.
Butler continued to write articles on art and science, he wrote
a cantata and an oratorio in Handelian form and, late in
life and late in his composing, began to study counterpoint.

But of equal importance were his relations with people.
His father—whose letters to him could contain sentences

like "I shall take your advice and not read your book. It would probably pain me and not benefit you"—died in 1886, this giving Butler, at a time when his finances were troublesome, financial security for the rest of his life. A year earlier had died Eliza Mary Ann Savage, whom Butler had met around 1870. An architect's daughter, she had met Butler at the School of Art, where they studied and where, he said, she had at first never missed "an opportunity of snubbing me." But an interest in literature and painting gradually brought them into a close relationship which was also a notably epistolary one, their exchange of letters between 1871 and 1885 constituting a record of decided interest. Miss Savage, who wrote newspaper and magazine articles and reviews, became a long-term and much-listened-to critic of Butler's work—she had very early in their friendship both criticized *Erewhon* in manuscript and reviewed it in print. In appearance she was rather dowdy and suffered from lameness; in intellect, on the other hand, she was remarkably acute, her abilities being very much complemented by her "sympathy and understanding." The personal relationship between her and Butler was a peculiar one which, from his never being attracted sexually—whether by her or by women in general—was devoid of sex. Though they met fairly often, they wrote to each other much oftener; and Butler's closest friend, Henry Festing Jones, who praised Miss Savage's "friendliness and good humor," felt that if, during the first years of their knowing each other, Butler had asked her to marry him she would have accepted, but that had he done so later, she probably would not. Such guesswork comes about as near to an explanation as any other; what is quite plain is that Butler never thought, early or late, of doing so, and that she was left with the short end of the stick—he being very self-centered, far from warmhearted, and to some extent given to exploiting her usefulness. Her death, however, left him filled with remorse and led him in time to write three sonnets about their relationship, this being the first of them:

> She was too kind, wooed too persistently,
> Wrote moving letters to me day by day;
> The more she wrote, the more unmoved was I,
> The more she gave, the less could I repay.
> Therefore I grieve, not that I was not loved,
> But that, being loved, I could not love again.
> I liked, but like and love are far removed;
> Hard though I tried to love, I tried in vain.
> For she was plain and lame and fat and short,
> Forty and overkind. Hence it befell
> That though I loved her in a certain sort,
> Yet did I love too wisely but not well.
> Ah! had she been more beauteous or less kind
> She might have found me of another mind.

In 1876 Butler had met Henry Festing Jones, a Cambridge graduate and unenthusiastic solicitor who became his closest friend, his fellow traveler, his literary executor, and, posthumously, his editor and biographer. Jones seems to have shared many of Butler's likes and dislikes, and was constantly consulted in the matter of Butler's writings; moreover, was his collaborator in composing gavottes, minuets, fugues, and other short pieces for the piano, as well as their cantata *Narcissus* and their oratorio *Ulysses*.

During the 1890's Butler became occupied with the two most majestic, and to a degree most mystifying, of literary figures, the one from before the Christian era, Homer; the other during it, Shakespeare. In terms of the disputed mystery of just who Homer was, Butler came up with the idea that Homer was a woman, a hypothesis which he developed into a sort of personal and textual biography, not without its ingenious and telling strokes, but without enough of them to make a convincing case. "Homeric commentators," Butler could not resist remarking, "have been blind so long that nothing will do for them but Homer must be blind too." Soon after, he published a colloquial prose translation of the *Iliad* and, two years later, of the *Odyssey*, both of which works he seems to have learned virtually by heart in the original. As for Shakespeare, Butler maintained, in the matter of the identity of Mr. W.H. of the *Sonnets*, that W.H. was a man of humble birth, a hypothesis not elsewhere regarded as tenable. After the century turned, Butler was to publish only one more book during his lifetime: *Erewhon Revisited*, which introduced the religion that the inhabitants of Erewhon had come to practice, and which is as satiric and ironic as its predecessor. Religion was perhaps a kind of sore tooth which Butler could not let alone, or a pesty insect he could not kill off: in any case, it had entered his blood before it exercised his mind; and it clearly influenced his prose, which has many biblical and Book of Common Prayer echoes. Yet if on the one side he could go to flippant extremes, such as suggesting that the Roman Catholic church have an eighth sacrament, divorce, on the other side he declared that though one could do little *with* faith, one could do nothing without it.

After 1900 Butler's health began to fail, which made him return from Sicily to London, only to go into a nursing home, where he died on June 18, 1902. After his death several books of his were published, books ranking with the most popular and valuable of his writings. The outstanding one, written much earlier and brought out in 1903, is *The Way of All Flesh*, his nearest approach to a real novel (the *Erewhon*s are satirical fantasies), or his sound enough claim to an auto-biographical novel, the Pontifex family of the book having a very great deal in common with Butler's own. (Earlier he had put together and written, in two volumes, *The Life and Times of Dr Samuel Butler*, his famous grandfather, much of it throwing light on the social and cultural world of early nineteenth-century England.) *The Way of All Flesh* is a cry from the heart, or perhaps more accurately, a growl from the spleen, in which the father, grandfather, and other members of the family are spitted, and Butler, as the young Ernest Pontifex, is subjected to all sorts of ultra-respectable and despotic sufferings, and grows up to suffer more—only at the end to inherit money enough to preserve him as a writer. Alethea Pontifex, the aunt from whom Ernest inherited, and a very likable character in this harsh satire on genteel and conformist cruelty, is based on Miss Savage. In its exposure of the hypocrisy, parental tyranny, pedagogical mistreatment, lip service, and materialism of the age, *The Way of All Flesh* became one of the most seminal and influential novels of the generation following its appearance. A certain dryness and overextendedness in the book has cost it something of its appeal, just as a certain datedness, or at any rate familiarity, about the theme has cost it a fraction of its importance; yet its power persists, and it must be found on any shelf that would represent significant nineteenth-century English fiction.

Two other posthumously published volumes, *The Note-books of Samuel Butler* (1912) and *Further Extracts from the Notebooks of Samuel Butler* (1934) hold a very valuable place in the Butler canon. If they quite lack sustained importance or carefully organized thought, they provide, peculiarly and abundantly, much to inform, stimulate, amuse, and instruct the reader, and to portray and characterize the man who wrote them. Butler, very early, began to keep a notebook and to set down in it many of his own thoughts and reactions, and many things that he was told or overheard. In due course, such a "museum" called for a catalogue, and later acquired an index; later still, Butler set about revising his notes while still adding to them, so that he left, at his death, five closely written notebook volumes, with enough unfiled and unindexed material for a sixth. The notations, anything in length from a short sentence to a short essay, are equally varied in content and tone—here Butler's great admirations, preeminently Handel, frequently reappear, and his much more numerous dislikes and *bêtes noires* are almost always in attendance; here stupid and silly remarks and entertaining and cautionary anecdotes abound. The *Notebooks* are also the birthplace of a number of Butler's ideas for expanded treatment, and are in particular the birthplace of many of his aphorisms.

In the face of all his diversified interests, Butler has been described as an amateur, and defended as a very rare kind of one, an amateur of great ability, disciplined training, and remarkable powers of concentration. He has equally been described and praised as an iconoclast who smashed all kinds of images and idols, whether religious, scientific, artistic, musical, critical, or archaeological; and most strikingly in terms of shibboleths and false pieties. "I am the *enfant terrible*," Butler wrote, "of literature and science. If I cannot . . . get the literary and scientific bigwigs to give me a shilling . . . I can, and I know I can, heave bricks into the middle of them." He hated cant as much as Dr. Johnson did—cant and hypocrisy, he declared, should be officially rechanneled, as lust and revenge had been by the institutions of marriage and law courts. He attacked tradition as Dr.

Johnson never did, but for two men who were not much alike, he and Johnson had a good deal more in common than a hatred of cant. They were both Tories—"Few radicals," said Butler, "have good digestions"; they were both, after a fashion, eccentrics, and they both commanded terseness and force. If Butler was more courteous than Johnson, he was much less compassionate: his treatment of Miss Savage, whom he called "the best and most remarkable woman I have ever known," argues something cold and unmagnanimous that must often have revealed itself elsewhere. He would not seem to have been a very likable man, and as a somewhat crusty old bachelor, his tics of personality can hardly have diminished or his tolerance grown greater. Plato, Virgil, Dante, Leonardo, and Blake among the dead, and Carlyle, Pater, Dickens, George Eliot, and Tennyson among his contemporaries, were just a few of his dislikes. His unfavorable comments are often amusing:

Mr Walter Pater's style is, to me, like the face of some old woman who has been to Madame Rachel and had herself enameled.

The difference between the Andrew Lang manner of translating The Odyssey and mine is that between making a mummy and a baby.

It was very good of God to let Carlyle and Mrs Carlyle marry one another and so make only two people miserable instead of four.

But satirists, to be sure, are not among the kindest or most sympathetic of men, and it is as a satirist or putter-down that, more than anything else, Butler has survived. *Erewhon* is satirical fantasy; *The Way of All Flesh* is satirical arraignment; and the *Notebooks* abound in observations, anecdotes, and aperçus that poke fun, or poke without fun, at something;

while the aphorist probes motives, roots out characteristics, and brings to life what mankind is ashamed of, or afraid of, or fatuous about, or ignorant about, or tends to mask, or to hide, or to deny. As a satirist, whether simply to make fun of things or to expose and excoriate them, Butler became one of the impudent Victorians who in due course helped to unseat the eminent ones. He was a nay-sayer to the era's sanctimonious and materialistic yea-sayings; he made his stuffy contemporaries uncomfortable as well as disapproving; and enlisted under his flag younger men, notably Shaw, who said he learned more from Butler than from any other writer. Today Butler's assaults survive, hardly as things in themselves, but from being assisted by talent; and his personality survives, not for what it was but for what, with wit and forcefulness, he has made of it in print. He played very well with words and very cleverly on them: "An honest God's the noblest work of man"; *"De minimis non curat veritas"*; "One touch of ill nature marks [sic] the whole world kin"; and from such linguistic toys it is but a step to some of his lighter aphoristic truths. "They say," Butler writes, "that the test of [literary power] is whether a man can write an inscription. I say 'Can he name a kitten?' " ("I," Butler adds, "cannot.") Or, he says, "All progress is based upon a universal innate desire on the part of every organism to live beyond its income." Or: "Life is one long process of getting tired." Or: "Five minutes delay in dinner now is more important than a great sorrow ten years ago." Or finally: "Words on many subjects are like trying to paint a miniature with a mop."

The *Notebooks* have their share of what, to be polite about them, might be called autobiographical comments—this for example: "Those who have never had a father can never know the sweets of losing one." (Better known, and better said, is Butler's comment that Melchisedec "was a really happy man. He was without father, without mother, and without descent. He was an incarnate bachelor. He was a born orphan.") Butler also copied down in the *Notebooks* odd and fatuous remarks of other people and bright ones of his own. Thus, at a railway station he heard one man ask of another: "Have you got sixpence?"—to be answered, "Yes, I have, and father and mother both living too." At the entrance to a building a woman came up to Butler and said: "Tell me, is this the place I came to before?" He overheard, on a bus, "She ought never to have been a mother, but she'll make a rare mother-in-law." A student asked Butler whether New Zealand wasn't the place where "hot water grows wild?" and a newspaper column which gave advice told an inquirer "We would not recommend you to write an epic poem on the National Debt." Of the Canadians, Butler said: "I found their jokes like their roads—very long and . . . leading to a little tin point of a spire which has been remorselessly obvious for miles"; and he recorded that at Charterhouse (the English public school) "if the son is flogged, the father is fined."

Along with such pleasantries and unpleasantries, the *Notebooks* are given to small insights and expeditions into thought; to reactions to places and people, and observations about all manner of things. Many of these are in the form of aphorisms and a fair number of them are concerned with rather worldly matters: "It is the sub-vicious who best understand virtue. Let the virtuous people stick to describing vice." Again: "Morality turns on whether the pleasure precedes or follows pain. Thus, it is immoral to get drunk because the headache comes after the drinking, but if the headache came first . . . it would be moral to get drunk." Again: "Money is the last enemy that shall never be subdued." Once more about money, and quite "relevant" today: "Death in anything like luxury is one of the most expensive things a man can indulge himself in"; and finally: "The gods are those who either have money or do not want it." Butler himself cared a great deal about money.

But, as aphorist, Butler can sound a very different note: "I care about truth, not for truth's sake but for my own"; "Conscience is a cur that will let you get past it but that you cannot keep from barking"; "To do great work a man must be very idle as well as very industrious." Here we encounter the imaginative scientist: "The father of geology was he who, seeing fossil shells on a mountain, conceived the theory of the deluge." And here we have the social observer: "Academic and aristocratic people live in such an uncommon atmosphere that common sense can rarely reach them." And here the voice of common sense: "There is no such source of error as the pursuit of absolute truth." And here an edict from a literary Beau Brummell: "A man's style in any art should be like his dress—it should attract as little attention as possible." Here a personal trait in aphoristic form: "I don't mind lying but I hate inaccuracy." Here Butler the Trinitarian: "The three most important things a man has are, briefly, his private parts, his money, and his religious opinions." And here the sage: "The world will only, in the end, follow those who have despised as well as served it."

A great deal of Butler's assault on Victorianism has, inevitably, become obvious, or outmoded, or done to death, and what has survived of it, as I have suggested, is not a matter of facts or theories, but of its approach, its satiricalness. *Erewhon* is in some sense the ancestor of a number of anti-Utopias; *The Way of All Flesh* is in some sense the progenitor of many antibourgeois, father-bullied, and autobiographically rebellious sons. The *Notebooks* strike me as more attractive today—they give us Butler as a common-sense eccentric;

they give us his perceptiveness and his prejudices, his sallies and his saber thrusts, many of these put with the agility of a master aphorist. With Butler, so rich in short and surcharged comments, it may well be that brevity is the key to survival.

Aphorisms

Logic and consistency are luxuries for the gods and the lower animals.

Nothing makes a man or woman look so saintly as seasickness.

It is death, and not what comes after death, that men are generally afraid of.

The history of art is the history of revivals.

Any class is all right if it will only let others be so.

To take away all animosity from a rivalry is like playing whist for love.

Conscience is thoroughly wellbred and soon leaves off talking to those who do not wish to hear it.

THE LAST WORD

If virtue had everything her own way she would be as insufferable as dominant factions generally are.

The great pleasure of a dog is that you may make a fool of yourself with him and not only will he not scold you, but he will make a fool of himself too.

Truth generally is kindness, but when the two diverge and collide, kindness should override truth.

A definition is the enclosing a wilderness of idea within a wall of words.

We can never get rid of mouse ideas completely . . . the best way to keep them down is to have a few good strong cat ideas.

I can understand anyone's allowing himself to be bullied by the living, but not, if he can help it, by the dead.

People care more about being thought to have taste than about being either good, clever, or amiable.

From a worldly point of view there is no mistake so great as that of being always right.

X

Nietzsche

FRIEDRICH WILHELM NIETZSCHE is one of the greatest—and most prolific—of aphorists, as he is one of the most brilliant, extraordinary, and in some ways misrepresented of men. A philosopher whose "philosophy has been popularly interpreted on the basis of two or three phrases and slogans," and given rise to something quite foreign; a thinker whose thought has been drowned in the daemonic intensity of his feelings; a German who has been bracketed with the most offensive German ideology while he often quarreled with it, Nietzsche was that mingling of the good and the bad, the balanced and the unstable, the inspired and mistaken, the rational and fanatical which attests true genius and can produce a madman.

Nietzsche was born in 1844 in Röcken, a small village near Leipzig, the son of a Lutheran parson who died when Friedrich Wilhelm—born on the birthday and given the name of Friedrich Wilhelm IV of Prussia—was not quite five years old. His family, all women—a mother, a grandmother, a sister, and two maiden aunts—moved soon after to Naumburg, where he grew up in a comfortable household surrounded by women who adored him, one of whom, his sister, could often dominate him as well. He later in life claimed descent, for which there seems to be no documentary proof whatever, from Polish noblemen; he very likely came of sturdy middle-class Germans. He was sent to a boarding school, where he was given a scholarship and from which he went to the University of Bonn to study classical philology; disliking Bonn, he proceeded to the University of Leipzig. There he stood forth, in the opinion of a notable professor of his, a very remarkable person:

However many talents I have seen develop . . . never yet have I known a young man . . . who so early . . . was so mature. He is the first one whom I have ever allowed, while still a student, to provide me with something . . . I prophesy that he will some day stand at the front of German philology . . . He is the idol and, without wanting to be, the leader of the entire younger generation of philologists here . . . You will say I'm describing a phenomenon. That's precisely what he is . . . He will simply be able to do whatever he wants to do.

On the basis of Professor Ritschl's glowing account—"This sort of thing," said Ritschl, "never, never happens in Germany"—the University of Basel in 1869 appointed a non-Ph.D'd, indeed an undergraduate Nietzsche to an *extraordinarius* professorship, promoting him the year after to an *ordinarius* one. At the time of his first appointment, Leipzig had conferred a doctorate on Nietzsche. Nietzsche would seem to have created the impression, or invited the belief, that during his student days he was a pretty lively fellow who went on wild sprees and sowed wild oats. He wrote home in some detail about drinking bouts; about women, then or later, matters are shadowy and unsubstantiated but just the tone he was after, and seem more a matter of talk than of action; more the product of what his too devoted sister said than what he himself did. Yet there seems no doubt that his future insanity was induced by paresis—and this, being the result of syphilis, suggests some knowledge of women, if only prostitutes.

The brilliant young man was not destined—nor did he desire—to win renown as a philologist; he had gone, not just at the Greek language, but at Greek literature and philosophy. While at Leipzig he had discovered in a bookshop Schopenhauer's *World as Will and Idea*, and had not been able to sleep for ten days after. "Here," he said, "each line cried out renunciation, denial, resignation; here I saw a mirror in which the world, life, my own mind were reflected," and he fell indeed under Schopenhauer's influence. During the same period Nietzsche met Richard Wagner casually at Leipzig. He so much admired him that he went to Triebschen, the Swiss village where Wagner was living with his friend von Bülow's wife, and his own future wife, Cosima, and where Nietzsche was well received by the master. Though Nietzsche worked hard at his teaching duties, teaching—and for that matter, the whole realm of Academe—very little enticed him. When the Franco-Prussian War broke out, Nietzsche—though compelled because of his Basel post to be a naturalized Swiss citizen—enlisted in the Prussian ambulance service from which, when invalided out, he emerged a man in shattered health. At Basel there were people whom Nietzsche got to know, particularly a very much older colleague, Jakob Burckhardt, the author of the classic history of the Renaissance. And though the best and the most loyal friend of Nietzsche's life was a young Basel professor named Franz Overbeck, the best-known and in time most notorious of Nietzsche's friendships was with Wagner. It began with Nietzsche becoming at Triebschen a disciple who not only sat reverently at the master's feet but also ran his errands; who sang his praises not just as a great composer but as a deliverer from a degraded Christian

Weltanschauung. Nietzsche signed himself, in writing to Wagner, "Your most faithful and reverential disciple and admirer"; and Wagner spoke of Nietzsche as "ever like a messenger from a higher and purer world." Wagner found his disciple brilliant, sympathetic, likable; here was, in any case, a disciple with a great, undisciplined ego of his own attached to a maestro with an even greater one—a maestro who proved a great lawmaker and teacher as well as an actor and charlatan. Music had always meant a great deal to Nietzsche, and here, more than a great musician, was a man who set philosophy to music; who, for that matter, set nationalism to music, religion to music, grandiosity and egomania to music. The classical philologist in Nietzsche had lost most of his interest in philology, and though his first book stayed to some extent within bounds, actually it was very far removed from the greatest German philologist of his time, Ulrich von Wilamowitz—and sharply castigated by him. It was, on the other hand, near to the greatest German composer of his time and much admired by him. In Nietzsche's book, *The Birth of Tragedy out of the Spirit of Music*, he traced the suddenness with which Greek tragedy first rose and then fell, so that what remained, however culturally superior it might be, was cast, as it were, in cold marble; was well conducted but no longer vital and alive. Against this removed-from-life Apollonian condition Nietzsche set—in one of his most famous contrasts—the Dionysian; set, very roughly, the romantic against the classic; and, hurdling the centuries, identified the New Dionysian with the dreaming but undestroyed German spirit and mythology, and the new Dionysos with Wagner. This, to be sure, is to reduce Nietzsche's subject matter to headlines—oversimplified, but scarcely misleading ones.

A year after *The Birth of Tragedy* Nietzsche, while continuing to teach, published the first two of his *Thoughts Out of Season*, one an attack on David Strauss, the author of the famous *Life of Jesus*, which George Eliot translated into English; the other on the *Sound Use and Ill Use of History in Human Life*—the stress being on the materialistic and corrupting nature of the modern world. A third *Thoughts Out of Season* was in praise of Schopenhauer as an educator; and two years later, in 1876, appeared the fourth and last of the *Thoughts*, entitled *Richard Wagner in Bayreuth*. It had actually been composed several years earlier as publicity and propaganda, as an effort to raise money for a center and shrine of Wagner's activities and art: his music dramas, as has been remarked, needed a theater and a general setting with a grander scope than previous operas did. Nietzsche had been chosen by the master to write this propagandist work, but he lacked the gifts of a publicity man and came in for the disapproval of the chief Wagnerites-in-residence. By 1876, however, it was Wagner who was beginning to win the disapproval of Nietzsche.

For by now Bayreuth, ultimately financed by the mad Ludwig of Bavaria, was completed; Wagner was surrounded by all sorts of fashionable, ambitious, and idolatrous people, and Nietzsche, invited to the opening Bayreuth Festival, found himself barely noticed. The general atmosphere, moreover, was quite unlike the Dionysian Valhalla that Nietzsche had envisioned—was, indeed, repellent and ugly, and the friendship with Wagner began its long, steep decline. Two such men of genius, who were also possessed of colossal German egos, could hardly preserve a balance, the less so, as Wagner was with tremendous acclaim storming the heavens, and Nietzsche brooding and suffering in the valley of despondency. In the years to come Nietzsche would first say unfriendly and hostile things about Wagner, and later write them; what best reflects their years of *rapprochement* can be found in their famous correspondence.

At the time of the Bayreuth disenchantment Nietzsche was once again suffering from ill health. He was granted a leave of absence from the University of Basel—he had already taken leave of it in spirit—and he set forth on what would become a reasonably well-regulated new life, something that would serve as a setting for continuous creative activity. Nietzsche went to Sorrento, and his entrance into Italy opened up for him a resplendent world that stood in pointed contrast to the ponderous gloom that darkened the north of Europe. In a different way, but to an even greater extent, Nietzsche experienced what Goethe had done before him: Goethe, when first bathed in Italian sunlight, had said: "I feel as though I had just come back from an expedition to Greenland"; Nietzsche now bathed himself in a physical, in an atmospheric, in a form of prophetic luminousness, hailing not a great past but the prospect of a great future: "We need the south . . . We need limpid, innocent, joyous, happy, tender intonations." Before the 1870's were out, Nietzsche would be retired from his Basel professorship and given a pension which, together with money he got from his mother, enabled him to live comfortably, and to find an odd but actual kind of home in the boarding houses and small hotels of various cities, spas, and resorts—Rome and Genoa, the Engadine and the Riviera, Marienbad and Stresa.

Though this was release and deliverance of a kind, Nietzsche was not delivered from the ill health that had stalked him from his early teaching days, that became a matter of grievous importance in his life, and is perhaps still open to speculation and subject to inquiry. In boyhood and youth he seems to have been normally healthy and even sports-loving —he swam, skated, and was much out-of-doors. A great detriment was his eyesight, his being "six-sevenths blind," so that when he worked, it was with his thick spectacles painfully close to the paper he was writing on. His constant overuse of his eyes in reading, often in a bad light, produced fierce headaches, which in turn led to sleeplessness, this in turn leading to drugs. As the years went by, Nietzsche's bachelor way of life did further damage to his health: he ate the wrong things, and at the wrong hours; he cooked, as it were, experimentally, following various self-contrived diets—or he just ate food raw. He "played doctor and patient with himself," trying all sorts of medicines for headaches, colic, spasmodic vomiting, and constipation; he became agitated when his books were critically attacked or his personal relationships were disrupted—all this creating a state of mind and body in which it is difficult to separate, or even distinguish between, actual ill health and hypochondria. "Pain," he wrote, "seeks out causes where pleasure never looks backwards"; and, by speaking of "holy suffering," he perhaps canonized his complaints. Though poor health and wretched eyesight conditioned his out-of-doors activities and affected, from a fear of ridicule, his social ease, he seems to have been always able to take long walks—these being, indeed, a part of his working routine, when he would create or clarify what he would later write down. If he was excited and inspired, the walks might go on for hours.

Stefan Zweig has drawn—in contrast to the image of Nietzsche as a "German superman . . . a Viking of the Teutonic North striding forward sword in hand"—a "real likeness of the man" during these many years. Here Nietzsche, living in what seem like mediocre boarding houses filled with nonentities—mostly elderly women—would grope his way, when the gong for dinner had rung for the third time, into the dining room, his face gloomy, his eyes melancholy, and sit down timidly at his place at table and all through dinner take no part in the conversation. He seemed outside human society; he examined every dish put before him, for fear it would hurt his digestion; he would ask whether the tea wasn't too strong or the food too highly spiced; he abjured coffee, beer and wine, cigars and cigarettes; and he went back, as soon as dinner was over, to his spare, chilly, typical boarding-house room—where, wearing an overcoat and a woolen muffler, his fingers half frozen, his eyes after a while burning or watering, he would write, often illegibly, for hours at a stretch. Some days, suffering painfully from one or another cause, he would spend entirely in bed. He lived, says Zweig, like Gulliver in Lilliput, a giant tormented by a thousand pigmy ailments; moreover, "an intimate relationship existed between his pulse and the atmospheric pressure, between his nerves and the degree of humidity in the air." However varied and changed the scene, this little chronicle, it appears, went always unchanged—whether in a boarding house at Turin or Marienbad or Nice. Nietzsche's "pilgrimage from one *chambre garnie* to another lasted fifteen years," a small epic of loneliness.

The loneliness was in good part the result of Nietzsche's makeup—of his frequent intractability and intolerance; of the eccentricity created by his actual or his imagined ill health; of his conception, or misconception, of aristocratic behavior. In view of his lack of society or, more to the point, his withdrawal from it, it is extraordinary—the aphorisms are one of the most telling proofs of this—how much about society and mankind the myopic Nietzsche observed, the solitary Nietzsche deduced, the overwrought Nietzsche called forth. In life generally, to be sure, a self-willed or socially shunned "outsider"—for example, a certain kind of old maid or handicapped person—stores up a certain kind of knowledge born of being neglected or going unnoticed, which in small degree Nietzsche may have done. The more feasible explanation is that, in addition to his brilliance, Nietzsche set himself up as a psychologist; and though he was nothing like so aristocratic, nor so clinical, nor—above all—so experienced of society as was La Rochefoucauld, Nietzsche, in putting the psychologist ahead of the philosopher, had something in common with La Rochefoucauld and learned something directly from him. (And where La Rochefoucauld disdained the middle class, Nietzsche detested it.)

In any case, Nietzsche's years of routine wandering were also very productive ones—as Walter Kaufmann points out, for ten years after 1878 Nietzsche would publish a new book every year. In 1878 he published—and dedicated to Voltaire —*Human, All Too Human*, a series of aphorisms. Though Nietzsche was clearly an aphorist born, he seems, after the Germanic Wagner relationship began to cool, to have turned for study and stimulation to a rationalist France and, as has just been suggested, to a ducal La Rochefoucauld and to other French writers. He perhaps absorbed some of their attitudes and, more plainly, he benefited by their skill as aphorists. "After virtue has slept," Nietzsche writes, "she will get up more refreshed." Again: "Often, when someone disputes an opinion, it is actually the tone of voice in which he does it that proves irritating." Here the form is pure La Rochefoucauld: "Convictions are more dangerous enemies of truth than lies are." Here the substance is pure Nietzsche: "A refined nature is vexed by knowing that someone owes it thanks; a coarse nature, by knowing that it owes thanks to someone." Here perhaps Nietzsche the philologist speaks: "It is neither the best nor the worst in a book that is untranslatable." Nietzsche followed up *Human, All Too Human* with two supplements, *Mixed Opinions and Maxims* and *The Wanderer and His*

Shadow. "Not joy," runs one of the aphorisms, "is the mother of dissipation, but joylessness." And another: "The greatest giver of alms is cowardice." Here the aphorism carries an element of autobiography: "Every master has just one disciple who becomes unfaithful to him, for he too is cast for a master's role." This also may breathe a bit of personal experience: "The worst readers of aphorisms are those friends of the author who are bent on ignoring his general statement, to track down the particular occasion that gave rise to the aphorism . . . they nullify, indeed, the author's whole endeavor."

In the early 1880's Nietzsche published, successively, *The Dawn of Day*, *The Gay Science*, and the first part of his best-known work, *Thus Spake Zarathustra* (the three further parts appearing during the next two years, Part IV in an edition of only forty copies). *The Dawn of Day* and *The Joyful Wisdom* are, among other things, the product of Nietzsche's ceasing to be a professor and of his discovery of Italy and delight in it. *The Gay Science*—a translation of the Provençal phrase *gai saber*—seeks a southern wit and warmth. Both works have more that is Italian and French than German about them, which is to say more that is bright and tolerant: they have been called Nietzsche's "best-tempered books." Largely written in parts of the world that Nietzsche particularly liked, these books, he said, "gave me back my life." *Zarathustra* scarcely reflects the clarity and sunlight of the south or, at any rate, the European side of the Mediterranean: it has a heavily prophetic, not to say biblical, air, a German *Langeweile*, and, to a not very informed reader, its virtue and value seem smothered in the rhetorical, the messianic, and the verbose. In it Nietzsche shouts the death of God and the arrival of the *Übermensch* (long and distortingly Englished as the Superman). As opposed to his early critics, who dismissed or ignored it, Nietzsche—whom Zweig described as "the greatest mind of the century"—thought *Zarathustra* "the greatest gift ever bestowed upon man"; and understandably moaned over the work's reception. "After such an appeal as my *Z*," he wrote, "a cry that came from my heart, it is terrible not to hear a responsive word, to hear nothing, absolutely nothing, to be surrounded by silence . . . Even the strongest might die under the strain . . . And I am far from being the strongest." It has been suggested that dissent would not have distressed Nietzsche, whose "bellicose temperament" would have thoroughly enjoyed harsh opposition, and even mockery; that only all lack of response could wrap him in gloom. Lack of response may have been the worse of the two; but in the light of Nietzsche's fear of ridicule and his intense emotionalism, he would scarcely have "thoroughly enjoyed" being attacked, let alone derided.

Though at times during these years his health seems to have improved, the headaches and sleeplessness persisted; what perhaps got worse was the sense of being abused and abandoned: "I have no comrades—no one knows when I need comfort, encouragement, or a grip of the hand." Like so many prophets and visionaries, he stood increasingly in need of the medical man. (Yet, a little like Baudelaire's Prometheus, he had learned to love his rock.) Still, he remained able to write, indeed to write very ably: *Beyond Good and Evil* appeared and, after it, *The Genealogy of Morals*, both valuable studies of human attitudes and behavior. In 1888 Nietzsche finished *The Twilight of the Gods* and published *The Wagner Case*. The old friendship with Wagner had by then not only withered but become toxic; introducing Bizet in contrast, as a composer with enchanting grace, lightness and style, whose music "does not sweat," Nietzsche attacked Wagner's music as all-too-damagingly German, all too top-heavy with sin

and redemption, while citing chapter and verse for strained
or laughable sin-and-redemption situations.

By now Nietzsche's regularized shifts of scene and boarding-house versions of home had, in conjunction with his disdain for most of humanity, made for an almost programmatic
loneliness; a loneliness increased and intensified by quarrels
with friends and members of his family; a loneliness stressed
by his lack of wide recognition. Some of his friends—which
was perhaps the unkindest cut—had dismissed his writings
with pointed silence or perfunctory acknowledgment; indeed,
only a few remained his friends. There had, over the years,
been one or two women—notably a very bright Finnish
Jewess, Lou Salomé, whom Nietzsche seems first to have regarded as a disciple. She was ready, she confided to him, to
sacrifice her life for truth; and though there was another man,
Paul Rée, in the foreground, Nietzsche—by way of the other
man—sent her a proposal of marriage. Perhaps it was not
delivered; certainly it was never answered. The three of them,
as devotees of truth, shared lodgings for a while, but on
Nietzsche's side nothing came of it except that, thanks to the
promptings of Nietzsche's meddlesome sister, he felt injured
and insulted by Lou, who may well have become the mistress
of Rée. In any case, he wrote to Rée: "I should very much
like to give you a lesson in practical morality with the help
of a few bullets" and speaks of Rée's concern with morality as
needing "clean hands, Herr Dr. Rée, not muckraking fingers
like yours."

In one way or another, from feeling lonely, from feeling
sick, spurned, sorry for himself, and from feeling vastly superior, Nietzsche had more and more taken to creating and
inhabiting a kind of private world. He escaped from it, in
varying degrees, managing sometimes to function with great
cogency and brilliance, and to keep on writing, sometimes to

an extraordinary degree. Indeed, the 1880's were his great decade. But as time passed, and before the decade ended, there were ominous and grandiose warnings. "I am not," said Nietzsche, "a human being, I am dynamite." "I have called together at Rome," he wrote to Strindberg, "an assembly of princes. I will have the young emperor [Kaiser Wilhelm I] shot," and signed the letter "Nietzsche-Caesar." He addressed the King of Italy as "my dearly beloved son" and signed a number of letters "The Crucified One." To Cosima Wagner he sent a five-word letter: "Ariadne, I love thee—Dionysos." He announced that with the publication of his *Antichrist* the Christian era would cease, and the years be renumbered. To his oldest and best friend, Overbeck, he wrote: "Right now I am having all the anti-Semites shot." This, and a letter Nietzsche sent to Burckhardt, decided Overbeck to hurry to Nietzsche's side.

Nietzsche had indeed gone mad, but Overbeck arrived in time to take hold of the situation and bring Nietzsche from Turin to Basel, from where his mother took him for examinations to Jena. The verdict was "incurably mad." In time his possessive sister took him to Goethe's old home, the capital of reason and culture, Weimar; there he lingered, half paralyzed as well as in mental darkness, until on August 25, 1900, he died.

Since his death, as during his lifetime, Nietzsche has doubtless been often misunderstood and misinterpreted. Clearly, he has been done least justice for what made him most notorious—for having been squeezed inside Nazi ideology, vicious anti-Semitism included. Also given glaring prominence are his attacks on Christianity and his fierce antifeminism: "Thou goes to women? Forget not thy whip!" Indeed, despite his having in one way or another attacked and excoriated

one belief after another, he has emerged in a maze of interpretations—a kind of blind-men-and-the-elephant procedure,
depending on what aspect of Nietzsche one touches. Certainly, for all his abuse of Germany and things German, and
his staying outside it for a great deal of his active life, his
image and identity remain Germanic. His insanity has also
contributed to his popular image; and his best-known work,
Zarathustra, with its prophetic and biblical tone, has exalted
him as a seer and associated him with a sect. But that he, for
all that was wrong with him, could be a far better psychologist than a seer, and a far better writer of brilliant prose than
of dithyrambic rhetoric, is very clear. Nietzsche's ultimate
importance as an intellectual, an iconoclast, a philosopher is
not nearly as clear, and could hardly be more controversial,
since appraisals of him are as much a matter of temperament
as of judgment. Thus, no one could be, so to speak, more
Dionysian in his approach to Nietzsche than, say, Stefan
Zweig, since his penetrating comments lie half-buried in
overheated and very repetitious prose; and no one could be
more Apollonian than, say, Crane Brinton, with his rational
and skeptical temper and his distaste for the rhapsodic in
Nietzsche. Although in this case two such extremes do not
meet, they both have something useful to contribute—Zweig
not least in elucidating Nietzsche's difficulties, Brinton in
elucidating the reader's.

Fortunately, despite *Zarathustra*, Nietzsche could command what might be called a non-Germanic style—indeed he
bracketed himself with Heine, prophesying that it would
someday be said that the two of them were by all odds the pre-
eminent wielders of the German language. Nietzsche's writing aphorisms early in his career, with French aphorists as
his model, undoubtedly helped shorten and sharpen and
lighten his prose, so that writing, for example, of George

Sand, he could speak of her "bright wallpaper prose" and say of her rigid writing habits that "she wound herself up like a clock—and wrote." (Nietzsche is borne out here by Gautier's famous anecdote of George Sand working each night from eleven till three, and on finishing a novel at 1 A.M., immediately starting another.) Nietzsche was a good critic of the arts, a classical critic, as Brinton says, along with being a romantic artist. "Romanticism," Nietzsche himself remarked, "is only an emergency exit from ill-functioning reality"; and in a good deal of his work, whatever the tone—classic, romantic, ironic, satiric, even prophetic—we find Nietzsche effectively aphoristic as well. Here, from the autobiographical *Ecce Homo*: "One must pay dearly for immorality: one needs must several times die while still alive." Here from *Zarathustra*: "Women understand children better than men do, but men are more childlike than women." Here from *The Genealogy of Morals*: "A married philosopher belongs to comedy." Here from *Beyond Good and Evil*: "Whoever fights monsters should make sure not to become one in the process."

But to indicate the whereabouts of Nietzsche's aphorisms, imbedded as they are in so many of his writings, is of little value; even to distinguish between those works which concentrate on aphorisms and those which merely contain them is no way of separating the wheat from the chaff. The aphorisms are so numerous as inevitably to exist at numerous levels—to be very often brilliant; sometimes in the sniffy phrase of pedagogues, brilliant but unsound; now startling, and now startling but also true; often able to stimulate thought if not satisfy it; on occasion, eccentric or outlandish, and now and then merely silly or dull. Among philosophers, only such few as Plato, Hume, Schopenhauer, William James, and Santayana had at all comparable literary gifts; and Santayana alone, aphoristic ones.

181

THE LAST WORD

Let us, while mindful of quality, set down a handful of aperçus and aphorisms which catch the nature and flavor of Nietzsche: "We use up too much artistic effort in our dreams, so that our waking life is often pale." Again: "He who despises himself nevertheless esteems himself as a self-despiser." Again: "Arrogance in persons of merit affronts us more than arrogance in those without merit, for merit itself is an affront." Once again: "When a man has been highly honored and has eaten a little, he is most benevolent." And again: "The idealist is incorrigible: if he is thrown out of his heaven he makes an ideal of his hell." And finally: "Our disciples never forgive us if we take sides against ourselves —to them this means we have not only rejected their devotion but have made a show of their judgment."

Nietzschean though these may seem in sentiment, there is about some of them the form and succinctness of the classic maxim-makers. Here in both form and substance Nietzsche is "classical": "Women learn how to hate in the degree that they forget how to charm"; and "Familiarity on the part of one's superiors induces resentment, for it cannot be returned." Again: "Shared joys, not shared sufferings, make for friendship." Or: "Some people never become thinkers because their memories are too good." Now and then Nietzsche offers a kind of satiric wisecrack: "A book calls for pen, ink and a writing desk; the rule today is that pen, ink and writing desk call for a book." And there are maxims—quite valuable ones—that we might characterize as all-too-Nietzschean: "So long as men praise you, you can only be sure that you are following in someone else's path, and not yet in your own." Or: "We have art that we may not perish from truth"; or: "To take upon oneself not punishment but guilt: that alone would be godlike."

That so many aphorisms or short sayings of Nietzsche

should clearly bear his signature is much less remarkable than that so many of his successful ones do not, but have rather an impersonal force and even a universal validity. We tend to think of the aphorism as particularly French for displaying a sense of form, a gift for polish, and a Gallic lightness and wit, and also for being, with the French, an established branch of literature. Yet, having to cope with one of the heaviest and most unwieldy of languages, three Germans stand among the very greatest of aphorists—Lichtenberg, Goethe, and Nietzsche.

Aphorisms

Men who have died are worse understood than those in our midst, but they are heard *better.*

No one lies so boldly as the man who is indignant.

When we are tired, we are attacked by ideas we conquered long ago.

The visionary denies the truth to himself, the liar only to others.

Theatrical poses don't consort with greatness . . . Beware of those who try to look picturesque.

THE LAST WORD

Beggars should be abolished. It annoys one to give to them and it annoys one not to give to them.

How good bad music and bad reasons sound when we march against an enemy.

It ill becomes a philosopher to despise mediocrity. Precisely for being the exception, he must uphold the rule.

The most vulnerable and equally most unconquerable of things is human vanity.

The thought of suicide is a great consolation; with the help of it one has got through many a bad night.

The man who sees little always sees less than there is to see; the man who hears badly always hears more than there is to hear.

What really makes one indignant about suffering isn't the thing itself but the senselessness of it.

The growth of wisdom can be accurately gauged by the drop in ill temper.

NIETZSCHE

Experience, as something sought after, doesn't work. We mustn't study ourselves in the midst of having an experience.

The lie is a condition of life.

Wit closes the coffin on an emotion.

XI

Oscar Wilde

THANKS TO BOSWELL, Dr. Johnson's talk has no equal in the English-speaking world; but Oscar Wilde's—very little of which has been accurately recorded, except as Wilde himself might repeat things he said in things he wrote—very possibly excelled Johnson's. Johnson clearly bears the palm for infusing into his talk a far greater impact of personality; and Johnson bears it, at his best, for the vital force of his comments and reflections. But where Johnson, from mistaking his prejudices for his principles, and from stopping people's mouths and trampling on their feelings, rather justifiably antagonized his hearers, Wilde seems in conversation to have charmed even those who disliked or disapproved of him; almost never trod on people's feelings or, like Johnson, pontificated or played the autocrat. Almost everyone entitled to pass judgment on Wilde's talk found it incomparable—found it Wilde's master talent, indeed his one real claim to genius. His talk could be playful, fanciful, nonsensical, sprinkled with insight, given to storytelling; truly perceptive, splendidly witty; and along with touchés and repartees, it spun countless epigrams and aphorisms, many of them woven into his writings. Perhaps no one else has ever uttered, in epigrammatic form, so many striking part truths and paradoxes—things that might be called halforisms—and few of even the greatest aphorists have excelled Wilde in pithy antithesis or conciseness of language.

OSCAR WILDE

If he, as perhaps both the greatest of English-speaking wits and the greatest of English-speaking talkers, must take a somewhat lesser rank as aphorist, he all the same takes distinguished rank, equally for substance and for style.

Oscar Fingal O'Flahertie Wills Wilde was, of course, Irish. He was born in Dublin in 1854, the son of William Wilde, a very brilliant, famous, and successful doctor—"the first, and in many ways, the greatest of English-speaking ear surgeons" —who was knighted, although it so happens, for his services to the Irish census. Oscar's mother, a professor's daughter, had been part of the Young Ireland movement, writing inflammatory newspaper pieces and verses under the names of "John Fenshaw Ellis" and "Speranza." She too had a brilliant side, but also an eccentric and nondomestic one, asking a servant, after one of her many parties: "Why do you put the plates in the coal scuttle? What are the chairs meant for?" Sir William became the center of a great scandal, involving a malicious woman he had had one of his many affairs with; and in 1876, while he was dying, another old flame of his sat, day after day without speaking a word, at his bedside. Oscar's mother accepted these and similar situations not, said Oscar, because she did not love his father but "because she loved him very much." Oscar in turn loved his mother very much.

He and his older brother Willie were brought up in a sophisticated atmosphere, being allowed as small children to dine with the family, even when there were guests. At school Oscar hated sports and took no exercise. He was not very popular; despite a love of clothes he looked—from being oversized—awkward and loutish, and he mostly read books of his own choosing, on the ground that "nothing that is worth knowing can be taught." In time he won an entrance scholarship at Dublin's famous Trinity College, where he spent three years and acquired a number of prizes and medals.

Here too he took very little part in undergraduate life and, with his "aesthetic" tastes, was again unpopular; but he proved sufficiently athletic when need be, his fists landing someone who taunted him on the floor. From Trinity he went on to Oxford, where the real Oscar Wilde assembled his personality and invented his poses: he displayed blue china, which he said he wished he could live up to; and when it was his duty to read from Deuteronomy in chapel, he announced a selection from The Song of Solomon. At times, it would seem, he "majored" in impudence; and he once again disposed physically of those who taunted him. He became interested, as he would continue to be, in the Roman Catholic church, and set forth on trips to Rome and Greece; he read a great deal, particularly admiring and being influenced by Keats, Pater (who was then at Oxford), and the Flaubert of *Salammbô*; he did brilliantly in his studies, gaining a double first; and he won the prestigious Newdigate Prize with a poem on Ravenna.

Going down from Oxford to London in search of immediate fame, he became—despite all the period's aestheticism of one sort or another—a kind of one-man Aesthetic Movement. He described himself as an art critic and professor of aesthetics; he dressed himself in velvet coats, knee breeches, silk stockings, and flowing pale-green neckties; he advertised himself with gaudy floral buttonholes; he insinuated himself into fashionable society; and he stationed himself, as it were, in or very near the Theater. He got to know Henry Irving, he wrote sonnets to Ellen Terry, he shouted "Vive Sarah Bernhardt" and threw lilies at her feet. He gave parties which attracted Lily Langtry and Modjeska along with ladies of title —women almost always responded favorably to him. He made witty and whimsical remarks that quickly got about, he fashioned flowery compliments that did no harm to his career, and he soon achieved the standing of a minor celebrity, being caricatured and satirized, by George du Maurier in *Punch* and by Gilbert & Sullivan in *Patience*. But though all this contributed to his fame, it did nothing for his finances; what money he had inherited from his father was used up, and though his first book, *Poems*, sold well while being reviewed badly, he was soon again out of funds. *Vera*, a play treating of Nihilism in Russia, at that time a very lively subject, was announced for production but permanently "postponed," perhaps because the Tsar of Russia was the brother-in-law of the Prince of Wales. *Vera* sported some of Wilde's first printed repartees and aphorisms, such as "Experience, the name men give to their mistakes"; the rather facile analogy between a good salad and a brilliant diplomat—"to know exactly how much oil one must put with one's vinegar"; and—an exchange in the play's dialogue—"We speak the truth to one another here." "How misleading you must find it!"

The blazing success of *Patience* in America gave D'Oyly Carte the idea of sending Oscar there on a lecture tour, a stunt that greatly enhanced Oscar's fame and Oscar's finances alike. Beginning with the newspapermen who met his ship and reported that Oscar was "disappointed with the Atlantic Ocean"; following this up with his telling the customs officials, when he was asked had he anything to declare, "I have nothing to declare except my genius," Oscar got himself immediately and widely talked about. His further "disappointment"—with American life—ran to such matters as its lack of ceremonies and pageants: "I saw only two processions: one was the Fire Brigade preceded by the Police, the other was the Police preceded by the Fire Brigade." He was swamped with invitations of every sort—dinner parties, theater parties, dances, receptions; and he was "tested" by a group of men who wondered how physically tough he was: he out-ate and out-drank every one of them, indeed he helped most of them, dead drunk, to their cabs and then himself strolled back to his hotel. In a later "test," it would seem, he proved as remarkable at brothels as at restaurants and bars. A doughtier physical challenge came in the course of his lectures out West, when he went to Leadville to talk to an audience of miners, who afterward took him to a dance-hall saloon with a sign on the piano which Wilde made famous: "Please do not shoot the pianist, he is doing his best"; and who then took Wilde, in a basket, to "supper" at the bottom of a mine. Each course of the supper consisted of neat whiskey, which seriously affected Wilde's hosts but not him. Similar feats won such cowboy tributes as "He can drink any of us under the table and afterwards carry us home two at a time." The lectures themselves—there were eighty or more of them—enabled him to pay his debts and live in comfort for some months after he returned from America. He had discoursed, in his own words, on "the decorative in art," one of his comments being that "to see the frock coat of the drawing room done in bronze, or the double waistcoat perpetuated in marble adds a new horror to death." Leaving the United States in December of 1882, for Paris, Wilde revised his opinion of the ocean: "The Atlantic," he this time remarked, "has been greatly misunderstood."

In Paris he met a number of distinguished Frenchmen—Verlaine, Mallarmé, Paul Bourget, Zola, Coquelin; he met also a young Englishman, Robert Sherard, who would be his loyal friend and biographer; and Wilde struck up conversations with thieves and other disreputables at sidewalk cafés. He was at work on a verse tragedy, *The Duchess of Padua*, which the famous actress, Mary Anderson, had made an advance payment on, but which she subsequently turned down:

in later life Wilde was to characterize the play as "unfit for publication" (though in 1891 it got a production in New York). When in May 1883 Wilde went back to London, he was so hard up that he got himself booked for what he was terribly tired of—a lecture tour; and delivered his most popular lecture, treating of his impressions of America, in Regency-style clothes. He was by now seeing a good deal of Whistler, who was close to twice Wilde's age and whom Wilde at this point admired; later, and very publicly, he would cross swords with the megalomaniac figure that Whistler had turned into. Wilde would become a much greater lion and—though Whistler could be in a malicious way very witty—a much greater wit.

It was during his lecture tour that Oscar became engaged to Constance Lloyd, a well-known Irish barrister's very attractive daughter whom he was "very much in love with" and who declared that "she worshipped him more every time she saw him." Their wedding in May 1884, at St. James's, Paddington, filled the church, collected a crowd outside, and had the appearance of a show. The wedding trip took them to Paris, where Wilde went out walking with Sherard and insisted on describing, down to physical details, "the marvelous night he had just spent with his wife." Back in London, the Wildes were soon installed, with the aid of Constance's dowry, in a Chelsea townhouse boasting various color schemes, Moorish, Venetian, and Japanese motifs, a writing table which had belonged to Thomas Carlyle, and a ceiling designed by Whistler. In this new house Constance gave numerous parties which aristocrats and artists flocked to, and where the hostess, to please her husband, was not very willingly got up in Grecian, Medieval, and Directoire toilettes. Over the years, as revealed in a book Constance kept, the guests included Ruskin, Swinburne, Browning, Meredith, Whistler, Sargent, Mark Twain, Oliver Wendell Holmes, Henry Irving, Ellen Terry, and Sarah Bernhardt.

In 1885 Constance gave birth to a son, named Cyril, and a year or so later, to a second son, Vyvyan. The coming of children for Constance to look after made for Oscar's going about a good deal without her. There were troubles over money, he himself making little and living far beyond what Constance's dowry permitted. He turned journalist, was editor of *The Woman's World* and a reviewer for *The Pall Mall Gazette*, where his criticisms were befriended by his witticisms. Of a novel by Charlotte M. Yonge and three others, Wilde remarked: "It has taken four people to write it, and even to read it requires assistance"; of the once famous author of *The Light of Asia* he said: "Sir Edwin Arnold has translated Sa'di, and someone must translate Sir Edwin Arnold." In 1888 appeared Wilde's *The Happy Prince and Other Tales*, a collection of fairy stories which differ in merit, and in style can approach the meretricious, but which deservedly survive at their best; and during these years Wilde continued to write, turning out, among other things, some of his best essays. He also wrote the *Portrait of Mr W.H.*, in which he contended that the shadowy and controversial Mr. W.H. of Shakespeare's *Sonnets* was a young actor named Willie Hughes. During the same period Wilde wrote the first of his really well-known works, and his only novel, *The Picture of Dorian Gray*. This story, of a young man who retains his youth while his portrait ages, with its "morbid" atmosphere and its "decadent" content, offended and scandalized most of the Victorian reviewers, who wrote of it as "dull and nasty," "stupid and vulgar," "unmanly, sickening, vicious . . . and tedious," "malodorous putrefaction," and "ought to be chucked into the fire." It aroused animosity in those who never read it, hostility in journalists and critics, and it would be used against Wilde at the time of the Queensberry trial.

These three or four years of miscellaneous writings were to give way, early in the 1890's, to a succession of plays which became Wilde's greatest successes and would be among the works he was best known for in the future. The first of the four plays, *Lady Windermere's Fan*—written near Lake Windermere in the summer of 1891 and produced in London in the following February—won him an ovation on opening night; and, though the critics, including Oscar's brother Willie, were for the most part unfriendly, the play was a hit, and the play's epigrams were quoted wherever one went. The second of Wilde's drawing-room comedies, *A Woman of No Importance*, opened a little over a year later and, though a far from good play, was an equally great success. No less great was the success of *An Ideal Husband*, opening in January 1895; and hardly more than a month later, Wilde's masterpiece, *The Importance of Being Earnest*, opened to fine critical reviews—Bernard Shaw was the one important dissenter—and enabled Wilde to boast of having simultaneously two hits on the London stage.

He had indeed restored to the London stage the glitter, the wit, the stylish worldliness that it had been denied since Sheridan's *School for Scandal* a hundred years earlier. The plays abounded in epigram, the best of it decidedly certifiable as aphorism—"The youth of America is its oldest tradition, it has been going on for three hundred years"; "When the gods wish to punish us, they answer our prayers"; "The greatest tyranny in the world is the tyranny of the weak over the strong . . . It is the only tyranny that lasts." The plays are also given to prattle and badinage—delightful at their best, indeed the best thing in Wilde's playwriting. As plays, all four are technically well put together; moreover, to the sheen of their wit might be added the sham luster of their high-society settings. The first three plays, however, are much less the classic comedies of manners they purport to be, than comedies of manners superimposed on melodramas of morals. Wilde's wit was spendidly his own, but his plots were in the stagy tradition of Scribe and Sardou, while his "morality," which had half an eye on box-office returns, was thoroughly and at moments absurdly Victorian. The scandalous and the shocking might dart all around the plays, but in doing so they bumped into the lachrymose and the maudlin; and any sin or wickedness that might darken the plot had always occurred many years before the curtain went up. The first three plays combine well-fashioned dialogue with old-fashioned "theater"; the fourth, *The Importance of Being Earnest*, stands not only far higher but almost alone on the English stage. It is brilliant high farce, or call it superb high nonsense, and can almost be summed up as Gilbert and Sheridan. It unfolds an absurd Savoy-opera plot in an elegant drawing-room setting, and goes at things in a drawing-room style: one complication, misunderstanding, entanglement emerges out of another; every detail in it counts, but nothing whatever really matters. In *The Importance* Wilde at last found himself, making use of his great special talents; in it he escaped from the realism he cared little about, but escaped, not as in the other plays, into melodrama, but into playfulness and civilized nonsense. It is the high point of his career.

In his own melodramatic way, he was to plummet, a few months later, to the low point of his life. For a number of years it had been known to a great many people—Wilde had indeed made small effort to conceal it—that he was a practicing homosexual. It was, however, Wilde's meeting and subsequent long relationship with Lord Alfred Douglas, the Oxford undergraduate son of the Marquis of Queensberry, that precipitated the scandal and the criminal proceedings which destroyed Wilde's career. Wilde himself did much to precipitate it: the ruffianly Lord Queensberry, who, with threats and prohibitions, had tried in vain to break up the relationship, at length left a card for Wilde at his club, which read: "To Oscar Wilde posing as a somdomite [sic]." Wilde, with insane foolishness, brought criminal proceedings against Queensberry, at whose trial Wilde's "past" became more and more apparent; and on the trial's breaking up in mid-air, Wilde himself was arrested. He had been urged on all sides to leave for the Continent but refused to go. At his trial, where he was indicted for "offenses under the Criminal Law Amendment Act," the jury failed to agree; but a new trial was immediately ordered, with Wilde released on bail and taken into the house of the well-placed Ernest Leversons, among the few people who stood stanchly by him. He was now beseeched to go abroad but again refused, possibly influenced by the mad, minority judgment of his mother, who said to him: "If you stay, even if you go to prison, you will always be my son . . . but if you go, I will never speak to you again." He stayed, was found guilty, and sentenced to two years at hard labor.

His life in prison—actually in several prisons—was harsh for the most part, and sometimes hideous: several of his warders or prison governors were brutal, the food made him vomit, and when he was so hungry he had to eat it, he developed diarrhea. For a long time there was very little that he was permitted to read, there were numerous punishments for trifling offenses, his health broke down, and, aside from visits from friends, what most helped him was the chance to talk— once he learned to speak without moving his lips—with his fellow prisoners. He helped some of them after his release; and thanks to a humane governor and warder, his last months in prison were relatively happy ones. His prison experiences deepened his own humaneness; while there, he wrote *De Profundis*, in places effective and moving, but marred by theatricalism; and his *being* there led to the writing, after his release, of *The Ballad of Reading Gaol*, uneven as poetry, but in many places vivid and powerful.

On leaving prison in May 1897, Wilde went to France, staying first at Dieppe, where a number of artists sojourned (and kept out of Wilde's way); then removed to Berneval-sur-Mer, some nine miles distant, where he was said to look very well, prison having rid him of puffiness; where he thought he would like to live permanently; where he wrote most of *The Ballad of Reading Gaol* and saw a number of his friends; but where he all too soon grew thoroughly bored. His wife had remained on good terms with him after his trial and had refused, as her family wished, to divorce him; but she *had* consented to a legal separation, which gave her the custody of the children, at the same time that it bestowed on Wilde, so long as he did not live with Alfred Douglas, £150 a year. A short while after Wilde's release from prison, Douglas got in touch with him and sensed that, whatever other people thought, Wilde himself had not turned against him. They met for some twenty-four hours at Rouen and agreed to meet again a month later in Naples. That reunion wore itself out, however, and they separated. Wilde's life thereafter—under the name he had assumed of Sebastian Melmoth—was all too frequently to be shabby, pathetic, painful: there was a constant need of money, often from its being squandered when he had it; there was a continuing exposure to snubs and insults; a craving for companionship, which drove Wilde out of a seedy hotel room to the bars and restaurants where he would not be asked to leave, and where he might even cadge drinks. There were desultory efforts at writing, and there were—usually as a tactful way of giving him money—a number of publishers' advances against something he was supposed to write. He saw friends and on occasion was his old self as a wondrous talker and master of impromptu. He retained his old interest in the life and person of Christ, and in the Roman Catholic church, going indeed to Rome, where he seven times received the Pope's blessing. *Salomé*, which he had written in the early 1890's, and had rewritten in French, was successfully produced on the French stage while he was in prison, and would become world famous as Richard Strauss's opera; and first *The Importance of Being Earnest* appeared in book form (though by "the author of *Lady Windermere's Fan*"); and a little later, *An Ideal Husband*.

As time passed, however, Wilde's health deteriorated: he suffered from headaches and required an ear operation, and he continued, despite the appeals of his friends, to constantly drink absinthe—until, as he wrote to his stanch friend Robert Ross, his throat was a lime kiln, his brain a furnace, and his nerves seething with angry adders. He died on November 30, 1900, of cerebral meningitis, probably aggravated by syphilis, having at the very end been received into the Catholic church. He was buried in Bagneux, but in 1909 his body was taken to Paris and to Père Lachaise, his grave to become by far the most sought-out of all those buried there, whether Balzac or Bizet or Chopin.

If a single adjective is to be attached to Oscar Wilde, perhaps the one that in the most ways applies is *theatrical*. His fame had the sharp glitter, and his notoriety the harsh glare, equally common to the footlights; his plays abound in stagy and overwrought effects. When not given to startling paradoxes Wilde tended to indulge in purple prose. His street clothes at certain periods resembled stage costumes—he never, said Vincent O'Sullivan, looked well dressed but always looked "dressed up"; his fairy tales often advance toward dramatic curtain lines; he made theater, wherever he went, of his travels; he made theater of his trial. He made it impossible to go unnoticed, so that he could not go uncommented upon. This doubtless accounts for how extremely often, after his downfall, people made an incident of his appearing in public places: not just restaurants and hotels asked him to leave; barbers refused to shave him. He for the most part lived within a kind of dream, a toy playhouse of emotions and attitudes, a dream he refused to abandon even when it became a nightmare: he possessed, or acquired, an irrational sense of destiny and a self-dramatized image of being fated to suffer. There Wilde's great interest in, and possible identification with, Christ may have played a part—may have kept him, in the face of ruin, from fleeing to the Continent. He shunned reality no less when it meant prison than when it spelled pleasure; he could resist everything but the limelight or the last word. Apropos of *Dorian Gray*, but applicable to much else, Wilde told Conan Doyle: "I throw probability out of the window for the sake of a phrase, and the chance of an epigram makes me desert truth."

The theatricalism tarnished his plays and his prose, as it did his physical image and his personal relationships—it made him take to using perfumed language, and turn into an unctuous flatterer. Some of his essays, a few of the fairy stories, the whole of *The Importance of Being Earnest* notably survive, with every right to; a fair amount in the remaining plays and the remaining prose survives—with every reason to—in Bartlett's and in other books of quotation. In even his least successful work an effective witticism or aphorism may crop up; and in the memoirs of numerous people, his spoken remarks, paradoxical or epigrammatic, are quoted at either first or second hand. Next to the brilliance of Wilde's conversation is the benevolence: though he might make monkeys of people, on the plea of *"C'est mon métier,"* he was seldom malicious: indeed, beneath his impudence there was unusual good nature. Even those he disliked became victims of wit rather than of waspishness. Of *Evelyn Innes*, George Moore's novel about singers and the opera, Wilde said: "I hear it has to be played on the piano"; and of Moore himself: "Do I *know* George Moore? Why, I know him so well that I haven't spoken to him for ten years." A number of Wilde's comments would survive for their wit or playfulness alone: "Meredith is a prose Browning—and so is Browning"; "The gods have bestowed on Max [Beerbohm] the gift of perpetual old age"; "Henry James writes fiction as if it were a painful duty"; and of Dickens's sentimentality, "One must have a heart of stone to read the death of Little Nell without laughing."

Wilde developed his own little formulas in being witty: one that he was very successful at, if overdone, was to reverse well-known sayings or clichés: "Punctuality is the thief of time"; "I am prevented from coming, owing to a subsequent engagement"; "Work is the curse of the drinking classes"; "old enough to know worse." Another trick was to make aphoristic hay of opposites: "There is only one thing in the world worse than being talked about, and that is not being talked about"; "In this world there are only two tragedies. One is not getting what one wants, and the other is getting it." Many of these sentences are more than merely clever, and most of them are legitimate aphorisms. Even some of Wilde's most delightful nonsense has the air of an aphorism: "To lose one parent may be regarded as a misfortune; to lose both looks like carelessness." Indeed, it was part of Wilde's inability to face reality that brought him such success in making fun of it; when he wrote seriously of reality, it ended in distortion or misrepresentation. Lady Bracknell in *The Importance* is a superb caricature, indeed a superb creation, where in the other plays his "seriously" treated aristocrats are for the most part mere pasteboard. Actually, the end of Act III of *A Woman of No Importance* is so incredibly bad as to be much more laughable than the death of Little Nell.

Yet, though to treat of life at all Wilde had to look at it through harlequin glasses, a great deal of humaneness underlay his excessive theatricality. He had always a very real feeling for the poor: "They are," he said, "ungrateful, discontented, disobedient and rebellious." And he added: "They are quite right to be so." Again: "To recommend thrift to the poor is . . . like advising a man who is starving to eat less." After speaking abusively of agitators for sowing the seeds of discontent, he continued: "That is the reason why agitators are so absolutely necessary." It is rather surprising that Wilde, in the Boer War, was pro-English; on the other hand, when Bernard Shaw asked writers to sign a petition to reprieve the Haymarket anarchists in Chicago, the only signature he got was Oscar Wilde's. "It was a completely disinterested act on his part," said Shaw, "and it secured my distinguished consideration for him for the rest of his life."

Like Chamfort a hundred years earlier, Wilde disparaged the rich and the grand while snobbishly cultivating and living among them, and like Chamfort he went to prison. But they were not too much alike, and their milieus were even less so. Where the 1790's in revolutionary France shattered an intolerably privileged society, the 1890's in Victorian England had still *their* Bastille, which is to say their fortress of Puritanism, their stronghold of hypocrisy. Even "normal" sex in any illicit form could be too much for the London stage of the nineties, which is one reason why in Wilde's plays sex is merely another word for sin. Indeed, not just Wilde but a number of writers and artists of the period went in for poses and self-display to dissociate themselves from the puritanical and the philistine; and drank and took drugs; and flaunted their defiances and their mistresses; and inhaled a foreign, French "decadence"; and came to sad or early ends. But theirs was not a climate, it was merely a small cult; it was not a true *fin de siècle*, but a *Lady Windermere's Fan de siècle*. The one man who in those years posed with real purpose—as a serious tactic—was Shaw. Wilde, whose writings and lecture tours and personal appearances were preeminently concerned with dress and décor and aesthetic surfaces, reveled in all such gaudiness and gilt, in italicized innovations and limelighted fashions, in epigrammatic self-advertisement. His protest against drab, timid, middle-class living suffered from being empurpled and monotonously outré, with what he advocated no better than what he abjured. His antics and his tactics might have a certain news value, fad value, refreshment value; but they relegated Wilde as a writer to an entertainer's level rather than an artist's. *That*, even today, is chiefly his role, though the artist is also present in the best of his work, as the psychologist and sage appear in the best of his aphorisms.

It is in his epigrams and aphorisms—in short, concise comments and statements—that Wilde is at his most perceptive and adult; is most the observing skeptic and least the dreaming romantic; and proves that out of the mouth of self-dramatizers both insight and truth may emerge. Hesketh Pearson sees Wilde as having matured intellectually very early and never having matured emotionally at all. Such a combination may well have brought about the role that Wilde assumed; a role, in the end, rather than a self—the role of showman, the rubric of *épater-le-bourgeois*, the dominator of glittering dinner tables and spinner of delightful yarns. To *be* all this one must be as dedicated to fantasy as are others to good sense; and to *do* all this, however minor it may largely be, one must possess a touch of the magician. That Wilde could not, even when confronted with harsh punishment, exchange fantasy for reality, playfulness for seriousness, is evidence of how much his dream world dominated him, and how life must have shocked and stunned *him* in the descent from high nonsense to hell.

He was very little resentful of those who snubbed or turned against him—perhaps his strongest epithet was to call Aubrey Beardsley "lache." Fortunately there were those with the character to stand by him from the start; and others who outgrew their cowardice or inconstancy. Still, his last years were too vagrant and—with his champagne tastes—too indigent, to bring more than fitful pleasure, or to produce— *The Ballad of Reading Gaol* excepted—any real writing at all. The last years were also in their own way punitive, and not till after his death would his place in letters be restored— and even then, far more on the Continent than in England. But, however much the fantasist in Wilde misgoverned, the aphorist had, from years back, all but foreseen his fate: "Misfortunes one can endure," Wilde had written. ". . . But to suffer for one's own faults—ah!—there is the sting of life." And again: "It is what we fear that happens to us." And a few words that Wilde wrote are perhaps autobiographical as well as aphoristic: "The basis of optimism is sheer terror."

OSCAR WILDE
Aphorisms

A thing is not necessarily true because a man dies for it.

To regret one's own experiences is to arrest one's own development.

One's real life is often the life that one does not lead.

Selfishness is not living as one wishes to live. It is asking others to live as one wishes to live.

Man is least himself when he talks in his own person. Give him a mask *and he will tell the truth.*

Man is a reasonable animal who always loses his temper when he is called upon to act in accordance with the dictates of reason.

The nineteenth-century dislike of Realism is the rage of Caliban seeing his own face in the glass.

Sentimentality is merely the Bank-holiday of cynicism.

Conscience and cowardice are really the same things. Conscience is the trade name of the firm.

THE LAST WORD

In Art, the public accept what has been because they cannot alter it, not because they appreciate it.

We teach people how to remember, we never teach them how to grow.

There is a luxury in self-reproach. When we blame ourselves we feel that no one else has a right to blame us.

Those who try to lead the people can only do so by following the mob.

It is only by not paying one's bills that one can hope to live in the memory of the commercial classes.

A community is infinitely more brutalized by the habitual employment of punishment than . . . by the occasional occurrence of crime.

XII

George Bernard Shaw

A KIND OF ENCYCLOPEDIC WRITER—his works incorporating everything from medicine to Methuselah, from prize-fighting to Nell Gwynn, from Ireland to Africa, from brothel keepers to supermen; his fields including plays, novels, essays, music criticism, art criticism, drama criticism, prefaces, and treatises —George Bernard Shaw would certainly not have ignored the aphorism, would have planted it in every field he plowed. Indeed, the aphorism would prove an invaluable tool in so wide a field of thought, where much that concerns mankind needs to be clearly and sharply articulated; moreover, the aphorism would be indispensable in terms of Shaw's personality, which insisted on having a capsule opinion about everything and on firing off, in succinct and pointed language, defiant, not to say shocking or iconoclastic "truths." Shaw dealt, in addition, with a number of figures of history into whose mouths he would put sharply phrased opinions characteristic of them; and here again the aphorism flourished. But Shaw did more than that; he composed, as an appendage to *Man and Superman*, a work entitled "The Revolutionist's Handbook," which consists of aphorisms—a compendium one may enjoy and profit from, without being, or being made into, a revolutionist.

205

THE LAST WORD

Shaw was born in 1856 in Dublin, of good family—there were hints of descent from Shakespeare's Macduff, and he was definitely the grandson of a prosperous lawyer-stock-broker who was ruined when his partner absconded. Accordingly Shaw's father was brought up by a hard-pressed widow with fifteen children: if likable and rather gifted, he was not destined to flourish in the business arena, and merely made ends meet by running a corn mill. Neither was Shaw's father notable in the domestic arena, having married at thirty-eight a woman of twenty-one who dominated an ill-run household: the father became a remorsefully genteel drunkard, which Shaw as a boy was unaware of until, on his saying to his mother, "I think Papa is drunk," she answered, "When is he anything else?" Papa, in his cups, would lose his temper and smash dishes, and his drinking destroyed the family's social life, and its social standing.

Perhaps the only thing the young George benefited from in so mismanaged a household was its concern for music: his mother had a good mezzo-soprano voice and started, in partnership with a neighboring orchestra leader, a voice-training school. From being a frequent auditor, Shaw, at fourteen, could sing and whistle, from beginning to end, leading works "by Handel, Haydn, Mozart, Beethoven, Rossini, Bellini, Donizetti and Verdi." This was not without future value. His schooling unimpressive, Shaw, also on his own, took to reading his father's books and to haunting the National Gallery of Ireland and becoming extremely familiar with its pictures. When, for business reasons, Mrs. Shaw's partner decided to move to London, she elected to go with him; breaking up housekeeping and setting forth with her two daughters, she left George at sixteen behind, along with his father, whom she saw only once again. While making his first efforts as a writer, young George did quite well working in a real estate office; but he had no mind to triumph in real estate and when, in 1876, one of his sisters died, he decided to go live in London with his mother and other sister: it would be twenty-nine years before he saw Ireland again.

If the move to London set Shaw on the right path, it was an extremely toilsome and uphill one. Between 1878 and 1883 he wrote five novels—*Immaturity*, *The Irrational Knot*, *Love Among the Artists*, *Cashel Byron's Profession*, and the unfinished *An Unsocial Socialist*. They were submitted to publishers in England and America, amassing a total of some sixty rejections. Shaw himself disliked the books and indeed wrote, with grim doggedness, exactly five pages a day, stopping at the end of the fifth page even in the middle of a sentence. Grinding out the books instilled in Shaw a reaction he put into one of his plays: "He who has never hoped can never despair." Eventually the books would be published, sometimes in America on a pirated basis; and they contained things that Shaw could later draw upon. Living with his mother, he contributed nothing to the needy household's upkeep except his share in an inheritance; he did, however, have his mother try to teach him to sing for a livelihood; he also got a job for several months with the Edison Telephone Company, going around and trying to get householders "to allow the Company to put insulators and poles and derricks and the like on their roofs"; and he once counted votes at an election. During these arid years he became a number of things: he became a vegetarian after reading Shelley; he became an atheist who told a Catholic Father trying to convert him: "It is as easy for me to believe that the universe made itself as that a maker of the universe made himself: in fact, much easier, for the universe visibly exists." He became a socialist and, just a little before this, became what he seemed hopelessly unfitted for—a speaker. Attending meetings that discussed and debated various issues, Shaw would stand up, so nervous that he could not read his notes, these held moreover in shaky hands, and would force himself to speak. Hearing Henry George speak, he became a Single Tax convert, only to be told to read Karl Marx: this, he said, "proved the turning point in my career" and "provided me with a purpose and mission in life."

He went forth preaching Marx in town halls, in parks, at street corners, becoming more and more effective and more and more in demand; and though he gradually discarded much in Marx, he continued making public speeches—which he greatly enjoyed doing—for fifteen years. He would often pass the hat for a cause, but in all his speaking never once took any kind of fee. His speaking and his socialism won him the friendship of such men as the drama critic William Archer, and Sidney Webb: Shaw joined the recently formed Fabian Society in 1884, as Webb did a year later. It was in writing one of the early Fabian tracts that Shaw first united his concern for socialism with his gift for aphorism, as in "The established Government has no more right to call itself the State than the smoke of London has to call itself the weather." Thanks much to Shaw—who made William Morris and Annie Besant members of the Fabian Society—and to Webb, the society would exert considerable influence in promoting Labour and, while doing so, in proscribing Marxism.

Through William Archer, Shaw in 1886 got the job of art critic of *The World* and also became a reviewer for *The Pall Mall Gazette*, these the beginning of a recognizable and remunerative career. In 1888 the famous T. P. O'Connor founded an evening newspaper in London called *The Star* and, having hired Shaw to write editorials, found them politically too advanced. When Shaw suggested that he write music criticism instead, "Tay Pay" was delighted, and for two

years, at two guineas a week, Shaw under the pen name of
Corno di Bassetto wrote happily, unconventionally, and
rewardingly as he pleased. From *The Star* Shaw moved to
The World for four years at five pounds a week: here he
"settled down" to becoming a far from sedentary and a very
Shavian music critic who made a kind of blazing manifesto of
his integrity and independence: "[The critic] should not
know anybody: his hand should be against every man and
every man's hand against his . . . It is the capacity for
making good or bad art a personal matter that makes a man
a critic." His greatest effort, indeed campaign, was his championing a much attacked Wagner; perhaps his greatest source
of appeal was writing music criticism in strong, straightforward, layman prose. His ridicule of opera performances
cost him his critic's seats at Covent Garden; his comments
generally could make a knife of his pen: "Dvorak's *Requiem*
bored Birmingham so desperately that it was unanimously
voted a work of extraordinary depth and impressiveness."
His music criticism remains remarkably fresh and cogent, not
least the great defense of Verdi that he wrote long after.

These jobs were to be followed, from 1895 into 1898, by
Shaw's drama criticism in *The Saturday Review* under Frank
Harris, where, given a free hand, he produced a notable body
of work. Most of the playwrights, players, and directors he
reviewed are totally forgotten, but what he said of them is
still extremely good, and sometimes very illuminating, reading. Of those whose names have survived, Sir Henry Irving
for example, Shaw is best remembered for knocking him off
his pedestal; or, for another example, Oscar Wilde: though
Shaw dismissed *The Importance of Being Earnest*, he elsewhere
recognized Wilde's gifts and almost alone, after Wilde's im-
prisonment, went on introducing his name and speaking his
praises. Perhaps the most eventful thing in Shaw's drama-

critic career was his "meeting" with Ellen Terry, which set going one of the greatest epistolary romances in history. Other people's performances called forth more characteristic Shavian, and often aphoristic, reactions: "I have never been able," he wrote, "to see how the duties of a critic . . . can be reconciled with the manners of a gentleman." He plainly had fun, and in turn provided it, in upsetting theatrical apple carts and reversing Establishment opinions; but, like many good drama critics—and Shaw was in many ways the best journalistic drama critic of modern times—he found the ordeal of endless dull and bad plays boring and wearisome; and in his "Valedictory," on retiring from *The Saturday Review*, remarked: "I can never justify to myself the spending of four years on dramatic criticism. I have sworn an oath to endure no more of it . . . The subject is exhausted; and so am I."

By now the retiring drama critic was very much a functioning playwright; and despite the countless other interests and activities Shaw spent time on, his playwriting was of course the great long-span occupation of his life, as it was the greatest single contribution to the modern English-speaking stage. During the 1890's Shaw turned out a succession of plays, first the more or less problem—and "unpleasant"—ones: *Widowers' Houses*, which was ill received; *The Philanderer*, which for a time went unproduced; and *Mrs Warren's Profession*, which was refused a license and not given a public production for a number of years. In his attacks on slum landlords and on brothel keeping as a successful business, Shaw spoke both too bluntly and too sharply for middle-class audiences; but he also spoke very didactically, giving small indication of the controversial comedy writing that would become his most individual and successful talent. Actually this was to begin with his very next play, *Arms and the Man*, lightly satirizing heroic views of war and romantic views of love: a failure when first produced, but eventually a favorite. It was followed by *Candida*, which did not get a production for several years and achieved success only several years later. This was a play that Shaw would let no producer read: "I always read it *to* them," he remarked, adding, "they can be heard sobbing three streets off." *Candida* has possibly been the most successful of Shaw's plays, and in a sense the slickest—an odd triangle story with all the fascination of a real triangle and very few of the traits. So early in his career as *Candida* Shaw clearly rebutted the accusation which, even very late in it, would be brought against him: that he was no playwright.

Between 1895 and 1899 he would turn out five more plays —the playlet *The Man of Destiny*, about Napoleon; *You Never Can Tell*, *The Devil's Disciple*, *Caesar and Cleopatra*, and *Captain Brassbound's Conversion*. *The Man of Destiny* was intended for Richard Mansfield, who refused it, and when produced it was a failure; *You Never Can Tell* was withdrawn during calamitous rehearsals and not successful until 1905. *The Devil's Disciple* became Shaw's first real stage success—but in America; in England this spoof of romantic melodrama which often comes close to reproducing it had, like other plays, to wait its turn at the box office. The generally very amusing *Captain Brassbound*, whose dominating heroine Shaw had written for Ellen Terry, had to be played by someone else at its only performance, though it was there that Shaw and Ellen Terry met for the first time in the flesh. All these plays stand at a decidedly lower level than *Caesar and Cleopatra*, which, at the very least, is one of the most durable and admirable plays Shaw ever wrote, and is quite conceivably the best of them all. In it Shaw had a hero who was altogether right for him, and in part resembled him—someone humane without being very human; showing mercy because unable to show love; believing in reason but also in the impotence of reason. Shaw's

Caesar isn't the great general and the prototype of dictators, but a man who cried out against war and who deprecated power, while realizing that Right Needs Might. "Murder shall breed murder," Shaw's Caesar cries, "until the gods are tired of blood and create a race that can understand"; and the tremendous final curtain, when his adoring soldiers shout, with swords upraised, "Hail Caesar!" is less his moment of triumph than of defeat—is, indeed, an "Ave Caesar!" that will very soon culminate in an "Et tu, Brute!" Over this play of a mature middle-aged Caesar who resists the charms, to escape the claws, of a young, passionate, feline Cleopatra hovers a rueful half-tragic mood: for all its tawny Mediterranean sunlight, the air in *Caesar and Cleopatra* can be very chill at times.

If, conceivably, Shaw had written his masterpiece before 1900, he had, well before 1900, spoken of what a genius he was, and how much greater a one he would be—having already become perhaps the greatest press agent of his own works in the history of authorship. If the press-agentry was at times blustering and vulgar, it was but one aspect of a much larger Shavian device—Shaw's showmanship. It was *necessarily* larger, since it would be applied to almost every facet of culture and every subject of controversy that confronted the public during half a century and more. If, as Shaw intimated, it was his shyness that fathered his showmanship, that may well be true on terms that one often finds true— that superior people who are shy are also very conceited. In any case Shaw, more successfully than any other man of his time, called attention to himself, paraded himself, promoted himself; made his beard a kind of trademark in person, his initials a kind of trademark in print, his heterodoxies a kind of trademark in polemics—these last proving a great source of aphorism. Furthermore, if Shaw made himself a subject of controversy, he was personally one of contradictions. He had a gay and witty mind and a gaunt and puritan body. When prankish, he very likely had a purpose; when pulpiteering, he might play the clown. The man of reason could turn mystical; the champion of socialism could exalt the Strong Man and the dictator; the man who wrote for posterity also wrote for Hearst. Shaw made a game of dialectics; and to a certain extent a career. He always took sides, doubtless as a way of being interesting as well as being honest. Hence we can't rubber-stamp Shaw in a phrase, as we can Montaigne in a *Que sçais-je?*; or Swift in a *cor laceratum*; or Voltaire in an *Ecrasez l'infame*, for so many-sided a G.B.S. has no precise GBessence.

Shaw was primarily and most brilliantly, however, a showman of ideas, which could be much more than a fashion parade of this or that generation's problems and questions, and much more than colorful sham battles. Under Shaw's generalship it could be a superb military spectacle where important issues crossed swords and drew blood and killed off one another—with the civilized Western world commanding a view of the battlefield. Moreover, the great showman of ideas most often chose the theater as his battlefield; his most brilliant dialogue as his gunpowder; and some form of dramatic surprise as his strategy. If he did not isolate or vindicate truth, he extremely often spotlighted error. As a great juggler of truths, he was necessarily a trickster as well, a master of dialectical trap doors. Shaw's showmanship succeeded in all ways but the final way: it entertained, it stimulated, it fumigated, it demolished, and frequently it shed light; but in any large sense, it decidedly failed to gain converts. The scintillating showman forgot that it is the solemn showman, who makes a ritual and a religion of his wares, that wins communicants and disciples.

THE LAST WORD

One other event in Shaw's life before the century turned was his marriage. He first met Charlotte Payne-Townshend at a Fabian house party given by the Sidney Webbs: she was wealthy, sick of social life, and interested in social problems; she and Shaw took to each other immediately and—as he wrote to Ellen Terry—he was going to "refresh his heart" by falling in love with Charlotte. She joined the Fabian movement, even though he thought she was "demoralized" by his ideas; she became for a time his secretary and, on hearing that Shaw was ill, hurried back from Rome to serve as his nurse. For several years he had trouble with a foot, which kept him on crutches, and during this period—on June 1, 1898—he and Charlotte were married at a registry office. "My wife," he wrote, "has been having *such* a delightful honeymoon. First my foot had to be nursed, and the day before yesterday . . . I fell downstairs and broke my left arm." The honeymoon might, without all this, have been an odd one, since the marriage, though thoroughly happy, boasted little if anything of sex: what with Shaw's showmanship-in-reverse, his very paucity of sex became as famous as an excess of it in a Rochester or a Casanova. Shaw once confessed that he thought the sexual act "monstrous and indecent" and best done, if at all, by groups of men and women meeting in the dark and coupling without ever seeing one another's faces. "The ideal love affair," he remarked, "is one conducted by post," such as his with Ellen Terry: an aphoristic statement that, for being so extremely remote a "truth," cannot qualify as an aphorism. "Only twice in my life have I been *sexually* infatuated," Shaw told Hesketh Pearson; and he had remained a virgin until he was twenty-nine. Then, it appears, a widow who took singing lessons from Shaw's mother asked him to tea "and virtually raped him." This became an affair of sorts, and there were apparently others, including one with an actress in a play of his; but Shaw's heart was not in it. He enjoyed "flirtations" and being constantly pursued, and he delighted in his postal apassionatas with Ellen Terry and later with Mrs. Patrick Campbell; and his marriage was, in a double sense, an ideal one.

Shaw's career during the first fifty years of the twentieth century—which were the last fifty years of his life—is a procession of many Shavian successes and of additional Shavian stunts; of his supporting causes that served humanity and protesting crimes that harmed it; of offering, in the theater, both an afterworld and a future life on earth; of dabbling in ologies and frisking with isms; and of still playing the showman long after becoming the most distinguished of living playwrights and one of the most newsworthy of living celebrities. Beyond the fact that the showman in him had become irrepressible, Shaw was doubtless aware that even the most popular products can decline in sales if they fail to be advertised. In any case, he became a great *éminence grise* without ever ceasing to be an *enfant terrible*.

But the great achievement of Shaw in this century, and almost certainly his most enduring one in the future, is the plays he wrote. As against the nine plays he turned out between 1892 and 1899, he would produce, between 1903 and 1912, nine more, these representing him at his most lively, most provocative, most diversified, perhaps most serious, and on two occasions most delightful. He was perhaps most serious in the two earliest plays, *Man and Superman* and *John Bull's Other Island*, and most delightful in the two latest, *Androcles and the Lion* and *Pygmalion*. *Man and Superman*, if chiefly famous for dramatizing in its heroine and hero Shaw's contention that it is the woman who actually does the courting, is most notable for its great interpolated Hell Scene, which is not only the century's most dazzling treatment of ideas in dialogue form; not only the most upside-down presentation of Heaven and Hell in theater annals; but the occasion of Shaw's championing of the Life Force, that evolutionary begetter of the Superman—someone, in my view, so totally dematerialized when he appears as to be a mere vibration in a void. *John Bull's Other Island* is Shaw's portrait of the Irish and his setting the Englishman against the Irishman, John Bull against O'Leary. It is admirably serious for refusing to go in for the kind of high-spirited farce or Irish–English wrestling match that Shaw might excel at, and for demonstrating each nation's faults. But high-spirited is just the word for *Androcles* and *Pygmalion*, for Shaw's dealing first with Christian martyrs and then with English phonetics; for humanizing both and giving a gay twist to two classic legends. Of the intermediate plays, *Major Barbara* is the most important and in many ways very good, but is peculiar for having Shaw, the champion of the Life Force, exalt, as it were, the Death Force only three years later. Shaw's great munitions maker, Andrew Undershaft, is a kind of poverty-hating blood brother of Alfred Nobel, full of practical humanitarian projects; but his source of income rather suggests that in order to clean up the slums man might have to blow up the universe. In Undershaft, Shaw's admiration for the Strong Man goes too far and perhaps explains Shaw's admiration for Stalin and Mussolini.

World War I interrupted Shaw's writing—or at any rate his making public any new plays. It made of him—through the well-reasoned pacifist pamphlet he wrote, *Common Sense About the War*—a very unpopular writer and an ostracized man. So high did feeling get, that the war was spoken of as "a struggle between Great Britain, France, Russia and Belgium on the one hand, and Germany, Austria, Turkey and Bernard Shaw on the other." Here the showman vanished, and courage ousted cleverness. When the war ended, Shaw quickly regained his old status, not least because a revived *Arms and the Man* delighted ex-servicemen. Two of his most impressive plays still lay ahead, along with his (and probably England's) longest play, *Back to Methuselah*. *Heartbreak House*, attempting a kind of Shavian version of Chekhov, was also "cultured, leisured Europe before the War." Offering a cross-section of English types, it is often thrusting and brilliant but, having sought to expose a drifting prewar Europe, it tended to become a drifting postwar play. *Saint Joan*, for many people Shaw's greatest play, appeared in 1923 and certainly contains—above all, in the trial scene—some of Shaw's greatest writing; and in the tragicomic epilogue, one of Shaw's greatest counterstrokes. Most of all, *Saint Joan* is serious and large-minded in its approach to its subject, without any Shavian fillips and folderol. Although, in the twenty-five years that lay ahead, Shaw would write two or three other plays that had their good points, *Saint Joan* crowns his theatrical career and really completes what he had to say of importance. The years ahead would, however, bring a great deal—the Nobel Prize; such books of his as *The Intelligent Woman's Guide to Capitalism and Socialism* and *The Adventures of the Black Girl in Her Search for God*; the publication of the Ellen Terry–Bernard Shaw correspondence; a visit to the USSR, a visit to America; the films made of several of Shaw's plays; various Shavian chuckles and rumbles and roars; the death of Shaw's wife in 1943; the celebration of his ninetieth birthday in 1946. His death came four years later: among the many commemorations of it, the lights along Broadway were lowered.

George Moore once said with his customary maliciousness that Tolstoy, in his desire to encompass all human life in *War and Peace*, must have waked up in the middle of the night screaming: "I forgot a yacht race! I forgot High Mass!" It would have been quite out of character for Shaw ever to wake up screaming; and in the way he sought to encompass all human life, not the least bit necessary—for he had no desire to pack everything into one very large and great piece of writing. He took a piece-by-piece inventory of the universe. How incredibly many things Shaw wrote or talked about, and sometimes pulled apart, and always reached an opinion on, are all the more incredible for how much of the time Shaw talked about himself. Yet most of this was done to charm, cajole, rouse, persuade, humble, threaten, and overpower the public concerning what in life he thought valuable and important, or intolerable and destructive. Eventually he became the most listened-to man alive, if far from the most agreed-with—this being fair enough, since over the years he by no means always agreed with himself. He was the most listened-to for being perennially lively, stimulating, and startling; and he could only be all this, of course, as a great wielder and master of language. He defended the way he would monopolize conversation at dinner parties by saying that people *expected* him to, and hence would not speak themselves; furthermore, social occasions buzzing with small talk bored him. At a high-spirited—and doubtless for everyone but Shaw a quite alcoholic—dinner of distinguished men, he broke in: "Gentlemen, we shall enjoy ourselves very much if only you will not try to be convivial." In much the same say, he exclaimed: "Holidays! I never took one in my life!" Witty, resourceful, clever at impromptu though he was, fun for fun's sake never attracted him: his forte, as has been said of him, was *purposeful* fun. On the actual basis of results, the serious element in Shaw's method might be the unsuccessful one: Egon Fridell once said that Shaw, being a sly fellow, always coated with chocolate the pills he made up for the public; but the public, Fridell added, was even slyer—it licked off the chocolate without swallowing the pills. And it is true, I think, that though Shaw commanded an enormous and expectant audience, he had, relatively, no lasting influence on its thinking. This would not be just because he was clever and impudent in his purposefulness—or call it his propagandizing; it could also be because he had *too many* causes and projects and protests; too many ideas and opinions. He could rally socialists much better than recruit them; hearten vegetarians much better than create them. And, of course, much that he advocated or deprecated was very unpopular with the public.

All this diverse activity has in a sense the same parent and leads to the same thing. Despite his reputed shyness Shaw seemed destined, like Voltaire and Goethe, to signify the writer as a great personage and a world figure, and very much as a sage. And for such a personage no form of writing is more public in style, or world-wide in application, than the aphorism. With his mastery of language, Shaw could turn the aphorism into a bugle for his propaganda, a bassoon for his satire, a trumpet for his proclamations, an organ for his principles, and a violin—not quite a cello—for his humaneness. His simplest statements often wear aphoristic dress: "Street arabs are produced by slums, not by original sin." His personal reactions seem to express aphoristic "truths": "When I have to relieve people financially, I hate them as heartily as they hate me." Indeed, he not only wrote, he also spoke aphorisms and caused them to be spoken. They were real-life comments in the mouths of his stage characters, truths in the midst of his stage fictions. As early as *The Philanderer* Shaw gives us: "The test of a man or woman's breeding is how they behave in a quarrel"; as late as *Back to Methuselah* we encounter: "Silence is the most perfect expres-

219

sion of scorn." Shaw can be as Wildean as he is Shavian in *You Never Can Tell*: "The great advantage of a hotel is that it's a refuge from home life"; in *Getting Married* he is very Shavian: "All progress means war with society." In *Man and Superman* Shaw gives us one of his typically light generalities: "An Englishman thinks he is moral when he is only uncomfortable," and one of his weightier ones: "The more things a man is ashamed of, the more respectable he is." In the prefaces to his plays, which can often be salted with his best writing, the aphorist is seldom absent: "When two people are under the influence of the most violent, most insane, most delusive, and most transient of passions, they are required to swear that they will remain in that excited, abnormal and exhausting condition continuously until death do them part." Or more briefly: "Fashions, after all, are only induced epidemics."

Shaw, in and out of his plays, was an aphorist about art. He could disparage: "Academic art is far worse than the trade in sham antique furniture." He could define: "The essence of art is recreation." He could distinguish: "It is ridiculous to say . . . that art has nothing to do with morality. What is true is that the artist's business is not that of the policeman." As for the "true artist," he will "let his wife starve, his children go barefoot, his mother drudge for her living at seventy, sooner than work at anything but his art." Shaw himself—as, for example, in his chocolate-coating of pills—was to a degree an artist of the middle classes and all the more, really, for his also being an antagonist of the middle classes. His chief subject is bourgeois life and thought, as his main object is to dissect and expose it. The second of these is of course the less aesthetic; is basically purposeful, basically problem play, basically pill. A generation after Ibsen, Shaw made an Ibsenesque assault on modern society, which became ultimately, by its often cockeyed approach and comic tone, a distinctly Shavian one: he amused the people he assailed, he came off as much a playboy of ideas as a propagandist. Aesthetically, he saw literature rather too much for what it had to say constructively, for what it stood for intellectually, so that Shakespeare was allowed nothing except his genius with words, and an *Importance of Being Earnest* nothing except its mere entertainment as nonsense. Shaw remarked somewhere to the effect that music meant more to him than literature, and certainly it both stirred and moved him more, and endowed him with finer critical judgment.

As Shaw had thoughts about almost everything, so, to almost the same degree, he had aphorisms—sometimes tossing them into his text as merely part of his prose, sometimes using them as part of his protest. From some of these we might quickly, or eventually, dissent; but most of them have at least enough vigor or individuality to make us think. That constitutes in many ways—including the playboy and poseur —Shaw's real intellectual value: he was much less a great thinker than a great distributor of thought and a great stimulator of thought; and not least in "middle-class" fields. Let us hear him on domesticity: "Home life as we understand it is no more natural to us than a cage is natural to a cockatoo." Or on bringing up children: "The best brought up children are those who have seen their parents as they are. Hypocrisy is not the parents' first duty." And again: "If parents would only realize how they bore their children!" Or about children: "A child hasn't a grown-up person's appetite for affection . . . They like a good imitation of it better than the real thing, as every nurse knows." Or on how we should behave: "The golden rule is that there is no golden rule," which is made clearer by "Do not do unto others as you would that they should do unto you. Their tastes may not be the same."

Here is Shaw on, perhaps, the mightiest and certainly most materialistic of themes: "Lack of money is the root of all evil." And one of the most weighty of problems: "Whilst we have prisons, it matters little which of us occupy the cells." Or on what today touches on the generation gap with great relevance: "It's all that the young can do for the old, to shock them and keep them up to date." And concerning humanity at every age: "Do you think that the things people make fools of themselves about are any less real and true than the things they behave sensibly about?" Or, apropos English snobbery: "Ladies and gentlemen are permitted to have friends in the kennel but not in the kitchen." Or a new La Rochefoucauldian twist: "What really flatters a man is that you should think him worth flattering." What is perhaps most urgent and hortatory in Shaw's maxim writing is that mankind should strive, work, do: "A life spent in making mistakes is not only more honorable but more useful than a life spent doing nothing." And again: "Use your health, even to the point of wearing it out . . . Spend all you have before you die, and" —said Shaw at fifty—"do not outlive yourself." He at any rate had outlived the equivalent of several lives before he outlived himself. And it is his whole career—as it is his total output, his *oeuvre*—that constitutes his importance. He was a great force, which to be sure might be misdirected; he was a kind of continent, which had its badlands as well as its mountain peaks; and he was an unforgettable personality, however much a contrived one, and a great playwright, however deficient in great plays.

GEORGE BERNARD SHAW
Aphorisms

Assassination is the extreme form of censorship.

Democracy substitutes election by the incompetent many for appointment by the corrupt few.

What we call education and culture is for the most part nothing but the substitution of reading for experience, of literature for life, of the obsolete fictitious for the contemporary real.

Marriage is popular because it combines the maximum of temptation with the maximum of opportunity.

Religion is a great force—the only real motive force in the world; but . . . you must get at a man through his own religion and not through yours.

Hardly any of us have ethical energy enough for more than one really inflexible point of honor.

All great truths begin as blasphemies.

Life does not cease to be funny when people die any more than it ceases to be serious when people laugh.

THE LAST WORD

There is nothing that people will not believe nowadays if only it be presented to them as science, and nothing they will not disbelieve if it is presented to them as religion.

A man's interest in the world is only the overflow from his interest in himself.

The reasonable man adapts himself to the world; the unreasonable one persists in trying to adapt the world to himself. Therefore all progress depends on the unreasonable man.

You have learned something. That always feels at first as if you had lost something.

In literature the ambition of the novice is to acquire the literary language; the struggle of the adept is to get rid of it.

You don't learn to hold your own in the world by standing on guard, but by attacking, and getting well-hammered yourself.

There are no secrets better kept than the secrets that everybody guesses.

Liberty means responsibility. That is why most men dread it.

Female murderers get sheaves of offers of marriage.

224

XIII

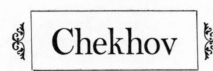

Chekhov

ANTON CHEKHOV was one of the great modern masters of two
forms of writing, plays and short stories. Both achievements
—the plays increasingly so—have gained for him a notable
reputation in many countries and languages, and in both
fields he has had much influence and been much imitated. The
last in a great line of Russian writers—Pushkin, Gogol,
Dostoevsky, Turgenev, Tolstoy—Chekhov, though not always so great, is as distinctive in manner, and can be as
distinguished in effect, as any of them. Moreover, he can be
pervasively Russian in atmosphere and intonation, and at the
same time, altogether unprovincial in approach and point of
view. Actually, Chekhov is a master of two other forms of
writing besides plays and short stories. For one of these he
has more and more become better known, has more and more
been read and esteemed—I am speaking of his letters; for the
other of these he is not, I think, much recognized—I am
speaking of his aphorisms. They are perhaps fewer than those
of our other aphorists, and they are, in good part, not so
carefully polished or handsomely given to antithesis; but
many of them seem to me peculiarly shrewd, apt, unexpected,
and at the same time sound, producing at their best a kind of
lightning that not only flashes but palpably hits something. If
Chekhov's is a slightly special place among aphorists, which
is to say that he has, as it were, no very traditional place, his

225

presence in this book is in some sense an effort to prove how much he deserves one.

Chekhov was born in 1860, the grandson of a man who, by working intensely as a serf, was granted his freedom at the rate of seven hundred rubles for each member of his family, with a daughter thrown in free. Chekhov's father spent his boyhood in serfdom but had a love of music and while still a slave could read music at sight and play the violin. Soon after being made free, he settled in Taganrog, in southwestern Russia on the Sea of Azov, started a grocery business, married a cloth merchant's daughter, was a leader in church music, took to painting icons, and fathered six children. Anton— baptized Antonius—was the third of five sons and grew up in a "patriarchal household" where the children formed a choir, played various musical instruments, and knew the whole church service by heart. From constantly having to read and sing in church and be overworked at choir practice, Anton felt, he said, "like a little convict, and now I have no religion." The father, something of a religious fanatic, would also, on feast days, wake his sons at 2 A.M. and take them to church for early mass. As a boy Anton got whipped by his father and had to work in his father's grocery store, which he hated. But though the pious father could be very strict and harsh, and would fly into a rage over trifles like too much salt in the soup, the family life was lively, given to sea fishing, "Russian tennis," amateur theatricals, and storytelling by their companionable mother. In time the two oldest boys were sent to Moscow, and not long after, the grocery business went hopelessly to pot, leaving the family impoverished. The father skipped town and went to join his sons and look for work in Moscow, the family house was sold and the furniture confiscated, the mother and the younger children followed the father to Moscow and left Anton for three years alone in

Taganrog, where he supported himself, while still at school, by tutoring pupils. He seems not to have been too unhappy: there were "French melodramas" to be seen, and "high-school flirtations": in the matter of sex, Chekhov once wrote that he had been initiated at "the age of thirteen"; also, that he "used to be a great expert about tarts."

At nineteen he followed the family to Moscow, bringing two school friends along to be boarders, and began his medical studies at the university. His father had a job away from home, and Anton became the recognized paterfamilias—"What will Anton say?" being the family's reaction to any problem or difficulty. Every member of the family was assigned some kind of work, with Anton becoming, and destined to remain, the only real breadwinner. He very soon started to write as a way of earning money, and between the ages of twenty and twenty-seven he contributed some four hundred stories, sketches, and other writings to various periodicals, much of this written under all sorts of pseudonyms, among them Ulysses, Antosha Chekhonté, A Man Without Spleen, and The Doctor Without Patients. "I attempted everything," Chekhov said, "except novels, poetry and denunciations." When he was twenty-four he had got his M.D., but disliked the idea of practicing, and it was only when a neighboring doctor went off on a vacation that Chekhov regularly began treating patients.

With their lively nature and open-house hospitality, the Chekhov family gradually accumulated a large circle of friends and acquaintances, including many people in the arts—among them, it is said, an actor as famous as Salvini, and a composer as Tchaikovsky. In Moscow, and during long summers in the country, Chekhov came to know many kinds of people, from sick lady patients to sportsmen and soldiers, all of whom would serve him as potential copy. By now he wrote regularly every morning, and had begun to make something of a name for himself with his stories and to work at them with a greater sense of purpose. His humorous writings prompted a Moscow producer, in 1887, to ask Anton, who had already done some writing for the theater, if he would write something for him. Chekhov's own account, as set forth in a letter to a friend, was that he said to the producer, "With pleasure," and to the compliment-paying prospective cast, "Merci"—while actually doing nothing about it; and he continues in his letter: "I don't want to have anything to do with the theatre or the public. To hell with them!" But he did write a play which, he joked, must be called *Ivan Ivanovitch Ivanov*: it took him ten days and he called it *Ivanov*. It had been promised ten rehearsals, but was given only four—two, really, Chekhov remarked, because the other two were "tournaments where the actors competed with one another in arguments and foul language." Despite such proceedings, and some damning conservative reviews, *Ivanov* got a reasonably favorable press and did rather well. But Chekhov thought that no one understood it, spoke of it as "my abortion" and set about making revisions, not only during the run of the play but after it closed. Produced later in St. Petersburg, *Ivanov* proved, in Chekhov's words, "a colossal success, a phenomenal success!"—which it was. Characteristically, however, the author told a friend that "Shakespeare himself never heard such speeches as I had to listen to!" and told another friend that St. Petersburg now had two heroes—a nude painting and a "clothed me." The important thing in all this was that *Ivanov* established Chekhov, in his own mind and in the public's, as a writer: the doctor's brass plate, though not taken down, would now pay obeisance to the author's writing table.

There was also, now, Chekhov the humanitarian sociologist and journalist. In 1890 he got hold of some treatises on prison management, became greatly absorbed in the subject, and decided to make a study of a penal settlement at Sakhalin, an island in Siberia. Unable, as a writer, to get the proper inspection credentials from the prison administration, he set off for Sakhalin simply as a newspaper correspondent, on a journey—there was then no Trans-Siberian Railroad—that abounded in hardships and that took three months. He spent a further three months on the island, observing the prison system in detail. He wrote of all this to a friend:

I have material enough for three dissertations. I got up every morning at three o'clock and went late to bed . . . there was still so much I hadn't done, and now . . . I have the feeling that I've seen everything, but failed to notice the elephants . . . I [made] a census of the whole Sakhalin population . . . went into every hut and talked to everyone . . . and I have already registered about ten thousand convicts and settlers . . . I was present at a flogging . . . I have talked to men chained to trucks . . . The upshot is that I've upset my nerves . . . We have destroyed millions of men in prisons: it's not the prison superintendents who are to blame, it's all of us.

Back home, Chekhov wrote a series of articles on Sakhalin and two short stories, which may have had some effect, for reforms dealing with penal servitude and exile were subsequently instituted.

Not long before going to Sakhalin, Chekhov had written several of his best, and best-known, short plays. Written in the tradition of the farcical "vaudevilles" which, beginning as French adaptations, had become Russian staples, these one-acters transcended the vaudeville form even when borrowing the formula, being not only lively but considerably more lifelike. *The Bear* was a great success, as was *The Proposal*; a third vaudeville, *A Tragedian in Spite of Himself*, though not immediately so successful, was to be constantly revived in Chekhov's lifetime; and a fourth one-acter, *The Wedding*, also came off well. However minor a vaudeville was in both form and content, Chekhov found writing "a good one" far from easy—it required "a mood brimming with high spirits." It was a mood that Chekhov, in those early years, was able to call forth and that, in the best of the short plays, still seems present.

Six of Chekhov's one-act plays were, in one way or another, adapted from short stories he had written, and in these years Chekhov was extraordinarily prolific at story writing, and often skillful. For all his professional productivity—and his social and physical animation—he was, even in early manhood, by no means well: when he was twenty-four, and again when he was twenty-six, he suffered from attacks of spitting blood; and though tuberculosis was clearly indicated, he refused to acknowledge it: to save his family worry and to further his medical and literary career, he all his life denied or played down being tuberculous. As soon as he recovered from hemorrhages, he would bounce himself back into a mood full of high spirits and into a routine at his writing table. In his little Moscow house, which looked "like a chest of drawers," he—interrupted only by his coughing—would work away while people swarmed in and out, talking their heads off and playing the piano. Summers in the country—the family once rented a country house where the rooms were so large that Anton's mother had to sit down and rest while crossing the hall—increased Chekhov's activity. He loved to walk and fish, and to gather mushrooms which, he joked, "stimulated the imagination"; and early in 1893 he satisfied a long-cherished desire: he bought an estate in the country.

He had grown tired of St. Petersburg, which he found cold and egotistical, while liking Moscow more and more; the country place at Melikhovo was in Moscow Province. In appearance, there was little to be said for it: the house was full of defects, the forest had lost its trees, there were all sorts of obstructive fences, and who knew what lay under the snow? Moreover, so many friends piled in that beds had to be placed in the corridors; but Chekhov did not mind all the inconveniences, and when spring came and the snow disappeared he set up a program assigning everybody duties: Anton himself, planting and caring for the trees, was up at four in the morning. Despite many obstacles, he soon had ninety of the estate's 639 acres under cultivation, almost all of it to be ruined by a dry summer. As time went on Chekhov did more and more to put the estate in shape—planting, rebuilding, laying out flower beds and a cattle yard, stocking the fish ponds, digging wells, and building guest houses. On top of his outdoor activities, Chekhov kept at his writing and treated sick people from all over the neighborhood. When, a little later, cholera was raging in the south of Russia, Chekhov took on, without pay, the sizable job of properly outfitting twenty-five villages and hamlets, and after several months of this, though still in good humor, he was altogether exhausted.

His cough persisted as did his spitting of blood, and though he made light of it, in 1894 he went for a time to the Crimea, where the climate was more equable; but came back to Melikhovo full of all kinds of plans, which he carried out for the neighborhood: a new highroad, new schools, a firehouse for the village, a belfry for the church. He looked haggard and sallow, the cough again persisted and there were intestinal complications; but he set to work, in the lodge he had built, on a new play which would be produced in St. Petersburg as *The Seagull*. The first night was a fiasco and Chekhov, as he put it, "flew out of Petersburg like a cannonball"—no one could find him, and indeed he had caught a train to Moscow.

"Never again," he vowed, "will I write plays or have them produced." But at later performances, when the actors knew their lines and better understood the play, *The Seagull* went off much better; and when it was revived by the Moscow Art Theatre in 1898, it proved a tremendous success.

In the spring of 1897 Chekhov had gone on a visit to Moscow, to suffer almost at once a serious hemorrhage and be taken to a hospital. There, lacking all his usual spirit, and looking extremely ill, he was forbidden to move or talk, diagnosed as having tuberculosis, and told (which for once he agreed was essential) to go to a warmer climate. In due course he went first to Biarritz, where neither the weather nor the fashionableness suited him, then to Nice, which he liked and where he met many Russians of distinction. He stayed in Nice for a good many months, during which he studied in detail the then raging Dreyfus case and became convinced that Dreyfus and his champion, Zola, were innocent. Further travel plans were upset by an agonizing malady picked up from a dentist's contaminated forceps; and, rather homesick by now, he made his way back to Melikhovo. When fall approached, Chekhov chose Yalta rather than Nice for his health, partly for wanting to see plays of his that were being produced in Moscow. At Yalta, where his health improved, he bought a piece of land with the intention of staying there, and began building a house; later he sold the Melikhovo farm and moved his family to Yalta. The next winter in the Crimea was fiendishly severe and the life there and lack of "interesting women" depressed Chekhov: he now dreamed of building in Moscow, where he had become very much involved professionally. *Uncle Vanya*, a remaking of an earlier play, *The Wood Demon*, had appeared in the provinces, "with," wrote Chekhov, "tremendous success," and was afterward produced by the Moscow Art Theatre. This was a period of great creative activity for Chekhov: not only for the writing of plays that would become famous but for some of his best and most famous short stories. But, though he remained in harness, his health grew worse—the intestinal trouble which kept him from eating, drinking, and writing being harder to bear than his coughing and hemorrhages.

The last few years of his life, however, were to be among the greatest in achievement. At Yalta in 1900 he wrote *The Three Sisters*, something he found "terribly difficult," but completed in about two months. After giving it to the Moscow Art people he was so appalled by Stanislavsky's proposed interpretation of it that he bolted out of the theater and came to blows with Stanislavsky, who dashed out after him. (Stanislavsky's "interpretations" of Chekhov's plays could differ greatly from Chekhov's intentions.) He took the script of *The Three Sisters* away with him and revised it, the Moscow Art Theatre producing it, not very successfully, early in 1901. Revived later in the year, it had, Chekhov wrote to a friend, "a wonderfully brilliant performance," though the Moscow Art's interpretation presumably established itself for years to come. In the interval between the play's two first nights, Chekhov had married Olga Knipper, a leading Moscow Art actress. "It was Chekhov's great tragedy," says David Magarshack, "that he should have met the only woman he wanted to marry . . . when he knew that he had not long to live." She was fond and devoted, but constantly urging him to "write something new." "Write, Anton darling," she would say, or "Don't be lazy, darling," or "Let me know what you are writing," or "I know you will write something nice." All this has its comic side in portraying the new wife of a celebrity; but if intrusive, it was largely Chekhov's fault, since he kept himself and his work, along with his ill health, away from her, and wrote to her affectionately, but often as one does to a child or an actress, addressing her in such terms as "My dear little fatty"; and since she did care, and did love him, she scarcely deserved to be constantly shut out.

After their marriage first Chekhov and then his wife became seriously ill (her illness entailed a miscarriage and there was never again, as Chekhov so much hoped, the prospect of a child), and he aggravated his poor health by not keeping to the right climate but going to Moscow, where he would be besieged and become worn out. He resigned from the Academy of Sciences when Maxim Gorky, who had been elected to it, was refused admittance; the next year Chekhov was elected temporary president of the Society of Russian Literature. In that same year, 1903, he wrote *The Cherry Orchard*, which the Moscow Art Theatre produced in January 1904, with Olga Knipper as Madame Ranevska; on the opening night Chekhov had to take so many curtain calls as to become exhausted. His condition was now hopeless, which was plain to all who saw him; and though he had gone back to Yalta, he went again to Moscow to become bedridden there, and later set out for Badenweiler, a spa in the Black Forest, where, though he wrote to everyone that he had all but recovered, he was actually dying. He died, less than a month after reaching Badenweiler, on July 2, 1904.

The last of the great Russian writers to become a world classic, Chekhov was also a very notable human being, whose understanding of human nature and response to human needs are reflected as much in how he lived as in what he wrote. I have said elsewhere, in suggesting a game dealing with which famous writers one would have wanted as house guests, that Chekhov might well have been the nicest and least troublesome, but also the most perceptive and observant. For this man of extremely humane and sensitive feeling was equally one with the sharpest possible eyesight. He could be wonderfully forgiving but was almost never fooled, could be gay and lively but never just pleasure-loving; was for the most part amiable, but could on occasion become irritated or angry. He clearly ranks with the great heroes of ill health, not least for refusing to be one. The ailing Robert Louis Stevensons and Marcel Prousts seem far more remote from him than such dynamic contemporaries as a Shaw and a Gorky. Thus, having had a little too much to drink, Chekhov, despite all his ailments, decides to climb Vesuvius. It takes three and a half hours to get to the top and his chief reaction is "I now believe in hell"; the descent is equally arduous, and he reports "You sink up to your knees in ashes." This escapade is done just for the hell of it—but this is at the same time a doctor who constantly needs doctoring, who is at the free-of-charge service of all kinds of needy or neurotic people, and who goes as adventurously to Siberia for months as he goes to Vesuvius for hours. This is a writer who fills his house with friends and acquaintances and strangers, who are so lively and noisy that he can scarcely write. This is the chief support of a largish family who, in addition, keeps all the members of it contentedly under one roof. This is a sophisticate in his reactions who loves the simplest of country pleasures and takes on the most taxing of country-house chores. This is someone who has a saw in hand as often as a pen, and who has farming projects in mind as often as four-act plays. As William Gerhardi put it, Chekhov's great distinction as a writer of genius derived from the perfect proportion of "ordinary human gifts" in the man. Chekhov himself, in the two-page "autobiography" he wrote in answer to being asked for one, felt that his being a doctor had been an important influence on his writings; it had, among other things, enlarged the range of his observations. "I don't belong," he said, "with those literary men who assume a skeptical attitude toward science, and I shouldn't wish to belong with those who rush into everything with nothing but their imagination to depend on."

Despite his own constant ill health, despite his insight into a good many of the trials of life, and his knowledge of the follies and deficiencies of people, there was something persistently affirmative in his way of looking at life and of living it. No foolish optimist, neither was he an unremitting skeptic; and the tone of affirmation also penetrates his writing (though many people, including critics, have only become aware of this rather recently). For a long time the prevailing impression of Chekhov was that he wrote of weaklings and futilitarians, of people who sighed over their fate and were too fiberless to alter it, who with inept nostalgia yearned for Moscow, and whose hearts fluttered while their hands remained idle. And it was because of this attitude that Chekhov's plays were produced in an atmosphere of lachrymose melancholy, so that the emotions were full of tremolo and the plays overcast with gloom. But though his characters might on occasion indulge in reverie and self-pity, Chekhov was never sentimental about them. Indeed, he more likely satirized their sentimentalism; indeed, he called three of the four famous plays—despite victimized lives in *Uncle Vanya*, a suicide at the end of *The Seagull*, and the "suicide" of a class in *The Cherry Orchard*—comedies. Nor were most of the characters themselves weaklings who gave in to their "fate" or proved unable to cope with their problems; most of them worked, many of them worked hard, and some worked well. And if they failed, they continued to hope, to have faith, to aspire; what may indeed have a genuine pathos is their persistent affirmation, their refusal to be *inwardly* defeated, to accept what seems like the end.

The plays themselves are among the most valuable in the

theater of the last hundred years, with, certainly in the twentieth century, nothing greater than *The Three Sisters*. Chekhov brought to the stage a method which at its best achieves an extraordinary evocativeness, truthfulness, and sensibility, enough to make up for a certain lack of vigorous movement and drama. It is a method that substitutes fluidity for force, and that to succeed requires great tact and talent not only in the playwright but in the director and actors as well. For what in Chekhov is sharp, eloquent detail diminishes among his imitators into mere naturalistic embroidery; what in Chekhov, and very tellingly, is atmosphere is in lesser playwrights fog. Chekhov's people are wonderfully—which can be woefully—human, neither villainous nor heroic, with his attitude toward them a combination of lynx-eyed perceptiveness and sympathetic understanding. He postulates that to err is human, not criminal; his sense of humor pleads for human nature, as his comic sense deflates its pretensions; his scene offers neither black pits of evil nor shining peaks of virtue, but a recognizable temperate zone. His lyricism gives his plays feeling and resonance, his humor frees them from self-pity, and his mercy seasons justice: he doesn't acquit his characters, he pardons them. And, from being so thoroughly life-sized, his plays achieve a paradoxical amplitude, an enlarging atmosphere of truth.

Chekhov's short stories—thirteen uniformly bound volumes of them, and some in addition, have appeared in an English translation—are one of the foremost literary achievements of modern times. Here again we encounter an insight and observation that can characterize, satirize, cut deep, expose; that yield a kind of reality far in advance of any period "realism." Here too an unfailing comic sense maintains perspective and a feeling for proportion, and serves as a social commentary and a moral agent in depicting presumption, philistinism, and vulgarity. But perhaps more than anything else—at any rate, counting more than anything else—is Chekhov's sense of compassion, all the greater for his refusal to sentimentalize, or to varnish or diminish the truth. Misunderstandings between people, that basis of comedy, are also in many of Chekhov's stories a basis of estrangement, frustration, even human fate. There are, to be sure, "ironic" stories of a minor sort, such as "Boots" or—more impressively— "The Chorus Girl," with a sharp touch or twist at the end; amusing satires, as of English behavior in "A Daughter of Albion," and biting ones such as "Sergeant Prishibeyev," with its needlessly brutal petty official. And there are many stories with more substance and more art, growing out of a particular relationship or predicament, as in the beautifully handled, touching comedy of "The Kiss" or the poignantly deepening emotion of "The Lady with the Dog." In "Enemies" the author's compassion never sidesteps the story's harsh truth; in "Misery" it movingly pervades a cabby's fruitless attempt to talk to his fares about his son who has just died; and there are those two very famous stories of Chekhov's, "The Bet" and—a favorite with almost everybody, including Tolstoy—"The Darling." One can open a volume of Chekhov's stories at random, and though what one hits upon may be quite unimportant, there will almost certainly be something that is fresh or striking about it; and one *may* hit upon something quite important, such as "Ward No. 6," at once a searing document of horrifying provincial medical incompetence and a masterly assertion—in the case of a superior doctor—of life's values smashed by the forces of life's villainy. In his stories, it seems to me, Chekhov can go deeper on occasion, and into regions that are darker, than in his plays.

If it is the artist in Chekhov that in terms of fame will make

Chekhov the man endure, the artist thus does us a tremendous service; but what must also be reckoned among Chekhov's talents are his letters and his aphorisms. Totally unillusioned without turning cynical, bathing his harsh verdicts in humor or bandaging them in irony, he lets fall his lively aphoristic comments like clues in a psychological paper chase. We are far from a La Rochefoucauld, formally and grandly probing, we are with someone who in conversational tones or with metaphorical humor mentions something he has learned about or lighted on. Here are bits of aphoristic counsel, concerning writers: "It is much easier," Chekhov remarks, "to write a play about Socrates than about a young girl or a cook." "Travel third class," he advises, "whenever you can. There you will sometimes hear remarkably interesting things." "You must never," says the dramatist, "put a loaded rifle on the stage if no one is going to fire it." Again: "To write a good play . . . one must possess a special kind of talent . . . but to write a bad play and then attempt to make a good one out of it . . . one must possess a much greater talent." Once more: "A writer must not be a judge of his characters but simply an impartial witness." And, to conclude: "A writer must . . . know that muck-heaps occupy a very respectable part in a landscape, and evil passions are as fundamental in life as good ones." But, as an aphorist, Chekhov is capable of quite different comments and insights. "There is no national science," he says, half echoing Goethe, "any more than there is a national multiplication table: what is national is no longer science." Or: "There are people whom even children's books will corrupt." Or: "Man is what he believes." Again: "If you cry 'Forward!' you must make altogether plain in what direction to go. Can't you see that if you don't, when you call out the word to both a monk and a revolutionary, they will go in diametrically opposite directions?" And here are aphorisms about family life: "We justify all our weaknesses, compromises, snobberies by saying 'It's for the children's sake.'" And: "I can't bear the crying of children, but when my child cries, I don't hear it." And: "Simple people suffer from mothers-in-law; intellectuals, from daughters-in-law." And, finally: "If you are afraid of loneliness, don't marry."

The writer and the man in Chekhov, though differently voiced, are not at odds with each other, and the letter writer acts to a considerable degree as a bridge between the two. The Chekhov who subtitled three of his famous plays "comedies" also gave a comic overtone, in his letters, to his irritations and dislikes. In his letters, moreover, he has the great gift of playfulness: "Excuse me for writing about nothing but food; if I didn't, I'd have to write about how cold it is, for they're my only subjects." Or: "Rejoice, O mother!" he writes: "I think I'll stop for twenty-four hours in Ekaterinburg and go see our relatives." He can also be playfully serious: "Medicine," he writes to a friend, "is my lawful wife and literature is my mistress. When I tire of one, I spend the night with the other." And there are small, half-smiled-at facts of life, as in commenting to a fellow writer: "You and I are fond of ordinary people, but other people are fond of us because they think we're not ordinary." And he adds that his sister is outraged that people only invite her because she's a writer's sister. But except where Chekhov himself is annoyed by how people exploit him, trying his patience, wasting his time, borrowing and never returning money, or where he is roused by injustice or enraged at human pettiness, the tone of his letters is much in tune with his other writing, and can be resonantly voiced and adroitly modulated. A subjective aphorism—"What upper-class writers have received, free of charge, from nature, plebeians acquire it at the cost of their youth"—precedes the idea he has for an autobiographical short story:

> . . . *how a young man, the son of a serf, who has worked in a shop, sung in a choir, gone to high school and college, been brought up to respect every one of higher rank and position, to kiss priests' hands, reverence other people's ideas, give thanks for every bite of bread; who has many times been whipped, trudged from this pupil to that without galoshes . . . write how this young man squeezes, drop by drop, the slave out of himself and, waking one fine morning, feels that at last he has no slave's blood in his veins, but the blood of a real man.*

It was a sense of personal freedom that Chekhov set at the head of his needs, and the autobiographical précis in one letter becomes a personal credo in another. Apropos of "trying" to pin down his politics, he writes

> *I am not a liberal, not a conservative, not a believer in gradual progress, not a monk, not an indifferentist. I should like to be a free artist and nothing more, and am sorry God hasn't given me the ability to be one. I hate lying and violence in all their forms . . . Pharisaism, stupidity and despotism don't only rule over merchants' dwellings, and prisons. I notice them in science, in literature, in the younger generation . . . That's why I show no preference for gendarmes or butchers, or scientists and writers, or the younger generation. I look on trademarks and labels as superstitions. I regard as sacred the human body, good health, brains, talent, inspiration, love and absolute freedom—freedom from violence and lying in every form.*

In these two passages the serious writer and man speak with one voice; but the general tone of most of Chekhov's letters is more informal, colloquial, conversational, and it is this natural, totally "unliterary" approach that contributes substantially to Chekhov's greatness as a letter writer. We also frequently find this colloquial turn or metaphorical pungency in Chekhov's aphorisms. One after another his fellow writers attested how totally lacking he was in pose and self-importance; how lacking—toward his fellow writers—in malice or envy; how much of his time he gave them, and of his praise; and how admiring he was of greatness (he wished that Tolstoy's every word had, like Goethe's, been written down). He not only tended to laugh at himself but could be amused at other people's gaffes about him, as when Tolstoy said to him: "I'm very fond of you and, as you know, I can't *bear* Shakespeare; but, all the same, his plays are better than yours." He could show anger, but not petulance; and be brutal, but not petty. Thus he could write to his "literary" brother: "The delicacy of feeling which you extol so much in your story . . . wouldn't keep you from slapping a man's face . . . You are a fellow who always consults his own interests first." If not without vanity, Chekhov made light, at least in public, of most of his achievements and successes—this possibly his one insincere and somewhat coy characteristic. He saw through people, but even where they were most foolish or selfish, he saw why; and it is partly because he was so observant at every turn, and so quick to catch on, that his aphorisms have an air of informality, of quick sallies and impromptus. All the same, they can equal, and often exceed, commentaries and truths carved out in marble.

CHEKHOV
Aphorisms

To a chemist the thought of dirt doesn't exist.

A writer is not a confectioner, a cosmetics dealer, or an entertainer . . . He is a man who has signed a contract with his conscience and his sense of duty.

The more refined one is, the more unhappy.

The stupider the peasant, the better the horse understands him.

A professor's opinion: not Shakespeare is the thing, but the commentaries on him.

It's a writer's business not to accuse or prosecute, but to speak up for the guilty once they are condemned and suffer punishment.

The lower ranks are as necessary in literature as in the army.

The most intolerable people are provincial celebrities.

We all give our hearts far more readily than our money.

243

THE LAST WORD

An artist must only judge what he understands: his field is just as restricted as any other specialist's.

If the Prince of Monaco has a roulette table, surely convicts may play cards.

It's not the number of nervous ailments and patients that have increased, it's the number of doctors who are trained to study the ailments.

A nice child's crying is ugly: just so, you may gather from bad verses that the author is a nice man.

An artist's flair is sometimes worth a scientist's brains.

People must never be humiliated—that is the chief thing.

You won't become a saint through other people's sins.

XIV

Chesterton

GILBERT KEITH CHESTERTON had conceivably the most consistent and demonstrable style among twentieth-century writers: a paragraph of his that lacked a paradox was much less the rule than the exception. Conceivably, again—Shaw or H. G. Wells might perhaps challenge him—Chesterton was the most prolific of recognized twentieth-century writers, the vast number of books he wrote treating of all sorts of subjects in a great variety of forms, but providing much the same positive qualities of style and gift of vivid expression. Pursuing a journalistic career, in which his liberalistic beliefs were asserted with aphoristic forcefulness, he would turn aside from the two great subjects that dominated his thinking—Christianity and democracy—to indulge a ready wit, a hearty sense of humor, an unapologetic opinionatedness, a pungent style of criticism, and a lusty band-concert style of poetry. All these qualities proceeded from a very fat man of Johnsonian assertiveness and appetites, wearing a huge cape and a floppy wide-brimmed hat, who—though he looked as if he might belong to some sect or order—was to a great extent *sui generis* in a very decided way.

Chesterton was born in London in 1874 of a father who headed an established firm of auctioneers and estate agents. With the "backwardness" of great talent, Gilbert did not talk till he was almost three, or learn to read until he was eight. When he was twelve, he was sent to London's famous school, St. Paul's, where his gifts as a writer—though at first it might rather have seemed as a draftsman or painter—were already apparent. Physically the boy was a bust: his fellow students used to get together to watch his strange performance on the trapeze or the parallel bars; near the end of his schooling his voice had still not changed, but his brain, said a doctor who examined him, was "the largest and most sensitive" he had ever seen. One of Chesterton's fellow students and friends was E. C. Bentley, the author of *Trent's Last Case* and the inventor of clerihews, a volume of which Chesterton would later in life illustrate. At sixteen, having previously started a debating club at St. Paul's, Gilbert helped start a magazine called *The Debater*, which he filled with his ideas, while more practical-minded students looked after the mechanical problems of getting the magazine through the press.

The young Chesterton was an early, and a lifetime, sufferer from absentmindedness, not least about his appearance; and he sat, we are told, at his school editor's desk, "a tall, clumsy, unbrushed, untidy scarecrow, drawing all over his blotter and his books," while being all the time deep in thought about the serious problems of life. The absentminded blotter drawings revealed, however, enough talent for Gilbert to be sent, on leaving St. Paul's, not to Oxford as had been intended, but to London's Slade School of Art, while simultaneously taking literature courses at the University of London. He never quite gave up drawing—many years later, he illustrated not only Bentley's clerihews, but his great friend Hilaire Belloc's novels—but in the matter of his capacities and his career, drawing soon gave way to writing.

In his pursuit of a career Chesterton did not sit, as at school, in front of his own writing desk; he sat at one desk after another in various publishing houses. He next began writing and editing in a number of journalistic fields, with the Liberal in Chesterton first being part of a Liberal magazine called *The Speaker*; and thereafter of a Liberal newspaper, the *Daily News*. In the same years, however, the poet in Chesterton was turning out a good deal of verse; indeed, the first two of his many books were volumes of verse, one of them, *The Wild Knight*, being particularly well received. This brings Chesteron to 1900, and close to two big events in his life. One was personal—his marriage the next year to Frances Blogg, whose Anglo-Catholicism affected his thoughts on religion; the other was political, his remaining—in the matter of the Boer War, and in opposition to many Liberals and his own brother Cecil—pro-Boer. He and his brother argued so much about it that the landlady of a seaside place they were staying in left them, after clearing away breakfast, seated at the breakfast table; found them there when she set the table for lunch, and still there when she set it for dinner. Chesterton not only sympathized with the Boers but saw an unjust imperialist war doing great harm to England, and felt his point of view due not to a defect, but to an excess, of patriotism.

During the years that followed, Chesterton published one book after another, on one subject after another, often taking issue with better-known writers, though he would soon be as well known himself. If, in *Heretics* he did a slashing attack on imperialists, he was to be better remembered for two literary books, the *Robert Browning* of 1903 and the *Charles Dickens* of 1906. Of the *Browning*, looking back long after at its inaccuracies, Chesterton said: "There is something buried in the book, though I think it is rather my boyhood than Browning's biography." In these books many of Chesterton's critical strokes reveal that the aphorist has already come into his own. The *Dickens* received a, so to speak, Dickensian appreciation and insight, and in later years, and in the opinion of such later critics as T. S. Eliot, Chesterton would be looked upon as a Dickens authority. In 1908 he published *Orthodoxy*, "not an ecclesiastical treatise," but "a sort of slovenly autobiography." Striving after an "ultimate attitude toward life," Chesterton resisted and rejected various trends and programs, in favor of Christianity, which, he felt, could alone provide an answer to all the problems, dilemmas, enigmas of life. For him, the point was not whether the Christian faith could be believed, but how personally he had come to believe it. "I tried," he wrote, "to be some ten minutes in advance of the truth. And I found that I was eighteen hundred years behind it." *Orthodoxy* has also its bright remarks: "Mr Blatchford is not only an early Christian, he is the only early Christian who ought really to have been eaten by lions"; and again: "We know that [Joan of Arc] was not afraid of an army, while Nietzsche, for all we know, was afraid of a cow. Tolstoy only praised the peasant: she was the peasant. Nietzsche only praised the warrior: she was the warrior. She beat them both at their own antagonistic ideals."

Chesterton's professional life continued, busily and many-sidedly as ever, but his personal life was somewhat changed by his moving from London to Beaconsfield, some miles distant, where he and his wife, first in a rented house and later in one of their own, settled down for good and all. They had, to their great regret, no children but apparently filled their house with other people's and fashioned all sorts of games and parties, along with "productions" in Chesterton's toy theater. Many grown-up friends were also visitors—Chesterton's good nature was proverbial, and his admiring friendly enemy, Shaw, pronounced him one of the "masters of the art of conversation." Maisie Ward has said of the argumentative Chesterton that "there are more ways than one of winning a battle: you can win the man instead of the argument, and

Chesterton won many men." Moving from London did not, in Chesterton's opinion, alter his Liberal outlook, but the aphorist put it: "More than ever did I believe in Liberalism. But there was a rosy time of innocence when I believed in Liberals." His social and political thinking largely boils down to democratic and humanistic feeling; thus, for Chesterton with his generous-spiritedness, family needs outmeasured any set economic philosophy, and a modest amount of property was the basis for a decent life. On the other hand, it was "the negation of property that the Duke of Sutherland should have all the farms on one estate, just as it would be the negation of marriage if he had all our wives in one harem."

Chesterton's ability as a critic was further demonstrated by his *George Bernard Shaw* (1909), one of the best books ever written about Shaw, and one of which Shaw himself remarked: "I liked it very much, especially as it was so completely free from my own influence." Chesterton's two-sentence introduction is in the spirit of the somewhat festive feud that he and Shaw maintained, and in its brash assurance it is almost as good Shaw as it is Chesterton: "Most people either say that they agree with Bernard Shaw or that they do not understand him. I am the only person who understands him and I do not agree with him." The two men differed inwardly as much as they differed in appearance: they were fat and lean, exuberant and puritanical, wine lover and teetotaler, believer and agnostic. Their many differences gave Chesterton many opportunities to make epigrams of Shaw's defects: "He is so much of an idealist about his ideals," cracked Chesterton, "that he can be a ruthless realist in his methods." As for Shaw the teetotaler: "The dipsomaniac and the abstainer are not only both mistaken, but they both make the same mistake. They both regard wine as a drug and not as a drink."

In 1911 Chesterton published *The Innocence of Father*

Brown, the first in a series of books—*The Wisdom* . . . ;
The Incredulity . . . ; *The Secret* . . . ; *The Scandal of
Father Brown*—centered in a Catholic priest who is also a detective, and whose prototype was a future Catholic mon-
signor, Father O'Connor. The "detective" originated when
Chesterton and Father O'Connor encountered some Cambridge undergraduates who disparaged the Catholic clergy as
"cloistered"—this coming on the heels of Father O'Connor's
all but shattering Chesterton with his "lurid knowledge of
human depravity." Yet, wrote Chesterton, "The face of
Father Brown . . . could shine with ignorance as well as
knowledge." As a detective, Father O'Connor could at the
very least detect when Chesterton had read a book—from the
awful condition he left it in. Another friend saw Chesterton
reading a book under a street lamp in pouring rain: his lack
of orderliness went along with his absentmindedness. Among
a number of anecdotal citations, there is the wire Chesterton
sent to his wife while away from home to deliver a lecture in
a town in the Midlands: "Am in Market Harborough. Where
ought I to be?" Even when he knew where he ought to be,
he consistently arrived late. He airily and aphoristically ra-
tionalized the virtue in this by saying: "Had St George not
been late, there would have been no story. Had he been *too*
late, there would have been no princess."

Having begun his literary career by publishing two books
of poetry, Chesterton continued to write verse till near the
end of his life, a good deal of it amusingly in praise of wine
and in dispraise of other liquids:

*And Noah he often said to his wife when he sat down to dine:
"I don't care where the water goes if it doesn't get into the wine"*

and

CHESTERTON

Tea, although an Oriental,
Is a gentleman at least;
Cocoa is a cad and coward,
Cocoa is a vulgar beast.

Even more amusing is one of the best of modern ballades, each verse ending with the refrain:

I think I will not hang myself today;

and in more martial vein, the spirited rhythmic beat of "Lepanto":

Strong gongs groaning as the guns boom far
(Don John of Austria is going to the war);
Stiff flags straining in the night blasts cold,
In the gloom black-purple, in the glint old-gold;
Torchlight crimson on the copper kettle drums,
Then the tuckets, then the trumpets, then the cannon, and he comes.

Chesterton's rousing gusto sweeps through his verse and prose alike, often enlivening the best of his *Victorian Age in Literature* (1913), which not only helps to shake the dust off the masters of a bygone era but, exhilaratingly, at times throws a little more on:

[The Victorians] were lame giants; the strongest of them walked on one leg a little shorter than the other . . . There is a moment when Carlyle turns suddenly from a high creative mystic to a common Calvinist. There are moments when George Eliot turns from a prophetess into a governess. There are also moments when Ruskin turns into a governess, without even the excuse of sex.

The First World War led Chesterton, unlike Shaw and others, to the patriotic rather than protesting side, less, as he said, because he thought England particularly virtuous than because he thought "Prussianism" vile. Early in the war he was taken very ill, from overwork perhaps aggravated by his being so tremendously overweight, and somewhat from the "horror" of the war itself. Both his heart and his brain were badly affected, and for many months he was often comatose or semi-conscious. When he was finally recovered, it was—or so it seemed—with a sense of being refreshed; he took over the editorship of *The New Witness*, which first Hilaire Belloc, and then Chesterton's brother Cecil, had edited as advocates of Distributism, something that sought to redistribute property so that everyone could have some, but was anti-Socialist and at best very eccentrically Liberal. Chesterton's own views about politics and economics having confused one of his readers, he answered by trying to frame simple concepts in plain language, such as

I say a democracy means a State where the citizens first desire something and then get it.

I say that where this is deflected by the disadvantage of representation, it means that the citizens desire a thing and tell the representatives to get it.

He had a real gift for putting things simply, as, apropos liquor: "Never drink when you are wretched without it . . . drink when you would be happy without it." Cocktails he detested, and they brought out his real gift for putting things amusingly. Ridiculing the "wholesome" belief that cocktails "give a man appetite," he asked at just what degree of intoxication "will a healthy grown-up man be ready to rush headlong upon a cutlet, or make a dash for death or glory at a ham sandwich?" As for Chesterton's girth, partly derived from his drinking, he once "gave his seat to three ladies in a bus." It was said that he "ate and drank absent-mindedly," presumably from neither happiness nor misery, but from simple huge hunger and thirst: for a while he was forbidden to drink, the *quantity* of liquid consumed (water included) proving more dangerous than the kind. Actually the amount of work he did was more remarkable than the amount of liquid he drank: his secretary, keeping tabs for a short time, found that he dictated 13,000 or 14,000 words a week, this "exclusive of his journalism, editing and lecturing." On a different occasion, his secretary also found that he had signed, with various publishers, contracts for thirty books. In 1920 he published three books, and in 1922, four.

In 1922 he also arrived at a decision that had long been in the making, which "overcame the largely physical problem posed for him by overwork, physical lethargy and the habit of depending on his wife for all practical decisions." He became a Roman Catholic, being received into the church by the prototype of his best-known fiction character, Father O'Connor. Another friend, Father Maturin, said after Chesterton's conversion that "for at least ten years the question had never been out of his mind for ten waking minutes." The next year Chesterton published a book on St. Francis of Assisi; ten years after that, he would publish one on St. Thomas Aquinas; other books, and much of his shorter work, had also to do with Catholicism. It would be difficult to overstate the importance and significance of his religion during the remainder of his life, which is also to say the comfort and peace of mind it seems to have brought him. His wife followed him into the church in 1926, and their close friends included a number of members of the clergy, among them Father Ronald Knox; and a number of Catholic writers, among them Maurice Baring and the name long-linked with Chesterton's, Hilaire Belloc. Belloc's and Chesterton's names are least happily linked in terms of their notorious anti-Semitism. Belloc's was certainly the more rabid; Chesterton's, in the light of his humane and kindly nature, the less explicable. He disclaimed being anti-Semitic, and his biographer Maisie Ward explains that he feared the Jews felt more deeply about a *patria* of their own than about being English; but various statements and lines of verse like "In English country houses crammed with Jews" scarcely bear out the explanation.

Under Chesterton's editorship, *The New Witness* became in 1925 *G.K.'s Weekly*, remaining so until his death. Though never out-and-out Catholic, the magazine stood for Catholic Christianity, as its social thinking stood for "small ownership, personal responsibility, and property," while opposing Socialism and Communism. Chesterton once put it that Shaw "wants to distribute money among the poor, we want to distribute power." Chesterton, in writing about religion, could be witty, trenchant, and Chestertonian:

The idea of birth through a Holy Spirit, of the death of a Divine being, of the forgiveness of sins, or the fulfilment of prophecies, are ideas which, anyone can see, need but a touch to turn into something blasphemous or ferocious. If some small mistake were made in doctrine, huge blunders might be made in human happiness. A sentence phrased wrong about the nature of symbolism might have broken all the best statues in Europe. A slip in the definitions might stop all the dances; might wither all the Christmas trees or break all the Easter eggs. Doctrines had to be defined within strict limits, even in order that man might enjoy general human liberties. The Church had to be careful, if only that the world might be careless.

As an editor, Chesterton had his good and bad points. *G.K.'s Weekly* was judged inferior to *The New Witness*; G.K.'s staff "adored" him personally, but a member of it said: "He was a bad judge of men. He never shirked an intellectual issue, but in a practical crisis he was inclined to slide out." *G.K.'s Weekly* had its chronic financial worries, and Chesterton confessed that he could only keep it going by writing mystery stories. "Many a shot," he wrote, "has rung out in the silent night, many a constable has hurled himself through a crashing door, from under which there crawled a crimson stain, in order that there might be a page somewhere for Mr. Kendrick's . . . exposition of the principles of Distributism."

Many an aphorism must also have contributed to Chesterton's exchequer, since aphorisms were always popping up in anything he wrote. Thus he wrote: "All men are ordinary men; the extraordinary men are those who know it"; less interestingly he had said: "A great classic means a man whom we can praise without having read." In the following statement we may fancy that the phrasing—or call it the imagery—is more rewarding than the fact: "There is but an inch of difference between the cushioned chamber and the padded cell." Chesterton is of course a master of phrasing; as for imagery, consider his "The wind came round the corner like a cab." Here is more bonbon than bombshell: "Music with dinner is an insult both to the cook and the violinist." Something that Chesterton said of Shaw is not difficult to generalize from, or to apply specifically elsewhere: "A man so eager to be in advance of his age that he pretended to be in advance of himself." And here we find Chesterton offering, in the most classical form, a crushing aphorism: "Silence is the unbearable repartee." Chesterton's gift of aphorism carried with it—like something the gods had bestowed at his birth—a small curse: the danger of being merely facile or clever. "The poet," wrote Chesterton, "only asks to get his head into the heavens. It is the logician who seeks to get the heavens into his head." As prose, this is nicely rhythmical; as contrast, it is acceptably sharp, and taken on the run, it is rather striking. But taken at a strolling pace, it offers little real substance and perhaps even less truth. If I am playing teacher for a moment, it is chiefly to drive home the fantastic ease—and the total lack of effort—with which Chesterton contrives shapely and fine-sounding aphorisms and epigrams, while clinging to antitheses and feasting off paradoxes. Chesterton's passion for them prompted Edward Anthony to write:

> O Gilbert, I know there are many who like
>   Your talks on the darkness of light,
> The shortness of length and the weakness of strength
>   And the one on the lowness of height

ending, verses later, with

> Some evening next week . . . I am going to speak
>   On the shallowness of the profound.

And occasionally Chesterton contrives something that seems worse than facile, that seems forced: "Every man is important if he loses his life; and every man is funny if he loses his hat and has to run after it." But though Chesterton is guilty of a number of such remarks, the proportion of what, were they a commercial product, would have to be labeled "defective" would be small compared with those that range from the acceptable to the exceptional, from the amusing to the brilliant. Here we have Chesterton in splendid form: "Nine times out of ten, the coarse word is the word that condemns an evil and the refined word the word that excuses it." Here he is at his most concise: "Progress is the mother of problems." And once more: "The man who sees the consistency in things is a wit . . . The man who sees the inconsistency in things is a humorist."

Whatever his record on the score of consistency, Chesterton was often enough a wit. He could also, as in the following remark which turns on his avoirdupois, be a humorist: "Everyone seems to know [who you are]," said an American, traveling about London with him. "Yes," said Chesterton, "and if they don't know, they ask." During the question period of a lecture that Chesterton gave in Toronto, someone inquired of him: "Is George Bernard Shaw a coming peril?" "Heavens, no!" said Chesterton. "He's a disappearing pleasure." And here is Chesterton's famous comment when he saw Broadway at night, illuminated with sky signs: "What a marvelous sight for some one who is unable to read!"

Chesterton paid two visits to the United States, coming away with mixed feelings; but, as he remarked, he found no greater fault with Americans than with his fellow countrymen. He put perhaps his most concise and considered reaction to America into "The real American is all right; it is the ideal American who is all wrong." He had his fun with America's habits, classifying its sense of comfort as "acute discomfort" and remarking that every American lives in an "airless furnace in the midst of which he sits and eats lumps of ice." But, among visits of various kinds, he found in one at Notre Dame, where he gave a number of lectures, what most impressed him in American life:

In a curious and almost creepy fashion the great presence of Abraham Lincoln continually grew upon me . . . A man of any imagination might look down these strange [Middle-Western] streets with their frame houses filled with the latest conveniences and surrounded with the latest litter, till he could see approaching . . . that long ungainly figure, with the preposterous stove-pipe hat and the rustic umbrella and deep melancholy eyes, the humor and the hard patience and the heart that fed upon hope deferred.

During his last years Chesterton did a good deal of broadcasting; "everyone," says Maisie Ward in *G. K. Chesterton,* "seems agreed that he was an extraordinary success." After the first talk, in November 1932, Broadcasting House assured him that he would "have a vast public by Christmas" and invited him to give a second series of talks after the New Year. One series of his had for theme "Literature lives by history. Otherwise it exists: like trigonometry." He was refused a program on Dean Inge on the score of "avoid religion," as though he ever could; and he debated with Bertrand Russell on "Who shall bring up our children?" no doubt because he had none.

Chesterton's very last years saw a good deal of traveling. In 1934 he and his wife went in Holy Year to Rome, and from there to Sicily, where illness prevented his continuing on to Palestine; and in 1935 he and Mrs. Chesterton went on a motor trip to France and Italy. Neither personal illness nor the acute cosmic illnesses of the 1930's destroyed his affirmation of life. Reading T. S. Eliot's *The Hollow Men*, with its then much-less-famous ending, he wrote: "I'm damned if I ever felt like that"; and he wished to say to the "young pessimists":

> *Some sneer; some snigger; some simper;*
> *In the youth where we laughed and sang:*
> *And they may end with a whimper,*
> *But we will end with a bang.*

During the year or so before he died Chesterton was at work on an autobiography, which he announced to a group of friends, early in 1936, that he had finished. He spoke in it of a life that had been "indefensibly happy," and wrote it with a good deal of verve; but a friend's chilly comment when Chesterton revealed that he had written his autobiography— "*Nunc dimittis*"—came close to the truth. He was tired from overwork, the overwork, one might say, of a lifetime. He still felt, and doubtless remained, loyal to his own individualistic Liberalism—denouncing, for example, the Italian invasion of Abyssinia; and he still traveled, though early in 1936 it was for his health; one of his trips included Lourdes and Lisieux. But though he seemed, on his return to England, the better for having traveled, he was given to falling asleep while at work and to not always being very clearheaded. His remarkable recovery in 1916 was not to be repeated in 1936, and he died at Beaconsfield on June 14. Two years earlier the Pope had made Chesterton, along with Belloc, a Knight Commander of St. Gregory, with star. At his death the Pope —Pius XII—in cabling his sympathy spoke of Chesterton as a Defender of the Faith, a title that is restricted in England to royalty, and hence was not cited about Chesterton in "the secular press."

Aphorisms

A figure of speech can often get into a crack too small for a definition.

A thinking man should always attack the strongest thing in his own time. For the strongest thing of the time is always too strong.

Powerful men who have powerful passions use much of their strength in forging chains for themselves; they alone know how strong the chains need to be.

CHESTERTON

Art is limitation; the essence of every picture is the frame.

The family is the test of freedom, because the family is the only thing that the free man makes both for himself and by himself.

The honest poor can sometimes forget poverty. The honest rich can never forget it.

Your next-door neighbor . . . is not a man; he is an environment. He is the barking of a dog; he is the noise of a pianola; he is a dispute about a party wall; he is drains that are worse than yours, or roses that are better.

Spring is never spring unless it comes too soon.

It is the test of a good religion whether you can make a joke about it.

A really accomplished impostor is the most wretched of geniuses: he is a Napoleon on a desert island.

A cosmic philosophy is not constructed to fit a man; a cosmic philosophy is constructed to fit a cosmos. A man can no more possess a private religion than he can possess a private sun and moon.

THE LAST WORD

He . . . met every kind of person except the ordinary person. He knew everybody, so to speak, except everybody.

Such professions [as] the soldier and the lawyer . . . give ample opportunities for crimes, but not much for mere illusions. If you have composed a bad opera, you may persuade yourself that it is a good one; if you have carved a bad statue you can think yourself better than Michelangelo. But if you have lost a battle you cannot believe that you have won it; if your client is hanged you cannot pretend that you have got him off.

Women prefer to talk in twos, while men prefer to talk in threes.

The man who cannot believe his senses and the man who cannot believe anything else, are both mad.

Dogma does not mean the absence of thought but the end of thought.

All slang is metaphor, and all metaphor is poetry.

There is more simplicity in the man who eats caviar on impulse than in the man who eats grapenuts on principle.

Index 🍂

INDEX

264

INDEX

INDEX

266

INDEX

INDEX

INDEX

INDEX

INDEX

INDEX